Sydney

Sydney

THE STORY OF A CITY

Geoffrey Moorhouse

HARCOURT, INC.

New York   San Diego   London

First published in England in 1999 by Weidenfeld & Nicolson

Library of Congress Cataloging-in-Publication Data
Moorhouse, Geoffrey, 1931—
Sydney/Geoffrey Moorhouse.—1st ed.
p.   cm.
Includes bibliographical references (p.) and index.
ISBN 0-15-100601-6
1. Sydney (N.S.W.)—History. I. Title.
DU178.M645 2000
994.4'1—dc21   99-044110

Designed by Lori McThomas Buley
Text set in Centaur MT
Printed in the United States of America
First edition
A C E G I K J H F D B

To Sally

Contents

Acknowledgments

This book could not have been written had I not been generously helped by a great number of friends and acquaintances
over many years. If I single out Ian and Joy Heads before any others it is not only because they are my oldest friends in Sydney, but
also because their fax machine spent an awful lot of paper in an-
swering questions that occurred to me when I was in my study on
the other side of the world. I'm also particularly grateful to Bridie
Henehan, who tirelessly arranged things for me before my most
recent visits to Australia, and who despatched vast quantities of
research material (about half a Jumboful at a guess) in my wake
after I'd flown out again; and to Patrick Gallagher, who smoothed
my path in all sorts of unobtrusive ways when he wasn't damaging
himself on distant cricket fields. The endless assistance of Alan
Ventress and his colleagues in the State Library of New South
Wales must also be emphasised, because I depended on it so much
for weeks at a time when I was in Sydney. But nobody ever said no
when I turned to them for help, and they include Margaret Allan,
Keith Barnes, Margaret Barrett, Neal Blewett, Fr Michael Bowie,
Stephen Brassel, Fr Edmund Campion, Michele Field, Shirley

Fitzgerald, George Franki, Phil Gardner, Robert Goldman, Kate Grenville and Bruce Petty, Richard Hall, Joyce Ingram, John Iremonger and Jane Marceau, Natty Jowett, Fr Ted Kennedy, Chris McGillion, Marshal and Theresa McMahon, Ern McQuillan, Sgt Larry Malone, Ann and Danny Meehan, Tony Morris, Tim Peach, Sandra Phillips, Julie Plummer, Barry Porter, Jim Pullin, Basil Sands, Alison Seale, Lindsey Shaw, Graham Silva, Peter Spearritt. My best thanks to them all, and I hope they think this book is worth the help they so unstintingly gave.

Sydney

CHAPTER ONE

'One of the Finest Harbours in the World'

As the sailor approaches them out of the great ocean, the cliffs appear to be impregnable. They run from north to south like a scrub-covered bastion, whose foundations are exposed as huge ledges at low tide. In a heavy swell, the Tasman smashes into these cliffs so violently that spouts of water rise almost three hundred feet to the top, but its other self sucks gently at the rock when the weather has calmed, so that wary fishermen are encouraged to clamber down to the ledges and there cast their lines into the surf. The impregnability is an illusion, whatever wind is blowing from the east, for presently the mariner discovers an opening in the bastion, between two headlands a mile apart. At 33° 45′ South, 151° 17′ 30″ East, he has found the entrance to Sydney Harbour, and no anchorage in all the seven seas has ever been safer or more beguiling than that.

As soon as he sails in between the Heads, our sea captain will be relieved to have a pilot aboard, for almost at once he has to squeeze past the Sow and Pigs, a nasty little shoal which is fully visible at the bottom of a spring tide and thereupon reveals a peculiarity of this haven: the fact that its shallowest water is close by the entrance, its greatest depth—twenty-six fathoms, or four times what's under the keel at the Heads—being sounded just above the Harbour Bridge, almost exactly five miles upstream. That stretch of water was described in 1788 by Arthur Phillip, the first Governor of New South Wales, as 'one of the finest harbours in the world, in which a thousand sail of the line might ride in perfect security':[1] he had just brought the First Fleet of convicts and their guards from England, and had swiftly concluded that this anchorage was a vast improvement on Botany Bay, which had been James Cook's recommendation eighteen years earlier.

From the Heads up to the Bridge, the Harbour is shaped like a boomerang, enclosed on either side by one promontory after another, which separate a series of rocky coves and sandy bays. As the pilot eases his newcomer into the main shipping channel, he can point out to port the most affluent habitations in the city, the posh part of its eastern suburbs, where the most valuable real estate in the southern hemisphere appreciates quite wantonly. To starboard, the foreshore of North Sydney, too, will shortly be littered with much wealth but, until Little Sirius Point is passed, enough of the primeval bush has survived to camouflage man's more expensive tastes and to hint at what was everywhere here before the Europeans came. On this side of the channel there is, moreover, the splendid entrance to what might be described as a fjord if only Sydney Harbour were enclosed within mountainously high ground, which it isn't; also the well-wooded slopes of Taronga Zoo, whose elephants doubtless enjoy the most exhilarating view in all captivity.

So our vessel plods steadily past Watsons Bay and an overpublicised restaurant, then past Rose Bay, where once the Empire flying boats berthed after almost weeks in transit from England, and which still sees seaplanes take off on sightseeing flights; past Reef Beach, where the nudists bathe, now well astern on the northern shore, with Chowder Bay also slipping by, its redundant military settlement quietly decomposing under the blistering sun.

And then, as our ship rounds Bradleys Head, Sydney's heart slides into view, more stunningly beautiful at this distance than any modern city centre has any right to be, with the Old Coathanger of the Bridge more than holding its own between two thickets of upstart skyscrapers, and a first sight of the Opera House, poised perfectly on the tip of Bennelong Point, confirming that this must indeed be the most excitingly graceful shape built in the twentieth century. Poised, what's more, beside the marvellous ellipse of the Botanic Gardens, possibly the most civilised mark that a colonial governor ever left on an imperial possession—for it evolved partly from Lachlan Macquarie's desire to please his wife in 1816.

Somewhere under the Harbour hereabouts is a coal seam which was mined in Balmain well within memory, until that robust enclave became somewhat more delicate and yuppified. The long wharf at Woolloomooloo, where generations of migrants—New Chums, Reffoes, Dallies, Ten Pound Poms and the like—invariably docked, has also seen the last of its workaday self, the triple-roofed shed of its old passenger terminal almost bound to be transformed into more luxurious premises soon. But, facing that wharf across the narrow strip of Woolloomooloo Bay, warships are parked nonchalantly alongside a main road, which makes Australia's principal naval base seem disconcertingly vulnerable, when anyone can hop off a number 311 bus and loiter with intent behind railings not fifty yards from frigates packed with the latest high technology (the submarines, however, are more discreetly tethered to HMAS *Platypus*, across the Harbour, beside the site of an old gasworks in Neutral Bay).

With the exception of the Navy's presence at Garden Island, and of the ferry terminal on Circular Quay, the workaday waterfront is almost entirely above the Bridge, amid oil tanks lining the edge of Gore Cove, in container facilities along White Bay and Glebe Island, and especially at the wharf leading into Darling Harbour, whose inner basin is now a rather pricey playground, much redeemed by its National Maritime Museum and its Aquarium.

Where that wharf turns a corner towards the Bridge, tools have been downed for the last time on Walsh Bay, whose jetties, like that at the 'Loo, were once the scene of bustling commerce, with hatches wide open here and cranes delving into holds, but whose buildings are quietly becoming derelict, having some time ago out-lasted their original usefulness.

The charts recognise several distinctly separate parts of this tremendous anchorage. If a seaman turns right on coming through the Heads he sails past the old Quarantine Station and up the North Harbour, with the seaside suburb of Manly ('Seven miles from Sydney but a thousand miles from care') curving round its upper end. If he goes straight ahead across the shipping lanes, he enters that fjord of Middle Harbour, which winds sinuously in-land past yet more well-heeled property, here nestling on steep hillsides smothered in bush, the fjord itself eventually fetching up in the wilderness of a national park; but not before it has negoti-ated the notorious Spit Bridge, whose roadway is raised periodi-cally each day to allow pleasure boats with tall masts to get past, to the great frustration of commuters who are anxious to be home in Manly, Queenscliff and Curl Curl in time for tea. If he turns left into the main channel, heading for the Opera House and the Bridge, he will be proceeding up the length of Port Jackson, so called by Captain Cook (though he never entered it) to remind posterity that the Fleet's Judge-Advocate at the time was Sir George Jackson—who shortly afterwards reinvented himself as a Duckett in order to secure the benefits of his second wife's inheri-tance. Once above the Bridge, there is still a great deal of water left, dozens of remaining coves and inlets and bays and other by-ways but, after Darling Harbour has been cleared, the main chan-nel is known as the Parramatta River, though it is mostly a tidal saltwater creek harbouring hundreds of pleasure craft along much of its length, and terminating in a weir so far from Circular Quay that it takes a jet-propelled ferry almost an hour to get there.

This entire waterway, something like twenty miles of navigation from the ocean to that weir, is studded with islands. Just past the Sow and Pigs there is Shark Island, to remind all-comers that Sydney Harbour contains other hazards as well as hidden shoals and rocks. Right opposite Bradleys Head is Clarke Island, where one of Governor Phillip's lieutenants had a vegetable patch, and where refugees from the city can nowadays relax among trees, with picnic areas and other amenities provided by the New South Wales Parks and Wildlife Service. Then comes Garden Island, which qualifies in name only, because it became attached to the mainland during the Second World War by the landfill and concrete required to construct the Captain Cook Graving Dock. Most famous island of all is Fort Denison, more familiarly known as Pinchgut, because convicts were sent there for punishment on very short rations, whose mid-nineteenth-century Martello Tower (one of the last, it's said, to be built anywhere in the world) is largely responsible for a strange hallucination when viewed from one of the near-by skyscrapers. At that range—so long as the island's caretaker hasn't hung his washing out, which spoils the effect— Pinchgut resembles nothing so much as a surfaced submarine, its Martello uncannily shaped like a gigantic conning tower.

Above the Bridge are other islands, all of them touched by something of Sydney's history. Rodd, which needs getting round during any passage up Iron Cove, was annexed for the training of US soldiers during the Second World War. More interestingly, it had been a bacteriological laboratory half a century earlier, when the state Government was desperate to eradicate the rabbit, then despoiling the sheep pastures of New South Wales. Consequently, this was where Sarah Bernhardt's pet dogs were quarantined while the French prima donna was playing a season at Her Majesty's Theatre ('her histrionic reputation is so high, her fame so worldwide' according to one obsequious local reporter, 'that the transplanting of this singular glory of the European stage to this part of the world must be taken as marking an epoch').[2] The remaining islands in this stretch of the Harbour are best remembered for their naval associations, and for the hard labour of convicts, who constructed many of their buildings. Goat Island, which stands square across the entrance to the Parramatta River, was a munitions dump from 1838 until 1893, when an explosion caused the authorities to shift the remaining contents to Spectacle Island, which was subsequently extended by recruiting landfill from the innards of the Balmain coal mine. The same source was tapped in the 1930s to upgrade a rocky outcrop off Birkenhead Point to Snapper Island, which serves as a base for the local Sea Cadets and houses a naval museum. Busiest of all for more than a century until 1991 was Cockatoo Island, once among the biggest shipyards in Australia, specialising in naval vessels, including the destroyer *Vampire*, which may be inspected at her mooring outside the National Maritime Museum, where she is on permanent exhibition.

The Harbour is the key to Sydney, its alpha and its omega. To some extent the same may be said of other ports around the world, but in no other case, perhaps, does a harbour so completely influence the lifestyle and the attitudes of its citizenry. This is so even among people who reside close by the Blue Mountains, which begin after thirty-odd miles of intervening suburbia, and were long thought of as an insuperable barrier between the new colony and the rest of the continent (you can see why in Augustus Earle's study of Wentworth Falls, with its two endless lines of vertical cliffs facing each other above deep chasms choked with bush, which the artist painted in 1830, only a few years after William Charles Wentworth and two companions, four convict servants, four packhorses and five dogs, had at last crossed the Great Dividing Range).* Inhabitants of Penrith, therefore, who live much closer to the mountains than to the Harbour, will still tell strangers that they come from Sydney, as adamantly as any taxpayer from Bondi or Darlinghurst Road, and will take the same

---

Wentworth Falls (*c.* 1830), National Gallery of Australia, Canberra.

proprietorial responsibility for the city's greatest asset and their spiritual home.

Other great harbours of the world do not generally so dominate the local psyche or, when occasionally they do, they are not often held in such affectionate regard. In New York you are scarcely aware of the harbour, unless you are disposed to inspect the Statue of Liberty or live in the borough of Staten Island. In San Francisco they have bridged their harbour wherever they are able to, in order to put it behind them as fast as possible, so that they may get on with the real business of the day. Wellington's harbour is as dramatic as they come, to be sure, but it seems to stimulate the often alarming maelstrom that gives the New Zealand capital its reputation as the tediously Windy City. Bombay is as important as any entrepôt on earth, as is Singapore, but in both places the lasting impression is not of beauty or great character, but of an armada of shipping riding at anchor in the roads. In Rio de Janeiro, in Cape Town, in Vancouver, the harbours are notable above all for some feature that upstages them, not for their own nature and activity: for the overpowering image of Christ, outstretched above Copacabana Beach; for Table Mountain and its attendant cloud, its Tablecloth; for an enclosing range of peaks which may not be as high as the Rocky Mountains but which are overwhelmingly close. There are no such distractions around Sydney Harbour, which is therefore allowed to be an incomparable presence at the very heart of this sprawling metropolis and which, in truth, goes a long way to defining Sydney. It establishes the local credentials as one of the most attractive cities of the modern world, which certainly didn't deserve to be patronised by clever, silly Neville Cardus, to whom it was a welcome refuge from the rigours of Europe in the Second World War, and who, when he was safely back home again after hostilities had ceased, wrote that 'Sydney is exactly like Manchester, except that you have the Pacific Ocean at the bottom of Market Street instead of the Irwell.'[3] (His compatriot and friend Sir Thomas Beecham was at least funny when he wondered aloud why they hadn't called the place Herbert instead.)

Only Hong Kong and Istanbul, perhaps, rival Sydney in this respect, for they, too, are chiefly characterised by their harbours, which linger in the memory more than any other single feature in their surroundings. In spite of its great antiquity, which makes for some obvious differences with which Sydney simply cannot compete, Istanbul comes closest of all to the ambience of the Australian city. And this is because its waterway, too, is perpetually criss-crossed by a multitude of ferry-boats, whose tall funnels billow black smoke across Galata Bridge and the Golden Horn, as they bustle off to Scutari, or tack along both sides of the Bosphorus, from one suburb to another, until the entrance to the Black Sea has been reached and the last passenger has disembarked.

The Istanbul ferry terminus is along a wharf just below Galata Bridge, while Sydney's is on Circular Quay, in the lee of the Old Coathanger. This was where Arthur Phillip's first settlement was established, because he found there 'a run of fresh water, which stole silently through a very thick wood, the stillness of which... and tranquillity... from that day were to give place to the noise of labour, the confusion of camps and towns, and the busy hum of its new possessors'.[4] The run of fresh water became known as the Tank Stream, using an Indian word for a small reservoir, imported from another British colonial experience. The spot was very well sheltered in what Phillip named Sydney Cove, after Thomas Townshend, first Viscount Sydney, Secretary of State for the Home Department and therefore a member of William Pitt's Government closely involved in the disposal of convicts to the southern hemisphere. And though the Tank Stream has long since disappeared under buildings and pavements, Circular Quay may still lay claim to being at the very heart of this community.

All the principal streets of commerce and government— George, Pitt, Phillip and Macquarie—slope down to the ferry landings, but Circular Quay is much more than a conduit through which hordes of people pass each day on their way to and from work. Except in the vilest weather—and it can pour buckets in Sydney when it has a mind to, with cloud scudding so low up the Harbour that the top of the Bridge disappears from view—these wharves and promenades are thronged with strollers. This makes the perpetual emptiness of Luna Park, a natural *alter ego* right opposite the Quay at the other end of the Bridge, all the more eerie; its Ferris wheel motionless, its sideshows silent, its hugely grimacing gargoyle inviting all and sundry to come and have a good time, when it knows perfectly well that the fairground gates are locked for some reason that nobody in Sydney seems quite to understand. Circular Quay is the antithesis of this, especially at the weekend, when it sometimes seems as if half the population has dropped by, and not necessarily in order to catch a ferry to somewhere else. People also fish from jetties here or over the concave wall that was built right round this part of the Harbour to prevent rats ever again coming off the tramp steamers into town, after a disastrous plague at the turn of the century; they slurp ice-cream as they watch the ceaseless traffic in vessels rumbling past; they linger over a coffee and a Danish while they read the *Sydney Morning Herald* or one of Mr Murdoch's publications; they queue for Travelpasses of varying denominations that will allow them to ride any ferry, bus or CityRail train without further ado; they amble along the eastern arm of the Quay, to sample bivalves in the Oyster Bar, and then continue strolling on to the Opera House where, on a shining day, scores of sun worshippers will arrange themselves lazily on its long cascade of steps.

Most of them have earlier paused at least long enough to appreciate some of the entertainments that are improvised around the Quay. For years on end an elderly Italian has been known to sit in the shade of an umbrella with his clamps and his jigs, his chisels and his saws, and there painstakingly fashion exquisite model sailing ships from the timber of the Lilly Pilly tree, perfect in every detail, and accurately scaled to the nearest millimetre; which, when triumphantly finished, he then presents to some charity. Young people busk enthusiastically and, more often than not, with high degrees of skill: a piper in full rig, bearskin, Black Watch tartan and all, puffing his way through complicated sets on a sweltering day in front of the Opera House; a beautiful blonde girl stroking a harp while she sings penillion as sweetly as a lark, with perfect counterpoint (which is virtually unheard of below Cerrig-y-Druidion); a lad with a violin, playing a Bach partita with an expression on his face which he may or may not have cultivated after watching Nigel Kennedy; a woman (I think) silvered from head to toe to resemble the Statue of Liberty, who poses on a stool without moving a muscle for minutes on end, then rearranges herself very slowly while children look on bemused; a cheerful Aborigine, his face painted with ancient significance, a didgeridu like a small tree trunk pressed to his lips, until the Quay reverberates to the beat of its hollow basso, and people begin to grin and tap their feet in time; a bowler-hatted young fellow on a clown's monocycle, pedalling deftly and high above his audience while he teases them relentlessly with a cheeky line in patter; an antique Chinese gentleman with a wispy beard, fiddling away at a stringed instrument which he holds above his lap vertically, making tunes that do not fall easily upon Western ears. All this is part of Circular Quay's stock-in-trade, as is the profusion of eateries, one of which boasts that it is the only place in town to stay open twenty-four hours a day, even though the last ferry of the night gets back from Mosman and Cremorne just after half-past twelve.

A variety of craft apart from the ferries tie up in the nook that was Sydney Cove. Down the western side and almost under the Bridge approach are the slots for vessels which have been rigged as period pieces in order to attract the tourists; a sternwheeler that might feel more at home on the Mississippi, and a replica of the HMS *Bounty* that was under William Bligh's command at the time of that unfortunate business with Fletcher Christian and his pack of mutinous dogs, long before Bligh became the fourth Governor of New South Wales, still irascible, still vigorous, still believing in firm discipline, but a man who did his best to rescue the little colony from the desperate straits it had fallen into after Arthur Phillip had gone home and the initial energy had been spent. Watch the pseudo-*Bounty* sailing slowly, diesels primed in case the wind drops, down the Harbour with Shark Island or Bradleys Head looming behind her, and you have an inkling not only of what it must have felt like to be aboard the First Fleet when it sailed through the Heads on 25 January 1788, but also how the individual vessels—HMS *Sirius* and HMS *Supply*, together with the transports and store ships *Alexander, Scarborough, Prince of Wales, Charlotte, Lady Penrhyn, Friendship, Fishburn, Golden Grove* and *Borrowdale*—would have been dwarfed by these bush-covered headlands and heights. They had just voyaged for two-thirds of a year and sixteen thousand miles across the emptiest seas in the world.

Other vessels make use of Circular Quay: swish jetboats which go throbbing down the channel loaded with sightseers; glorified houseboats that tend not to sail until dusk, full of youngsters doing their disco thing afloat, under strobe lights and to deafening sounds; water taxis that scuttle here and there around the Harbour, bearing twosomes embarking on special occasions, or businessmen who have suddenly remembered that urgent appointment; a launch that is reserved exclusively for the patrons of Doyles, whom it carries off dashingly to Watsons Bay where, they hope, they can get stuck into something a bit more sophisticated than fish and chips. An updated passenger terminal along this length of the Quay is where the cruise liners berth between spring and autumn, to the chagrin of another restaurateur, because they blot out a classic view of the Opera House which would otherwise be enjoyed by his customers.

But it is the Sydney ferries that set the pace on Circular Quay. For nineteen hours in every twenty-four they shuttle to and fro between the Quay and comfortable destinations on either side of the Harbour, above and below the Bridge—down the water to Watsons

Bay, via Milsons Point and Double Bay, or upstream to Woolwich (Valentia Street) with intermediate stops at Balmain, Balmain East and Balmain West: then there's the short trip across to Cremorne and Mosman, and the shorter still (thirteen minutes flat, including stops at Kirribilli and North Sydney High Street) to Neutral Bay. The longest journey is up to Parramatta by that jet-propelled catamaran, which drops people off at eight staging points first, and the biggest deal of the lot is a non-stop ride to Manly, which can be done swiftly in another jet, or more traditionally in a double-ended steamer which is much bigger than any other conventional ferry in Sydney because the Heads have to be traversed *en route:* and when the full force of the Pacific Ocean is propelled through that gap by an onshore wind the trip can be less than tranquil for ten or fifteen minutes, as the *Freshwater,* the *Queenscliff,* the *Narrabeen* or the *Collaroy* lurches and rolls in the heavy swell, sometimes pitching so heavily that their screws race madly with not enough water under the stern. There is an alarming photograph *of Freshwater,* which appears to be rising at an angle of thirty degrees from the sea-bed in a tumult of white water and foam, her bows well clear of the surface, her for'ard screw and rudder completely exposed, together with a great length of keel.

There is an even more heroic painting of the ferry *Burra Bra* which, one June morning in 1923, left Manly Wharf with 500 passengers aboard for the 8 a.m. run to the Quay, in a winter gale which was blowing so fiercely that many people had decided to go to work that day the long way round, by other forms of transport which would deposit them in Cremorne for a shorter and much easier ride across the Harbour.

> The *Burra Bra* was lifting to the swell before she was halfway to Smedleys Point. Passengers could see the huge rollers sweeping in through the Heads and breaking heavily on the rocks at Dobroyd and Middle Head. The entrance to Middle Harbour between Grotto Point and Balmoral was a continuous line of breaking surf.... *Burra*

Bra was dipping, rising, then burying her nose into the swells, spray flying over the bridge and water running all over the lower deck. She was halfway across the Heads when one mighty sea slammed into her on the port quarter, a massive wall of solid water disintegrating with an explosive roar. The ferry shuddered and slumped under the weight of water. Dozens of windows were broken, seats with passengers sitting on them were wrenched from their fastenings and slid across the rolling decks, the sliding doors on the port side were stove in and shattered, leaving the sea to pour into the lower decks as the doors burst open.... Four people were injured, one badly. Several women fainted as water flooded the deck downstairs.... The signal master at South Head estimated that at the time of the incident the gale was roaring in from the south-east with a force of 80 miles an hour. Somebody watching from the shore said the ferry disappeared from sight completely in the trough between enormous seas halfway across the Heads.[5]

The Manly ferries are, in fact, traditionally so substantial that they have been known to sail all the way from a Scottish shipyard, before it became axiomatic that they should be built much nearer home. The rest of the Sydney flotilla is much stockier than that, butty little boats that, even so, are in some cases bigger than the eleven vessels of the First Fleet which crossed the world two centuries ago; and eight of them do proudly bear the names of their gallant (and infamous) predecessors. In their distinctive livery of dark-green hull and cream superstructure (which may well induce more homesickness among Sydneysiders exiled in Earls Court than almost anything apart from the gum trees of the Australian countryside), the *Golden Grove* and the *Fishburn* back off from their wharves at the city terminus and execute a smart half-circle with water boiling under the counter, so as to be pointing the right way for the outward journey, while *Scarborough* and *Borrowdale*, inward bound from Birchgrove or Darling Harbour, pause on their way into the Quay so as to let their sisters pass, which they do more often than not with a grateful burp on the horn, before steaming away under the Bridge or round Bennelong Point; just as, like as not, *Sirius, Charlotte, Alexander* or *Friendship* is heading for the Quay with a slight list to port because all the out-of-towners aboard want to take photographs of the Opera House.

Sydney and many of its suburbs have been held together, as it were, by ferries ever since the paddle steamer *Surprise* chuntered upstream to Parramatta in 1831; and for a quarter of a century afterwards all such craft were built like her, running what might be better described as excursions rather than regular services. The great expansion into a timetabled local transport system can be dated to 1854, when the Manly ferries began to run; and the rest of the nineteenth century saw the settlements which were spreading around the inner Harbour increasingly served by conventional steam launches and double-enders as well as by paddle boats. At the end of 1904, when Sydney's population was touching half a million, it was announced that nineteen million passengers had used the ferries that year, a statistic which reached its highest point when forty-seven million took to the water in 1927, largely because North Sydney was then expanding fast and the Bridge linking it to the city centre was still five years away. By then, the ferry service had become an ineradicably memorable part of the local culture.

Part of the memory has consisted of mishaps and, on two occasions, of absolute disaster. The mishaps have generally been hailed with some glee by everyone except those most closely involved; like the ferry master who overshot the Musgrave Street wharf, where people were waiting—vainly, it transpired—to clamber aboard, then very nearly hit a moored yacht before crashing into the Old Cremorne wharf and abusing passengers who had started to complain. Several skippers have run their boats aground, usually in thick fog, none more embarrassingly than the captain of *Freshwater*, which climbed on to the beach at Manly a few years ago, taking the swimming pool net with her when she was finally able to refloat and go astern again—but not before she had been there long enough for many photographs to be taken by fascinated onlookers, some of which were published as souvenir postcards. Curiously enough, her sister *Narrabeen* did likewise in the same spot twelve months later, and again the swimming pool net was the worse for wear. Then there have been the occasions when Sydney ferries decided to take on the Navy, like the celebrated old-timer *South Steyne*, which avoided running down some clueless yachtsman off Garden Island by ramming an aircraft carrier instead; and like the *Bellubera*, which so hurt HMAS *Parramatta's* dignity when the frigate failed to see what was behind her and backed into the ferry, that the Navy refused to speak about it to the press. The biggest cock-up of the lot occurred during, of all occasions, the Bicentennial celebrations in 1988, when a floating platform had been constructed in the middle of the Harbour, from which a *son et lumière* display including fireworks was to be realised. People were supposed to watch this from a safe distance ashore, but hundreds of pleasure craft had decided to take a closer look and effectively blocked the Harbour with their hulls, their anchor cables and their other gear, quite ignoring the fact that the ferries were expected to provide scheduled services at the same time. To make matters worse, many of the yachties didn't even display the correct riding lights, to the greater confusion of ferry captains who were trying to find a way through or past the obstruction. Cables began to snap, and so did tempers, as vessels were bumped and their expensive paintwork was scratched, wire became wrapped round propellers, and homeward-bound passengers crossly demanded that captains bash a way through the various impediments. Boarding parties of irate pleasure-boaters made matters even worse, and the only people to benefit from the mayhem that ensued were the lawyers who enjoyed the next few months profiting from the various litigations that were brought to court.

A shudder can be the only response of anyone who recalls the two disasters. Pleasure craft were again involved in 1938, when the

American cruiser *Louisville* was leaving the Harbour after a courtesy visit, and half the boaters in Sydney decided to sail with her towards the Heads before seeing her off. Among these craft was the almost brand-new ferry *Rodney*, licensed to carry a couple of hundred passengers, but with only half that number booked for an excursion to bid farewell to the Americans. One of the visiting ship's company took a photograph of *Rodney* as she came in close, and by then the distribution of her load was obviously perilous, with the majority of passengers lining the upper deck and very few down below: among the people topsides was an Australian naval rating, who should have known better than to stand posturing upon the wheelhouse roof. The almost predictable result was that as the ferry came round *Louisville*'s stern, and people rushed from one side of her upper deck to the other, she capsized and sank, later to be raised, refloated and refitted, and to work the Harbour for another fifty years under a different name. But nineteen of her passengers were drowned that day.

Even worse was the accident which befell the *Greycliffe* in November 1927, when she was on a late-afternoon run to Watsons Bay, carrying among others many children on their way home from school. She had paused once at Garden Island to pick up more passengers who worked at the naval base, and was steaming away to her next stop just as the 8,000-ton Union Steamship liner *Tahiti*, outward bound for San Francisco, came pounding down the Harbour, set to pass the much smaller boat on the ferry's port side. But, instead of overtaking, she sliced right through the *Greycliffe* amidships, so that the two halves of the ferry foundered on either side of the liner's bows. A subsequent board of inquiry, which heard conflicting evidence about the relative speed of the two vessels, concluded that the *Tahiti* was at fault for not keeping out of *Greycliffe*'s way as the Rule of the Road at Sea required: but when Sydney Ferries later sued the Union Steamship Company, another judge found *Greycliffe*'s captain mostly to blame for making 'an unexpected and unnecessary turn'[6] which had cost forty-two people their lives.

Yet tragedy is the last thing that comes to mind when you stand on Circular Quay and watch the activity there as the ferries arrive and depart, with bells ringing to warn would-be passengers that they must now hurry up and get on board, and horns announcing that the ropes are being cast off, or when, one glorious summer's day, just as the sun is rising like a molten disc beyond the Heads, you glance out of your apartment and see the gleaming tranquillity of the Harbour disturbed as the first green-and-cream vessels come butting in line ahead towards the Bridge and the Quay from their depot on Mort Bay, where they have spent the night; or when, loafing amid the modest upholstery of *Lady Street*'s upper lounge, you watch the Opera House, the Bridge, Pinchgut and the rest of this marvellous display slip by. For the Sydney ferries are essentially genial as well as purposeful in their comings and goings, jaunty craft that give you a small lump in the throat when you remember them and their setting from twelve thousand miles away. Lucky the businessman who goes to the office this way, smartly turned out in immaculate shirt and tie, above a pair of freshly laundered and sharply pressed short pants, with enough long stockings on his legs to expose just a healthily sunburned pair of knees. Occasionally, just such a character is still to be seen, though he is no longer the commonplace of thirty or forty years ago.

It is, or at least it ought to be, a matter of astonishment that James Cook did not recommend this haven to London, but nominated instead Botany Bay, about nine nautical miles further down the coast. He was, after all, not only the greatest navigator of all time and one of the greatest seamen, but possessed of enormous curiosity, interested in everything that crossed his horizon, from icebergs to bird life, from the behaviour of native peoples to the nature of coral: and although it was the Admiralty which had instructed him to find something that would prevent scurvy from decimating a ship's company, as it often did, it was Cook who carefully experimented with various vegetables and liquids until he came up with the right formula of lemon juice, sauerkraut, malt, carrot marmalade and similar substances, to be taken regularly instead of an unvarying diet of salt beef, salt pork, dried pease and ship's biscuit infested with weevils. The Admiralty instructions were, of course, chiefly to observe the Transit of Venus from mid-Pacific (where the night skies were almost guaranteed to be clearer than over the Thames),* for astro-navigational purposes, but, after that, the first priority was to discover *terra australis incognita*, the Unknown Southern Land of maritime fable. The principal reason for this was not to find somewhere on the other side of the world where convicts might be imprisoned—not until the American colonies rebelled five years after Cook's great voyage, and refused to accept the dregs of British society any longer, did it become necessary to establish penal settlements elsewhere—but to see if such a country might be useful in a global strategy which always had one eye warily cocked for the equally aggressive French, and the other sparkling with greed at the prospect of an oriental trade that might be wrested from the similarly acquisitive Dutch. The East India Company was doing business with China and India, and there was no telling what additional benefits might accrue from a foothold in *terra australis*, if such a place really existed.

HMS *Endeavour* sailed into Botany Bay on the last Sunday in April 1770, and a couple of days later her crew buried Forby Sutherland, one of their number who had died in the night. The vessel stayed in the bay for a week, by which time Cook had concluded that 'it is Capacious, safe and commodious'[7] with a number of other attributes that commended it to him. One of these was the great quantity of fish in the Bay, which very nearly caused him to name it Stingray's Harbour, after the *Endeavour*'s yawl had landed a pair which weighed nearly 600 lb. That it acquired the

---

*The Royal Society, which sponsored the scientific research on Cook's voyage, had also arranged for observations of the Transit to be made on Hudson Bay and above the North Cape of Norway.

name by which it has been known ever since was largely because the two scientists who sailed with Cook—the dilettante Fellow of the Royal Society Joseph Banks and the Swedish botanist David Carl Solander—were highly enthusiastic (and over-optimistic, as it turned out) about the natural history they studied ashore, especially the local flora. 'Our collection of Plants was now grown so immensely large', wrote Banks, 'that it was necessary that some extraordinary care should be taken of them.... Dr Solander and myself were employed the whole day in collecting specimens of as many things as we possibly could, to be examined at sea.'[8]

On 6 May *Endeavour* weighed anchor and sailed north until 'at Noon we were by observation in the Latitude of 33° 50′ S about 2 or 3 Miles from the land and abreast of a Bay or Harbour wherein there appeared to be safe anchorage which I called Port Jackson...'.[9] Then Cook sailed on in a light southerly breeze, without even attempting to pass between the Heads, an uncharacteristic puzzle about a man whose great successes occurred largely because he meticulously checked everything.

And so it was left to Arthur Phillip to discover properly one of the greatest natural harbours on earth. Phillip was a semi-retired naval captain of forty-eight when he received the most important commission of his life, living as a gentleman farmer in the New Forest of Hampshire, with an unhappy marriage over and done with by then and not a great deal ahead of him in job prospects. He was the son of a German language teacher from Frankfurt who had married a naval widow, and he went to sea at the age of sixteen, was promoted lieutenant within three years, but was making so little headway in the Royal Navy by his mid-thirties that he was given permission to join the Portuguese fleet as a mercenary in a war against Spain. Five years later he was back in command of a British ship, but his career never managed to escape the doldrums for long until a crisis in the penal system, occasioned by the American reverse and the consequent overcrowding of prison hulks in London and other seaports, caused a Parliamentary committee to seek an alternative dumping ground to the plantations of Virginia. Joseph Banks—by now celebrated for his labours with Cook, President of the Royal Society and soon to be Sir Joseph—appeared before the Honourable Members, and vouched for the suitability of Botany Bay as a penal colony. Arthur Phillip doubtless got the job of establishing it because someone in the Admiralty noted that, during his mercenary period, he had once shipped 400 Portuguese convicts across the Atlantic to Brazil without losing a single one.

The first British prisoners to be transported to Australia—736 of them, mostly Londoners—could have been even more unfortunate than they were had someone else been in charge, for Phillip was as sympathetic as anyone from his station in life at the time could be expected to be: this may be no great commendation, but much more vicious men than he were let loose on the convicts, and some of them sailed in the First Fleet. Phillip, in fact, had an unusually imaginative vision of the colony's future, believing that at least some of his charges were capable of reformation and therefore of participating in a free antipodean society at some stage. 'As I would not wish convicts to lay the foundations of an empire,' he wrote, 'I think they should remain separated from the garrison and other settlers that may come from Europe, and not allowed to mix with them, even after the 7 or 14 years for which they are transported may be expired. The laws of this country will, of course, be introduced in New South Wales, and there is one that I wish to take place from the moment his Majesty's forces take possession of the country: that there can be no slavery in a free land, and consequently no slaves.'[10] The old lags were, in short, to remain an underclass of helots for the rest of their lives: but some of the people who had sent them to the other side of the world, as well as some of their captors there, would have been much happier had their only future been to rot in chains.

The voyage of the First Fleet took as long as it did—eight months and a week, or six months' sailing time—because it travelled by way of Rio de Janeiro and the Cape of Good Hope in order to revictual and replenish the water butts, as well as to repair some of the vessels, which were not in prime condition even at the outset of the journey: but before the eighteenth century was finished, the direct passage from England had been made in three months and fifteen days. Phillip's flagship *Sirius* dropped anchor in Botany Bay on 18 January 1788 but very soon the Governor had decided that this was not the place for them: he made a careful examination of the bay,

> from which it appeared that, though extensive, it did not afford shelter from the easterly winds: and that, in consequence of its shallowness, ships even of a moderate draught would always be obliged to anchor with the entrance of the bay open, where they must be exposed to a heavy sea that rolls in whenever it blows hard from the eastward. Several runs of fresh water were found in different parts of the bay, but there did not appear to be any situation to which there was not some very strong objection. In the northern part of it is a small creek, which runs a considerable way into the country, but it has water only for a boat, the sides of it are frequently overflowed, and the low lands near it are a perfect swamp. The western branch of the bay is continued to a great extent, but the officers sent to examine it could not find there any supply of fresh water, except in very small drains ... no place was discovered in the whole circuit of Botany Bay which seemed at all calculated for the reception of so large a settlement.[11]

Something better awaited him just up the coast and inside the Heads. 'Here all regret arising from the former disappointments was at once obliterated. ... The different coves of this harbour were examined with all possible expedition, and the preference was given to one which had the finest spring of water, and in which ships can anchor so close to the shore, that at a very small expence quays may be constructed at which the largest vessels may unload.'[12] On this premise was Sydney founded, and, as soon as the rest of the convoy had come up from Botany Bay, the business of settlement in *terra australis* began. King George III and his ministers, in fact, had been calling it New South Wales ever since Cook annexed the entire eastern seaboard under that name—which he chose for no clear reason that even his most distinguished biographer, the late and great J. C. Beaglehole, ever managed to work out.

We have an excellent eyewitness account of the first few years in the new colony, because Arthur Phillip's Judge-Advocate, David Collins—a captain of Marines by trade, without legal training—was clearly fascinated by his new surroundings and everything that went on in it, had a fine eye for detail and wrote very decent prose. He tells us a great deal about the treatment of the convicts (and we shall return to that topic later) in an almost daily record of what generally happened in and around Sydney Cove. It is through Collins that we know precisely what livestock and vegetation were packed into the First Fleet, so that the colonists might take the first steps towards self-sufficiency: one bull, one bull-calf, seven cows, one stallion, three mares, three colts, 'together with as great a number of rams, ewes, goats, boars and breeding sows as room could be provided for.... Coffee, both seed and plant; cocoa, in the nut; cotton, seed; banana, plant; oranges, various sorts, both seed and plant; lemon, seed and plant; guava, seed; tamarind; prickly pear, plant with the cochineal on it.... The fig tree; bamboo; Spanish reed; sugar cane; vines of various sorts; quince; apple; pear; strawberry; oak; myrtle.'[13] The animals were acquired from the Dutch colony at the Cape, which also provided some of the plants, to supplement what had already been procured in South America. The new settlement's other great necessity, fresh water, turned out not to be as freely available as Phillip had at first supposed, 'only a drain from a swamp at the head of it',[14] where Hyde Park would one day be laid out. It was therefore decreed that no trees should be felled within fifty feet of the Tank Stream, in order to protect it from the sun and prevent vaporisation.

For this place was hotter than any of its new inhabitants could ever have experienced before leaving Europe, with shade temperatures often in the eighties for days at a time, rising at least once to 105°; whereupon the settlers had their first experience of bush fires, which have periodically threatened Sydney ever since. There was also the slight shock of an earthquake in the first six months, lasting only a few seconds but accompanied by a noise like a cannon firing somewhere in the south. The strangeness of everything most certainly included the aboriginal natives, who were clearly uneasy at the arrival of so many aliens but seemed at first to be biding their time in the hope, perhaps, that the newcomers would go away again, as Cook's expedition had quickly departed the last time the white man came visiting. The local fauna captivated David Collins with their novelty, though he may already have been familiar with the sperm whale that surfaced in the anchorage and was unsuccessfully hunted by boats with harpoons: until 'a few days afterwards a punt belonging to one of the officers was pursued by a whale and overset; by which accident a midshipman of the *Sirius* and two soldiers were unfortunately drowned'.[15] But the Judge-Advocate had never in his life seen anything like the wombat before, and spent several hundred words describing the marsupial comprehensively and with commendable accuracy—'a squat, thick, short-legged and rather inactive quadruped, with great appearance of stumpy strength, and somewhat bigger than a turnspit dog. . . .' [16] He was also enchanted by the kangaroo, 'a small bird of beautiful plumage' and the emu, though not enough to deplore the fact that, like the kangaroo, it was regarded as fair game 'and the flesh was very well flavoured'. [17]

Through his eyes we can watch Sydney begin to take shape as a segregated community (a home from Home, in fact), an encampment under canvas for a start, with the officials on the east side of the Tank Stream, the convicts and Marines on the west. The convicts did the donkey work—some of it highly skilled carpentry—in putting up the first buildings around the cove. Bricks were made in a clearing about a mile away and timber from the cabbage tree was hauled from lower down the Harbour, perfectly good material

for making temporary huts, less useful for anything permanent because it tended to rot in a local version of the monsoon, which
broke not long after the First Fleet arrived; likewise the grass of
the gum-rush, which was utilised for thatch. There was good
building stone in the vicinity but no limestone to make mortar, so
that stone and brick alike had to be bonded with clay, which too
easily washed away in the rain: not until an aboriginal midden of
seashells was discovered and pulverised to yield lime did matters
improve. Dwellings were obviously the first requirement and this
meant tents or huts for the Marines and the convicts, cottages for
the officers. Arthur Phillip had brought his own domicile with
him, a prefabricated canvas house which had cost £125 but was neither rain nor sun-proof, also ten thousand bricks and window
glass, to construct something more substantial. This soon went
up, and for the next twenty years Government House was the only
two-storeyed building in the colony, containing the only staircase.
It had its own windmill, and eventually the landscape around Sydney Cove would be dotted with these appliances. One other building appeared quite quickly, given the construction difficulties. The
Board of Longitude in London had provided a complete set of
the most up-to-date scientific instruments because a comet was
scheduled to appear in 1789, and so an observatory was built on a
little hill, where its nineteenth-century successor still stands today,
hemmed in by traffic at an approach to the Harbour Bridge. All
else had to wait until other priorities had been attended to, though
some semblance of normality was maintained in even the most
trying circumstances. Eighteen months after their landfall, 'in a
little hut fitted up for the occasion',[18] a group of convicts put on
the first theatrical performance in Australian history, a spirited
rendering of Farquhar's comedy *The Recruiting Officer*, to celebrate
King George's birthday.

Difficulties were plentiful during the five years of Arthur
Phillip's governorship, and there were times when the colonists
faced starvation *en masse*. To everyone's consternation, the first

breeding cycle of the livestock produced far more males than fe-
males, and many of the animals were lost to pilfering Aborigines,
struck by lightning or savaged by dingoes. Much of the seed
brought from Rio and the Cape had rotted on the way to New
South Wales, and that which had survived frequently failed when
planted in soil that was sometimes too wet, often too dry, but
seemed rarely conducive to thriving agriculture. The stores that
had travelled from England steadily went down and strict rationing was imposed, which Phillip shared with everybody else.
One of his officers had a breakdown which caused him to row
round the harbour for a couple of days, and he was eventually sent
home, as mentally unstable. A surgeon described the plight at Sydney Cove in his diary one day.

> It is now so long since we have heard from home that our clothes are
> worn threadbare. We begin to think the mother country has forsaken
> us. . . . In this deplorable situation famine is staring us in the face.
> Two ounces of pork is the allowance of animal food for four and
> twenty hours, and happy is the man who can kill a rat or a crow to
> make him a dainty meal. We have raised some excellent vegetables
> but such food does not supply strength, but keeps us lax and weakly.
> I dined most heartily the other day on a fine dog, and hope I shall
> again have an invitation to a similar repast. The animals that were
> meant to stock the country are almost all butchered.[19]

Only six months after the landfall, HMS *Supply* was sent in desperation to Lord Howe Island, four hundred miles to the east, in
the hope of bringing back turtles, which were rumoured to breed
there in quantity, but they had evidently gone elsewhere and *Supply*
returned with nothing. HMS *Sirius* then embarked on an epic voyage to buy food from the Dutchmen at the Cape, effectively cir-
cumnavigating the globe by sailing eastabout all the way, and
returning seven months later with enough provisions to keep
everyone fed until the autumn of 1789. After that, famine stared
them in the face again and, as Geoffrey Blainey has suggested,

rebellion and bloodshed or a systematic retreat from the colony could not have been far away when a leaky old tub, *Lady Juliana,* which had lost some of her cargo overboard in a storm, sailed through the Heads on 3 June 1790 and brought sustenance as well as the first news from England that anyone in Port Jackson had had since leaving home; also more mouths to feed, because she carried two hundred female convicts as well. By the end of that month, four more vessels had arrived, and the crisis was over, even though a large part of the Second Fleet's cargo consisted of yet more convicts, whose voyage from Portsmouth 'turned out to be the worst in the whole history of penal transportation'[20]: a quarter of the thousand or so prisoners who began the journey never completed it. And although enough stores were landed to tide the colony over until its first really successful harvest, the population was almost doubled in those few days.

By this time Arthur Phillip was worn out with his endeavours in establishing the settlement, and with the perpetual anxiety about its chances of survival. He submitted his resignation to London and sailed for home in December 1792, taking with him two Aborigines who had become attached to him, one of whom he had forgiven for attacking him on their first acquaintance. Various botanical and other specimens were also on the *Atlantic*'s manifest, including four kangaroos. What Phillip left behind, with all its penal inequities and worse, was the makings of a great city, linked by toll road to a second settlement sixteen miles further inland at Rose Hill, which later inhabitants would know by its aboriginal name of Parramatta, 'the place where eels sit down'. He had not seen the first free settlers arrive from England, but he had been instrumental in emancipating some of his prisoners, thereby taking the very first step towards transforming New South Wales from a penal colony to a more civilised society. He was an honourable man and, by the standards of the time, an extremely humane one: the only convicts to hang while he was Governor were those found guilty of theft, which was a sin against the entire community when it was starving to death and in other ways deprived. The colony, remarkably for a place whose *raison d'être* was punishment, had such a tolerable reputation during Phillip's term that seven sailors from the transport *Royal Admiral* went missing when she sailed, and didn't come out of hiding until she was well over the horizon. They were eventually deported, because no one was allowed into New South Wales without permission: but, as Marjorie Barnard remarked, 'That they should want to stay is the interesting point.'[21]

Men much crueller and more self-serving than Phillip would be in positions of authority after he had gone. His immediate successor was Major Francis Grose, the military commander, whose most notable act was to tolerate a trading monopoly enjoyed by fellow officers who were indifferent to the general economy of Port Jackson, wishing only to line their own pockets. John Hunter, another naval officer, who ran the place from 1795 to 1800, was a pleasant man but no match at all for the commissioned soldiers of the New South Wales Corps, who constantly outmanoeuvred him until he was virtually powerless and the colony was in dire straits again. Phillip King (1800–4) took on the military and succeeded in curbing some of their excesses in his efforts to stabilise the settlement, but he also promoted the appalling Major Foveaux, a sadist who was given command of the penal colony on Norfolk Island, one thousand miles offshore, whose brutal reputation soon terrified the most recalcitrant criminals. Commodore Bligh came next and, although he did his best to steer his new command in the right direction in the increasing friction between Government House and a rising class of roughneck entrepreneurs, he succeeded only in putting everybody's backs up, and retired exceedingly hurt. Not until Lachlan Macquarie arrived in 1809 did light begin to appear at the end of the tunnel. Humourless and vain, with a dislike of delegating his powers and a mania for installing clocks in all public buildings in order to encourage punctuality in the workforce, he was nevertheless a decent and thoughtful man who genuinely believed that the reformed convict should be readmitted to society, that even while serving his sentence he might conceivably be allowed to participate in its development. Macquarie had a vision of what might ideally be on this other side of the world. It was he who produced Sydney's first currency, Spanish coins with a disc punched out of the middle, which created an instant circulation of two denominations. And it was he who recruited the architect Francis Greenway, who had been transported for forging a contract in 1814, to design buildings that would last and be admired; as they have lasted and are much admired in Sydney to this day—the Hyde Park Barracks and St James's Church for a start—probably the finest early architecture in the whole of the continent.

The last convicts to be transported from Europe reached Western Australia in 1868, thirty-two years after the highest annual figure for new arrivals, when four thousand were deposited in New South Wales alone; and the original colony received its last consignment in 1840. By then, Sydney was on its feet at last, with the threat of starvation no more than a memory, and the provision of durable housing for a growing population—131,000 New South Welsh by 1841—the biggest problem in sight. For this was no longer a mostly convict society: instead it also included those who had served their sentences and had been allowed to start their lives afresh, together with a growing proportion of free settlers, who in 1837 for the first time arrived in greater quantity than prisoners. Among the earliest migrants was a friend of Joseph Banks named Gregory Blaxland, who had sold up his properties in Kent to come out and farm four thousand acres in 1805, both the land and a workforce of forty convicts being granted by Governor King as soon as Blaxland's ship dropped anchor in Sydney Cove.* Thereafter, word had filtered back to Europe that a better life was possible in *terra australis*, for those

---

*Blaxland was one of the men who made the first European crossing of the Blue Mountains in 1813. See p. 6.

who had the necessary energy and health, than ever they could have achieved at home, where the opportunity for improvement was generally denied the lower orders, however dutiful and law-abiding they might be. And because the British Government soon became anxious to populate its new holding in the southern hemisphere, for the aforesaid strategic and commercial reasons, it was prepared to ferry potential settlers to the colony at its own expense when, as was more often than not the case, they simply didn't have the resources to pay their own way to Australia. Three-quarters of all of those who came freely between 1832 and 1851 did so on assisted passages.

By then, other colonies were coming to life around the edges of Australia, each with its own idiosyncratic and topographical differences from the first settlement at Port Jackson. Van Diemen's Land (which wouldn't be known as Tasmania until 1855) was first settled by Governor King as an outstation of New South Wales in 1803, and became a convict overspill from the parent colony. Yet the principal reason for breaking new ground there was to frustrate the French, who in the last four decades of the eighteenth century had sent no fewer than three 'scientific' expeditions that far south. King's vanguard followed orders by possessively running up the Union Jack and leaving forty-nine souls to get on with it, which these men managed to such good effect that Hobart for a few years was second only to Sydney in its sophistication, hailed somewhat improbably—in spite of its splendid setting beneath Mount Wellington—as 'the Athens of the Southern Ocean'.

No one was ever likely to nominate Brisbane for that title, with its sopping climate and its origins in the dreadful Moreton Bay penal colony, which was established when Thomas Brisbane was Governor of New South Wales immediately after Lachlan Macquarie. Incorrigible recidivists were first sent there in 1824, to a re-settled Norfolk Island the following year, and there was nothing to choose between these two hell-holes, either in brutality or in the sense of hopelessness they engendered among their prisoners.

Brisbane's destiny, moreover, was to be forever playing second fiddle to Sydney, smouldering with resentment at neglect and other indignities inflicted by the authorities further south, even after Queensland separated from New South Wales in 1859: and it really could have done without its principal crossing of the Brisbane River eventually being a Sydney cast-off, having been rejected from the competition to design the Harbour Bridge in 1924. The resentment palpably persists to this day, in politics and on the sports field, where nothing is more grudging (or more brutal) than State of Origin rugby league matches between the two old adversaries. To stand on the terraces at Lang Park, when that xenophobic ground was still used for big matches, and to hear the Brisbane crowd baying for New South Welsh blood was to be shocked by how deeply some sports followers can hate.

The extreme isolation of Western Australia caused it, too, to be earmarked for penal settlement in 1826, when twenty prisoners and their guards were unloaded on that barren coast. Convicts survived there for the best part of five years before being withdrawn, because it had been decided that the Swan River and its immediate hinterland had much greater potential if it were exploited differently. It had an obvious strategic value to anyone wishing to control the Indian Ocean, and it might well have a future as a re-victualling base for the East India Company, as well as an entrepôt where cargoes could be unloaded by Company vessels outward bound for China (the cargoes thus becoming a local currency for trade with much nearer tropical neighbours). In the end, the making of Perth was as a land-grant settlement, the land coming from the New South Wales Government, the funding from private investors, with the settlers having to meet strict requirements if they were not to forfeit their holdings. The first of them were landed amid sand dunes during a wet and windy winter in 1829, and the topography as much as the isolation ensured that the settlement had a long struggle ahead of it: Sydney in its first two years had more inhabitants than Perth in its twenty-first, but gradually the new outpost took shape, named after one Scottish city (the Colonial Secretary's Parliamentary constituency) and modelled on another (the 'New Town' in Edinburgh). Its future would eventually depend most of all on the prosperity of the Western Australian sheep farmer, but the strategists have maintained their interest still, at the turn of a new millennium: Fremantle is second only to Garden Island as a naval base.

The decision to settle the very coast on which Jonathan Swift cast Lemuel Gulliver into the kingdom of Lilliput also assumed that from the start its population would be relatively law-abiding. South Australia's origins have been seen in the social upheaval which followed the passage of the British Reform Bill in 1832, in the aspirations of Jeremy Bentham and his followers for a new order based on free trade, religious tolerance, workers' rights, an end to nepotism, and various other ideals; and in the eagerness of many to make a fresh start in some place that had not been contaminated by its past. The National Colonisation Society and the South Australian Land Company were two manifestations of these urges, followed the year after the Reform Act by the South Australian Association, which was formed in the wake of Captain Charles Sturt's explorations along the course of the Murray River, and his report that this was a bountiful land. As a result, fifteen ships full of migrants arrived in the second half of 1836, to find the association's Surveyor-General, Colonel William Light, almost single-handedly plotting the grid pattern of streets that would become Adelaide (named after William IV's wife, some old habits being quite unreformed). And the city prospered from the start, its wealth deriving from its fertile surroundings which, by 1850, had become the granary for the whole of Australia.

Gracious is the word that most naturally comes to mind nowadays as you walk Adelaide's spacious thoroughfares, in which no building has yet been allowed to dominate the rest, unlike some places that we all know and usually deplore. It has a certain faint hauteur, and it does not feel as if it could be even distantly connected with the manufacture of something as, well, as *common* as the motor-car.* Instead, as you contemplate handsome King William Street, with its grassy strip running down the middle, accommodating flagpoles and their bunting at short intervals, there is a more than faint suggestion of a European spa, an antipodean Montpellier, perhaps, or a Baden-Baden under Capricorn. There is also the leisurely flow of the Torrens River, where pelicans glide above the supple backs of the coxless pairs; and the view across Pennington Gardens to the Cathedral from the Bradman Stand in Adelaide Oval which, as anyone knowledgeable in such matters will confirm, is indeed the loveliest prospect from any major cricket ground on earth.

Canberra, of course, is a creation of the twentieth century, chosen as the site of national government after the federation of the states in 1900, when Australia as we know it today was born;† but beyond that it is entirely the result of a long-standing tetchiness between Sydney and Melbourne. So intense has this been since Victoria separated from New South Wales in 1850 that the first decade of this century was spent in a fierce running argument over the location of the federal capital, to the exclusion of almost every other topic in Australia. An early suggestion that an independent district (as in the case of Washington DC) should be set up was rejected by Sydney on the grounds that an Australian Parliament must obviously be located in the country's senior city; whereupon Melbourne cheekily nominated its own suburb of St Kilda. A compromise began to emerge when Sydney extracted an undertaking from the other states that the capital should be situated somewhere in New South Wales, which was promptly modified to meet Melbourne's

---

*Australia's own Holden took its name from that of an Adelaide firm which started by making saddles and worked its way round to producing car bodies. But the main Holden plant has always been in Melbourne.

†New Holland, the name Dutch navigators had given to Australia's western coast in the seventeenth century, was officially used for the land mass as a whole until Governor Macquarie in 1817 asked London's permission to call it Australia instead.

demand that this should not be within 100 miles of its rival: the Victorian capital was also to be the temporary home of the Australian Parliament until a federal base was established. The arguments didn't end there, however. Disputes followed about where in New South Wales the new federal district should be. Sydney favoured Bathurst, almost exactly a hundred miles away and (more to the point) four times as far from Melbourne, but a dozen other places had their supporters. One of them was Dalgety, high in the Snowy Mountains, backed by a member of Parliament who claimed that 'cold climates have produced the greatest geniuses'.[22] This did not commend itself to either Sydney or Melbourne, and so a final compromise was reached in the choice of Canberra, then no more than a scattering of small settlements along the Molongo River, 177 miles from Australia's oldest city—and four hundred miles from Melbourne.

Like Adelaide, Melbourne is proud to think that it started life without penal associations, which rather overlooks the fact that the first two ships to arrive at the bay of Port Phillip in 1803 carried nearly three hundred convicts, who were only transported elsewhere after less than a month because conditions were deemed unsuitable; and that some 150 convicts were brought in permanently from New South Wales to do some hard manual labour for the Government a few years after a lasting settlement had been started at the head of the bay, beside some falls in the River Yarra. This was given the name of a British Prime Minister who was in and out of office so frequently that sometimes he couldn't have known whether he was coming or going. The idea of a settlement here was yet another instance of paranoia about the French, but Melbourne's proper beginnings followed from a treaty that the squatter John Batman had made (off his own bat, so to speak) with the local Aborigines in 1835 when, seeking more pasture for himself and some friends who also raised sheep, he crossed the Bass Strait from Van Diemen's Land and bought 600,000 acres in exchange for an annual disbursement of one hundred blankets, fifty knives, fifty tomahawks, two tons of flour and some trade goods, the lot being worth £200 a year.

With such a start in life, it is scarcely surprising that Melbourne swiftly acquired a reputation for being the most businesslike city in Australia, a solid place with very sharp commercial instincts, quite often more enterprising than its flamboyant neighbour. Within three years of its beginning, four banks had opened there and foursquare bluestone buildings were going up everywhere in the spirit of free enterprise: twelve months later the first ship sailed for England directly from Port Phillip, without bothering to call at Port Jackson on the way. Incorporated as a city responsible for its own affairs in 1842, the same year as Sydney (which had half a century's start), Melbourne shortly afterwards drafted a Building Act that took account of local needs and conditions, instead of simply imitating the custom of London: and in that same year its citizens were treated to a public lecture on architecture, which had never yet happened in the older community. Sydney's educational first was the more important, though, its university opening its doors twelve months before Melbourne's students were able to enrol in 1853. Australia's first train ran from Melbourne to its port, a year before Sydney acquired a railway of its own in 1855, and its town hall opened at the junction of Collins and Swanston Streets, twenty-one years before Sydney completed its own civic centre at the top end of George. And then there was the matter of the international exhibitions, in 1879–80. Sydney built a timber and glass pavilion on five acres of the Botanic Gardens, to show off the expertise of the world to its citizens and to attract overseas businessmen, and it included Australia's first mechanical lift, an American contraption which finished up in Toohey's Brewery. The exhibition was an unprecedented and unsurpassable show of High Victorian endeavour, as everyone agreed until Melbourne soon afterwards built an even bigger pavilion for its own display, which was also a tremendous success; and in due course Melbourne was able to claim that it, and not Sydney, had installed Australia's first electric elevator. So the competition and the pique developed, exacerbated by the gold rushes that had followed one another in mid-century, from which Victoria enjoyed much greater prosperity than New South Wales; so that Melbourne, long patronised by the other place, rapidly overhauled Sydney as the country's biggest city, which it remained for the next fifty years.

A consequence of this nitpicking tradition is that it is impossible for an outsider to contemplate either city without consciously comparing it with the other; and maybe only the citizens of Glasgow and Edinburgh can comprehend the subtle ramifications of the municipal feud that still quietly smoulders on the other side of the world. You therefore notice very quickly that more of Melbourne's main thoroughfares are better off for trees than Sydney's; that Flinders Street Station with its thirteen clocks is a class act which makes Sydney Central look tacky, but that Sydney Town Hall makes Melbourne's version look dingy; that Larry Latrobe, a small brass dog with a pig's head set into the pavement on Swanston Street, is clearly Melbourne's waggish response to Il Porcellino, a bronze boar outside Sydney Hospital on Macquarie (which was faithfully copied from a seventeenth-century original in Florence); and that both cities exasperatingly and repeatedly run out of maps that would help you make the best use of their public transport. Sydney dispensed with its trams in 1961, though it is probably beginning to wish it hadn't, but would die rather than admit envy of Melbourne, which notoriously has held on to its own fleet: and very appealing as well as useful the Melbourne trams are, though this isn't the most obvious thing about them if you find yourself driving in fits and starts behind the one that lumbers for miles into town from the end of the line in Coburg.

The two places have much in common, not least in their resemblance to American cities when seen from some distance. It's the clump of downtown skyscrapers that does it in both cases, Melbourne's when observed from the sweeping curve of the West Gate Bridge, Sydney's from the front lawn of the University. But there is one feature by which Sydney so far outstrips the old enemy that in this respect there is no contest. Instead of a glorious harbour, Melbourne has an almost featureless bay, with weed drifting to and fro amid the ripples at St Kilda Beach, until the black Jetcat goes thundering over the horizon to Hobart, eight hours away at some speed, setting up a wake that eventually breaks powerfully along the Victorian shore. So Melbournians make the best of their Yarra, which the citizens have lately rediscovered in much the same way that Glaswegians have rediscovered the Clyde. There is now a lively waterside café life, with *bateaux mouches* plying their trade so that you can imagine yourself beside the Seine— until a gondola comes downstream with a couple sitting romantically on its bench, and a boatman in a straw hat poling them along, whereupon you are transported to someplace else. But this isn't at all the same as sipping a Chardonnay with a plate of rock oysters just round the corner from the Opera House, while the ferries come steaming past on their way into and out of Circular Quay.

Many writers have tried to describe Sydney's great and defining asset, have wanted to say what it is about the Harbour that captivates us from that first glimpse and holds us forever in its thrall; and probably not one of us has been satisfied with what we've said. Anthony Trollope came as near as possible to getting it right when he wrote, 'I despair of being able to convey to any reader my own idea of the beauty of Sydney Harbour. I have seen nothing equal to it in the way of land-locked sea scenery, nothing second to it.... It is so inexpressibly lovely that it makes a man ask himself whether it would not be worth his while to move his household goods to the eastern coast of Australia, in order that he might look at it as long as he can look at anything.'[23]

Trollope wrote that something over one hundred years ago, and I know exactly how he felt. Much has changed in the years between, but not that instant recognition of inexpressible loveliness which man, astonishingly, has not yet destroyed.

CHAPTER TWO

In the Beginning . . .

T his is not the way they look at things in Eveleigh Street,
where stories of European settlement are dismissed with irritation or disdain, and the rivalry between Sydney and Melbourne
is regarded as an irrelevance. Eveleigh Street lies in the middle
of Redfern, which, once upon a time, when Sydney was beginning
to spread its wings not far into the nineteenth century, was an
outskirt of the city where its newly landed gentry were settling
down, including William Redfern, one of the noblest figures ever
to reach Australia, either in chains or as a freeman. He was a naval
surgeon who had been transported (and was lucky not to have
been hanged from the yardarm) for merely exhorting the muti-
neers at the Nore to stick together in their demands for better pay
and conditions, but after serving no more than two years of his
colonial sentence he was pardoned, was put in charge of the Sydney Rum Hospital, and became Governor Macquarie's family doctor. Because of his efforts to reform all aspects of his profession,
he has been seen as the father of Australian medicine, who ran a
special clinic where he took care of convict ailments as tenderly as
those of everybody else.

Gradually, as the city expanded, the well-to-do forsook this part of town and moved further out, the district's own future being settled in 1855, when Sydney's first railway ran from there to Parramatta, and railway workshops were among the first of many industries that became established near the street where Dr Redfern had lived. It remained the city terminus until Sydney Central was opened in 1906, an increasingly plebeian area with lots of boarding houses (but enough affluence within reach, ten years earlier, to justify many hansom cabs awaiting passengers, according to Arthur Streeton's painting of Redfern Station).* Inevitably, a working class moved in as labouring and artisan jobs appeared, and life became a bit of a struggle for its new inhabitants, as it has remained ever since. Seventy-five years after the coming of the train, Redfern was one of Sydney's most notorious slums (we refer to it evasively as an inner-city area now), in which Lebanese and Greek and Italian immigrants had at various times tried their luck: there was a Maronite and an Antioch Orthodox Church there as early as 1900. Thomas Keneally caught part of the local flavour in a novel he wrote about a post-war migrant family, and a rugby league footballer who is involved with their daughter:

> There was always ferocity in the air at Redfern. They called this team the Rabbitohs, after the Depression days when the unemployed of South Sydney used to hunt rabbits in that low country of sand dunes and sell them from door to door. Half the crowd seemed to have the toughness of Depression survivors, old men with the shadows of a hard life on their faces, old women who knew their football backwards and wore green and red beanies on their heads. And then, lots of dangerous kids, the kind you saw rioting on English football fields in the evening news. It was exactly the sort of fierce crowd Delaney welcomed that Sunday.... As he ran onto Redfern Oval, down the wire-caged walk placed to prevent the crones of South Sydney

---

*Redfern Station (1893), Art Gallery of New South Wales.

from attacking players or referees, his jaw was retracted, his teeth slightly parted, his mouthguard tight in his fist.[1]

Off the football field, the ferocity is usually suppressed, but something intimidating is certainly in the air as you emerge from Redfern Station to find a couple of drunks watching you blearily from a bench, and are then accosted by a girl who demands money with the menacingly urgent manner of someone who probably needs a fix. On the brickwork of the railway bridge, amid a swirl of distinctively indigenous patterns, someone has painstakingly painted a heartfelt solemnity: '40,000 years is a long, long time. 40,000 years is still on my mind.' This is not graffiti, as we have come to understand the word, a graphic way of rejecting society and saying Up Yours. It is the art of protest, and an infinite sadness lies at its core.

Being a little uncertain of your bearings, you approach a police van which happens to be parked nearby, and politely ask the two constables inside the whereabouts of a certain address. 'What are you going there for?' asks one of them coldly; and doesn't warm up much even when you have satisfied him that your intentions are not nefarious. 'It's down there,' he says, 'where those Abos are.' He nods in the direction of some youths who are throwing a basketball about amid a detritus of broken bottles and squashed tin cans, with two rows of decaying terraces sloping beyond them, further down from the station road. Discarded furniture and other sorts of garbage lie in front of some houses, and people lean against doorways, whose paintwork peeled so long ago that the occupants either can't afford to fix things or have simply given up. The place carries the odour as well as the marks of decay, and in this it has something in common with the stews of Calcutta or Bombay. But this is Australia and here is Eveleigh Street.

It is part of the Block, together with the neighbouring Vine, Louis and Caroline Streets, which are noted for several things apart from the general decay of the properties. Here is a ghetto of mostly aboriginal Australians, one of two areas in the Sydney region where they are chiefly congregated nowadays: the other is at La Pérouse, a settlement just inside the northern arm of Botany Bay, which was founded in the 1880s and which, within fifty years, had become a tourist attraction where 'the blacks are always ready to entertain visitors by Boomerang throwing, and they sell some cleverly made shell work in imitation of flowers'.[2] At least the people there have a beach to enjoy, and bush-clad dunes by the entrance to their bay. At Eveleigh Street, the dunes Keneally mentions are much too far away to reach on foot and there is not so much as a sniff of the sea: instead there is noise, as the double-decker trains go rushing past, between Central and distant destinations like Campbelltown, Cronulla and all stations to Wollongong; and there is the claustrophobia that comes from being hemmed in by factories, warehouses and other buildings that have seen much better days. This is not what the aboriginal natives of this land were ever accustomed to until recently, which means only the tiniest speck of time in the long memory of their past. That cry for help on the railway bridge tells how long it is.

The figure of forty thousand can obviously be no more than a matter of informed guesswork at best, and at least one expert has concluded that 'The timespan is more likely to be at least 75,000 years, perhaps much longer.'[3] At such distances, bearing in mind that white settlement is only a little over two hundred years old, it is of no more than academic interest where the Aborigines originated, though it is accepted that in some unimaginably remote age they arrived in Australia by sea: they have variously been linked with the Munda tribespeople of India, the Veddahs of Sri Lanka and the Ainu of Japan, the final stages of their migration conceivably being by a drift voyage through Melanesia, or from South China via Taiwan, the Celebes and New Guinea, with a final landfall somewhere in the north of Western Australia. From there they presently spread across their new continent and from that time, whenever it was, a distinctive culture took shape. Theirs was from the outset a nomadic existence, because, although the Australian landscape is everywhere very beautiful, most of it is perilously harsh for most of the time.* It was necessary for those first inhabitants always to be moving, at least with the seasons, in order to find food; and because mobility was of paramount importance they deliberately kept their tribal numbers small by various devices which included protracted initiation rites for their young men, in order to delay their breeding, and even in some cases infanticide if the presence of small children was likely to retard the whole tribe when it was engaged in a desperate search for sustenance. Sometimes the tribes fought each other in the struggle for survival, which was never less than precarious.

They developed distinctive rituals and ceremonies, some exclusive to women, some for men only, others including both; some intended to attract partners, others to produce fertility; dancing or chanting with or without musical instruments, re-enactments of myths, totemic rites which related humans to other creatures and may be described as religious. They had their doctors and their sorcerers, who were sometimes one and the same person, and who were initiated into their vocation by arcane procedures in which the creator-god Baiami 'sang' into their bodies a number of gifts and attributes which they would need in order to practise—wings with which they might fly, a crystal to give them X-ray vision, a thick cord of sinew which could be used for a number of purposes; and after that the postulant was placed under the tutelage of an experienced doctor, to receive other gifts in due course, and to meditate in seclusion. One of a trained sorcerer's functions was to bring rain in times of desperate drought, and it is said that in the Great Victoria Desert even today an aboriginal tribal doctor may be identified by a little bag attached to his beard, containing

---

*Many would say that it is seen at its most beautiful from thirty-three thousand feet above the harshest and most barren tracts of the Outback, when the late-afternoon shadows throw everything into relief and Australia seems to be a series of primevally sculpted ridges and valleys stretching away to infinity, in a unique spectrum that runs all the way from bronze to ochre under a still burning and heavenly blue sky.

objects required for rainmaking ceremonies—quartz crystal, pearlshell, australites. Among the ways of making rain, 'one is by scraping a pearlshell, mixing the powder with fresh grass, and spitting in the direction from which rain is required—all to the accompaniment of singing. The other is through a special rite in which participants wear pearlshells: this is said to attract the rain, and as a few drops fall the *gingin* (doctors) beckon it to come. There is a shower. That evening there is another ceremony, and the participants wear Wonambi snake headdresses.'[4]

The basis of everything was their concept of the Dreaming, in which:

> the past, present and future were regarded as a continuing and uninterrupted stream. Spirit children were intermediaries who brought life from out of the Dreaming, conferring this precious substance upon aboriginal people as on all natural species. The Dreaming was the source of all life, and anything which touched it was, virtually by definition, sacred. Sacredness was, therefore, a condition of living. The intermediate period between the emergence of physical life and its disappearance on death was permeated by a concern for retaining or enhancing sacredness. All initiation was a re-introduction to the sacred, and death merely another form of initiation—creating or re-creating life out of physical death. Aboriginal religion was oriented around two basic issues. One was physical survival, the other spiritual survival. The key to both was believed to rest in the Dreaming. Together, they pervaded all aspects of human living.[5]

A distinctive art emerged from this culture, though no aboriginal language has ever contained a word which translates as 'art', only expressions which indicate techniques. Each part of the country, sometimes each tribe, had its own idiosyncratic style, whether the art was painted on wood or bark or stone or skin, or whether it was carved into rock surfaces. Arnhem Land was where painting on stringy bark reached its highest development, and the same area produced the most intricate body painting of all. North of Broome, in Western Australia, human figures unlike any others were painted in caves, each outlined on a white ground, with an emphasis on the face, which generally had no mouth. Up in the Wadaman country of the Northern Territory are drawings on several rock sites which depict the mythical Lightning Brothers, one of whom has lines radiating from his head, the other boasting a penis as long as his legs. Everywhere, much of this art had mythological significance, but the experts reckon that in the south of the continent the painters and carvers more noticeably reproduced scenes from contemporary life than was the habit in the north: and so on ... Everywhere, too, the art is highly stylised, with dots and whorls and circles recurring time and again, whether the subject is an animal, a human being or some abstract shape that requires an interpreter to describe it. Implements also were fashioned and decorated in local patterns: the boomerang in New South Wales tended to be much less angular than those made in South Australia and Victoria, and whereas shields generally were elongated and slender, those made in the rainforests of North-east Queensland were much wider and without exception asymmetrical, because they were carved from the native fig trees rather than from more malleable timber.*

It has been estimated that when the British dropped anchor at Sydney Cove in 1788 there would have been about 750,000 Aborigines in Australia, divided into maybe five hundred tribes—the Adnjamatana, the Bigambul, the Djinnang, the Gunavidji, the Kanang-Worimi, the Mulluk Mulluk, the Turrbal, the Wanamara, the Wurunjerri and all the rest. In the Sydney region were several tribes, whose common denominator was the Dharuk (or Dharug)

---

*You can see some of the art in a dozen public and private Sydney galleries, as well as what purports to be art in a hundred tourist traps: and while the latter is usually crude and mass-produced rubbish, the former is no less authentic than a small gouache by a contemporary Indian artist in Udaipur, who has just produced a perfect miniature in the manner and to the scale of something painted during the Mughal period two hundred years ago. Both are simply derivative, just like neo-Gothic architecture, which also varies in quality.

language, which was spoken in different dialects as far inland as the Blue Mountains. From Sydney Cove to the sea at South Head was Eora territory, while the northern side of the anchorage, between the Lane Cove River and Middle Harbour, was the stamping ground of the warrior Camaraigal. North of Manly was the land of the Gayimai, with the Walumeda to the west of them. A line drawn from Port Jackson to Botany Bay would have crossed the Cadigal lands, with the Wangal on their landward side; and from Botany Bay down to Port Hacking a tribe of swamp dwellers could be found, the Gwiyagal.

It is still, but only just, possible to appreciate what *terra australis* looked like round here when the Aborigines had it all to themselves. To do so you need to go up the Parramatta River, where there are still small mangrove swamps in Homebush Bay and near Rydalmere, where duck and pelican, cormorant and sandpiper flourish, just as they did when they were hunted to keep aboriginal hunger at bay; or you must go some distance north of the city, where the Hawkesbury River winds down to the sea at Broken Bay, through hundreds of square miles of national park and its blessedly unexploited bush. In fact, the people lived well in this part of the country, for roots and fruits were abundant here, together with witchetty grubs which could be found in rotting tree trunks and were regarded as a great delicacy when lightly grilled (witchetty grubs are the wood-boring larvae of the longhorn beetle or two varieties of moth). Fish were plentiful as well as birds, and these were sometimes caught at night by the light of flares, on hooks made of polished shell, more usually during the day with spears. The fishermen sought their quarry from canoes made from sheets of bark which were tied at the ends and sealed with gum, and sometimes they even cooked their catches while still on board, a little mound of earth in the bottom of the boat serving as their fireplace.

They, too, were artists, who have left behind them in stone a remarkable testimony to their presence here. There are caves in the vicinity of Sydney which were decorated by aboriginal painters, and one of them has no fewer than sixty-nine pictures in the usual pigments of red, yellow, white and black, showing people, animals, weapons, which are the most common subjects in all the rock art executed in this area. But it is the rock carvings on the local Hawkesbury sandstone (which is great for the engraver, but the despair of many a Sydney gardener) that are truly sensational, both in their quality and in their extent. There are possibly two thousand of them, only half of which have been logged. The oldest are thought to have been with us for about five thousand years, and the most recent were certainly cut no more than two hundred years ago: we know this for a fact because they depict eighteenth-century sailing ships. Many were doubtless connected with initiation rites, and they were frequently carved on boulders overlooking superb views across the bush-covered land and intervening expanses of water. But they are liable to turn up almost anywhere: there is one beneath a garage at Point Piper, another in a front garden at Beacon Hill, a third in the middle of a fairway on North Bondi Golf Course.

Towards the middle of the nineteenth century, some Europeans asked an old body they knew as Queen Gooseberry, whose late husband had been chief of the Eora when the First Fleet arrived, to show them some rock carvings and explain them. 'At first she was reluctant, saying such places were forbidden ground and that she must not visit them. Later she was persuaded to take the party to several sites on the north side of Sydney Harbour. Queen Gooseberry said that she had been told by her father that "black-fellow made them long ago" and that the tribespeople kept away from the area except for special occasions, in which dances or ceremonies took place, because "too much debble walk about there".'[6]

It is not necessary to have the rock carvings explained to you in order to sense their extraordinary significance. Just ponder the engravings at your feet—the platypus, the man stepping into a canoe, the kangaroo being hit by several boomerangs, Baiami with his two wives—and feel in your bones the great and mysterious antiquity of man's first presence here. Or stand on the heights of West Head, where some of the finest carvings have been incised across a plateau of tessellated sandstone within sight of the Hawkesbury's majestic estuary, and allow a great and unsuspected paradox to dawn. For it occurs to you then that Sydney, one of the youngest cities in the world, numbers among its riches probably the greatest wealth of prehistoric art to be found in any one place on earth.

We have, alas, no detailed aboriginal description of what the natives saw when the white man came, though we know that at first they were convinced the newcomers were the returned spirits of the dead, pale because they had been drained of all life. This belief would account for the fact that the first reaction of the Aborigines was generally a mixture of fear, suspicion and curiosity with, occasionally, apparent indifference instead, which might have been a form of wait-and-see: above all, they evidently had no collective response to their visitors, whether or not these were ghostly figures, for individual natives reacted to the same event in different ways. We know very well what the Europeans made of the Aborigines from the outset because they kept journals, none more meticulously than Joseph Banks, who was one of the first two or three Englishmen to clap eyes on the native Australians. At Botany Bay, he tells us,

A small smoak arising from a very barren place directed our glasses that way and we soon saw about ten people, who on our approach left the fire and retired to a little eminence where they could conveniently see the ship; soon after this two Canoes carrying two men each landed on the beach under them, the men hauld up their boats and went to their fellows on the hill. Our boat which had been sent ahead to sound now aproachd the place and they all retird higher up the hill; we saw however that at the beach or landing place one man at least was hid among some rocks who never that we could see left that place. Our boat proceeded along shore and the Indians followed her at a distance. When she came back the officer who was in her told me that in a cove a little within the harbour they came down to the beach and invited our people to land by many signs and words which he did not at all understand; all however were armed with long pikes and a wooden weapon made something like a short scymetar. During this time a few of the Indians who had not followed the boat remaind on the rocks opposite the ship, threatning and menacing with their pikes and swords—two in particular who were painted with white, their faces seemingly only dusted over with it, their bodies painted with broad strokes drawn over their breasts and backs resembling much a soldiers cross belts, and their legs and thighs also with such like broad strokes drawn round them which imitated broad garters or bracelets.

Each of these (Banks continued) held in his hand a wooden weapon about 2½ feet long; the blades looked whitish and some thought shining insomuch that they were almost of the opinion that they were made of some kind of metal, but myself that they were no more than wood smeared over with the same white pigment with which they paint their bodies. These two seemed to talk earnestly together, at times brandishing their crooked weapons at us in token of defiance. By noon we were within the mouth of the inlet which appeared to be very good. Under the south head of it were four small canoes; in each of these was one man who held in his hand a long pole with which he struck fish, venturing with his little imbarkation almost into the surf. These people seemed to be totally engag'd in what they were about: the ship passed within a quarter of a mile of them yet they scarce lifted their eyes from their employment; I was almost inclined to think that attentive to their business and deafned by the noise of the surf they neither saw nor heard her go past them. At 1 we came to an anchor abreast of a small village consisting of about 6 or 8 houses. Soon after this an old woman followed by three children came out of the wood; she carried several pieces of stick and the children also had their little burthens; when she came to the houses 3 more younger children came out of one of them to meet her. She often looked at the ship but expressed neither surprize nor concern. Soon after this she lighted a fire and the four Canoes came in from fishing; the people landed, hauld up their boats and began to dress their dinner to all appearance totally unmoved at us, tho we were within a little more than ½ a mile of them. Of all these people we had seen so distinctly through our glasses we had not been able to observe the least sign of Cloathing: myself to the best of my judgement plainly discerned that the woman did not copy our mother Eve even in the fig leaf.[7]

Eighteen years later our principal eyewitness is the excellent David Collins, whose long contact with the Aborigines enabled him to leave behind a much more comprehensive record than any of Cook's voyagers could have done. His investigations included his discovery that the Dharuk language contained variations, in which the word for 'head' among the coastal natives was Caberra, which became Coco further inland, 'buttocks' were either Boong or Bayley, 'moon' could be Yennadah or Dilluck, and the laughing jackass (or kookaburra, a rather large kingfisher) was Gogennegine if sighted round Sydney Cove but Goconde in the lands of the Wangal and the Walumeda. Collins also noted some of the native rituals, including an initiation ceremony at which he was present, together with 'a person well qualified to make drawings of every particular circumstance that occurred'.[8] This event took place at the head of Farm Cove in 1795, when several boys 'were now to be made man' by having one of their front teeth knocked out. After a week of tribal dancing, each candidate was seized by a warrior and made to sit in an excruciatingly painful position throughout a whole night, while 'mystical rites' went on around them. Next morning 'the poor dismal looking boys' were showered in sand and dust by men who circled them on all fours, 'imitating the dogs of the country', before the same fellows acted out a pantomime of hunting the kangaroo; during all of which the boys were completely motionless. Other mimicry followed before the climax was reached, when each boy (and one of them was only eight or nine years old, according to Collins) had the gum above one of his front teeth pierced by a sharp bone, after which a pointed stick was used as a lever in the wound so that the tooth could be loosened enough for it to be knocked out of the jaw with a stone. 'During the whole of the operation, the assistants made the most hideous noise in the ears of the patients, sufficient to distract their attention and to drown any cries they could possibly have uttered; but they made it a point of honour to bear the pain without a murmur.' The little lad who is undergoing this process in one of the engravings published with Collins's text, does not look as if he is enjoying his introduction to manhood very much.

Arthur Phillip himself was as observant as anyone and his intentions towards the Aborigines were unexceptionable. His instructions from London, indeed, had included the following charge: 'You are to endeavour by every possible means to open an intercourse with the natives, and to conciliate their affections, enjoining all our subjects to live in amity and kindness with them. And if any of our subjects shall wantonly destroy them, or give them any unnecessary interruption in the exercise of their several occupations, it is our will and pleasure that you do cause such offenders to be brought to punishment according to the degree of the offence.'9 This was a needless injunction, given Phillip's temperament, which was shown at its best in his dealings with the native whose name is commemorated in the point of land on which Sydney Opera House now stands.

By the standards of our own more knowing and more censorious age, Phillip's actions may be seen as, at best, well meaning but wrong-headed. At the end of the eighteenth century, they were as innocently sympathetic as anything Rousseau had lately pronounced about the noble savage. Phillip was so determined to have some form of collaboration with the native Australians that, when they were slow in coming forward voluntarily, he ordered the capture of an Aborigine, who would be trained to act as an interpreter between his own people and the Europeans. The first attempt to achieve this was disastrous, because the young native died of smallpox within six months. Then two others were secured (the First Lieutenant of HMS *Sirius,* who carried out the operation, described it as 'the most unpleasant task I was ever ordered to execute'),[10] and, although one of them escaped shortly afterwards, the other was to spend the rest of his life as a cultural go-between.

He was Bennelong, a twenty-six-year-old Cadigal when he was captured, with half a thumb missing and other scars acquired in combat, probably with the Camaraigal, who were the Cadigal's sworn enemies. He was treated royally by Governor Phillip and his staff from the outset, rapidly developed a taste for European food and drink (preferring, on the whole, wine to spirits), sometimes stayed the night after dinner at Government House, and eventually persuaded his new masters to build him a brick hut on the tip of land that David Collins promptly dubbed Bennelong Point. For his part, Bennelong introduced his patron to the corroboree and a number of other aboriginal customs, demonstrated some aboriginal skills (he could throw a spear almost a hundred yards against a strong wind) and taught the Governor some rudimentary Dharuk, including Beenena (father) and Doorow (son), which were the words they applied to each other. His relationship with Phillip was obviously one of mutual self-interest, and it was so far developed by 1792 that, when the Governor sailed for home, he took Bennelong with him. In London the young man met George III, but almost nothing else is known about his time there before he returned to Australia in 1795. There, again, he lapsed into semiobscurity until he died in 1813 at the age of forty-nine. His obituary in the *Sydney Gazette* was not generous: 'Of this veteran champion of the native tribe, little favourable can be said.... His propensity to drunkenness was inordinate; and when in that state he was insolent, menacing and overbearing. In fact, he was a thorough savage, not to be warped from the form and character that nature gave him by all the efforts that mankind could use.'[11]

The conciliatory approach of the first settlement was on its way out by then. Arthur Phillip had invariably blamed his own people, sometimes unjustly, when things went wrong between them and the natives; when he was wounded by an aboriginal spear, he forgave the man who threw it and within a week arranged a reconciliation beach party on the north shore, at which presents were given to the Aborigines, Bennelong collecting a hatchet and a fish. Later Governors attempted the same policies, none more assiduously than Lachlan Macquarie, who in 1810 promulgated an order that 'The natives of the territory are to be treated in every respect as Europeans; and any injury or violence done or offered to the men and women natives will be punished according to law in the same manner and in equal degree as if done to any of His Majesty's subjects or foreigners residing here....'[12] By then, this view was not much applauded outside official circles, where the military, the convicts, the ex-convicts and the free settlers on the whole preferred to see Aborigines kept firmly in their place at the bottom of the pile. One such man was Thomas Watling, a native of Dumfries, who had been transported for forging notes on the Bank of Scotland and whose skills were turned to better use in drawing some of the earliest pictures we have of life around Sydney Cove. Bitterly he noted that 'Our governors, for they are all such, have carried philosophy, I do not say religion, to such a pitch of refinement as is surprising. Many of these savages are allowed what is termed a freeman's ratio of provision for their idleness . . . and they are treated with the most singular tenderness. . . . Irascibility, ferocity, cunning, treachery, revenge, filth and immodesty are strikingly their dark characteristics—their virtues are so far from being conspicuous that I have not, as yet, been able to discern them.'[13]

With such a cast of mind prevalent in the colony from its earliest days, the decline in aboriginal fortunes was inevitable from the moment the white man stepped ashore in New South Wales, with his superior armaments at the ready to enforce his claims to territory. Convicts stole aboriginal fishing tackle and were occasionally killed in retaliation, which led to punitive expeditions in which natives died. Frustrated by the white man's occupation of a tribal hunting ground through which the Tank Stream flowed, the Aborigines attempted some small-scale guerrilla warfare to recover what had been theirs, but this was invariably repulsed, and more of them died. Fighting between Aborigines was encouraged by whites, for whom it became a spectator sport, often fuelled by careful distributions of booze to the combatants beforehand: rum was a common inducement for anything the European required of the native. And then there were the deadly sicknesses the white man brought in. Smallpox was only one of these maladies that took their toll of the native population, but it alone is thought to have wiped out maybe half the local Aborigines during an epidemic in 1789; and, because white men coupled with any available aboriginal women from the outset, venereal diseases were also imported where there had probably been none before; David Collins, at any rate, was one who thought so. Sensing early on that they were powerless to prevent the spread of the colony from the shores of Sydney Cove, the Aborigines presently lost the will to resist and they were effectively pacified before Governor Macquarie's term of office ended in 1820. Some remained to become caricatures of their former selves; like Bungaree, the native who played Bennelong to Matthew Flinders's Arthur Phillip in a circumnavigation of the continent, but finished up as an overdressed buffoon who was endlessly on the cadge, humoured on the streets of Sydney as a pathetically risible character. Those of his compatriots who had more dignity—and it was most of them—retreated further and further away from the white man into a Never Never that was still their own: the Botany Bay tribe, which was 400 strong in 1796, had been reduced by 1845 to a lonely quartet. Bloodshed, victimisation and contempt were all that the vast majority of white Australians offered their aboriginal compatriots until well into the second half of the twentieth century. The death rate among blacks in police custody at one stage rose to thirteen times the level reached under South African apartheid. [14]

This is the view from Eveleigh Street, where the ancestral hero is not Bennelong, and certainly not Bungaree, but Pemulwuy, the Rainbow Warrior whose insurrection against the incomers began when he speared Arthur Phillip's 'gamekeeper', the convict John McEntire, thus provoking the first punitive expedition against the natives. For a dozen years afterwards, Pemulwuy and a band of followers harried the colonisers and killed a number of them, while a myth developed among the Aborigines that he was impervious to European musketry, which endured until the day he was shot dead by a couple of settlers. The legend of his resistance has been revived in recent years, as the people on Eveleigh Street have desperately sought some figure who can be invoked to represent the proudest part of their past, who can symbolise their present and future aspirations. So they drop his name into conversations, to see if you recognise it, and when you only just do, they carefully fill you in on all the heroic details of Pemulwuy's life, omitting only to mention that after he had been shot, the local Aborigines, wishing to prove to the authorities that he was no longer a menace, cut off his head and sent it to the Governor, who forwarded it to England, where it finished up on the desk of Sir Joseph Banks.

On Eveleigh they also have other local models, canonised more recently, like the boxer Dave Sands, who was the Empire middle-weight champion in 1949 and is commemorated by a statue in Glebe; and Arthur Beetson, who was a bruising rugby league forward for Balmain and Australia in the 1960s. Then there is Charlie Perkins, who was born on a table at the old Alice Springs telegraph station and in 1966 became the first Aborigine to gain a university degree, a Bachelor of Arts from Sydney. Twelve months earlier, he had led a group of students on a freedom ride through New South Wales in order to draw attention to the abysmal living standards of most Aborigines on or off the special reservations where they dwelt in the Australian version of apartheid (and if they didn't live on reservations, local citizens invariably made sure that they were segregated at swimming pools and in cinemas). Perkins was also protesting against the entire history of the aboriginal Australian since the coming of the white man, which had not improved as the nation became notionally more civilised, but had further declined to the point where some could see racial extinction looming shortly ahead. The wholesale massacre of natives who happened to get in the way of nineteenth-century land-grabbers had been succeeded by mass evictions and destruction of property in the twentieth: one such episode in 1963 had produced widespread misery on the Cape York Peninsula, where police cleared the area to allow bauxite mining to start. There was also the matter of the 'stolen children', thousands of whom were forcibly separated from their indigent parents between 1901 and 1940, and more often than not they never saw each other again. In New South Wales, boys were given rudimentary training as farmhands, before being indentured to distant sheep and cattle stations, where they were paid next to nothing throughout their working lives; girls were turned into domestic servants at a special school in Cootamundra, before being hired out to the Australian middle classes, who simultaneously affected to despise such European notions of servitude. Two entire generations of Aborigines, and their descendants, have been grieving ever since over the matter of the stolen children alone.*

The fear of racial extinction has not been fanciful, though aboriginal statistics are notoriously imprecise. Nevertheless, the assumed native population of Australia in 1788 had been reduced by almost two-thirds when the 1966 census was taken, and to approximately one-seventh if people of mixed blood are discounted. Since then, no attempt has been made to distinguish between the

---

*It has been estimated that there may be a hundred thousand people of aboriginal descent who do not know their families or original communities; and that in New South Wales alone ten thousand children may have been taken from their parents by the Protection and Welfare authorities.

two groups, so that it is now difficult to say what the relevant proportions are: the estimate for New South Wales as a whole in 1966 was of no more than 130 'pure' Aborigines, with twenty-three thousand people claiming part descent. But, mixed or unmixed, on Eveleigh Street they adamantly feel kinship as one persecuted people. Sometimes they refer to themselves as blacks, sometimes as Kooris, which has long been the local aboriginal word for all the people related to each other in varying degrees of descent from the Sydney tribes; and for some mystifying reason they now insist on using 'aboriginal' as a noun instead of an adjective. They do not speak of European settlement in 1788, or even of colonisation; they simply call it an invasion.

And there is unmistakable desperation in this part of town. An old lady who has lived in Redfern almost all her life, and who has been a battler for aboriginal rights since she can't remember when, tells one by one of the things that have afflicted Eveleigh Street since she came into it as a child, before the Great War. The racket in legally abducted children may have ended half a century ago, but the roughness of the police towards the aboriginal community has persisted to this day: then it was breaking and entering in search of children; now it is much the same process in order to discover drugs, which have been pushed in the area recently by criminals in, it is thought, Sydney's Vietnamese community. Mrs Ingram is even more despondent at this turn of events than she is about the traditional hostility of the police. Crack hasn't arrived yet but, she says, 'when it does come here, you can say goodbye to the Abo'. She is mindful of her people's historic weakness for al-cohol and the widespread damage this has done to them. Mindful also of their inability to pull together as often as they might, she herself remarks that the inhabitants of adjacent Louis Street 'think they're better than Eveleigh Street folk', and goes on to lament the lack, among Aborigines, of the leadership that she sees on the other side of the Tasman, where 'The Maoris stick to-gether; they have a chief.'

Her most scathing criticism of her own people, however, is reserved for the Kooris who run the Aboriginal Housing Corporation, which was given title to this part of Redfern in 1973, in order to ensure decent and affordable accommodation for the inhabitants. Whatever the rights and wrongs of this dispute, it is obvious that the fabric of Eveleigh Street has been shockingly neglected over a great number of years. Joyce Ingram reckons that the people who run the corporation are colluding with the authorities to render the place uninhabitable, so that its population can be evicted and dispersed elsewhere, in a political manoeuvre designed to stifle a growing self-confidence among the local Aborigines. Such a clearance would also make it possible for cosmetic improvements to be made in Redfern before the millennium dawns, so as not to offend visitors to the Olympic Games.

All this is not to say that the people of Eveleigh Street fail to recognise the existence of good friends among white Australians. A number of Roman Catholic priests and other clergy have battled alongside Joyce Ingram and her neighbours for many years, and some of them have been driven close to similar despair at their apparent inability to halt the continuing decline. One man who never knew despair, however, whose name is reverenced among Aborigines everywhere, was Herbert Cole Coombs, more generally known as Nugget because he was only 5 foot 3 inches from start to finish. Born in Western Australia in 1906, he died in Sydney ninety-one years later, and spent much of his life close to the seat of federal government in Canberra. He started work in his native state as a rural schoolmaster, who startled parents and the school inspectors by teaching children 'The Waste Land' as well as Henry Lawson and Banjo Paterson. His destiny, however, was to become a polymathic economist, who at one time or another was wartime Director of Rationing, Director-General of Post-war Reconstruction, Governor of the Commonwealth Bank (its youngest, at the age of forty-two), head of the Royal Commission on Australian Government Administration, Chancellor of the Australian

National University, Chairman of the Elizabethan Theatre Trust, Chairman of the Australian Council for the Arts and President of the Australian Conservation Foundation: had the advice of the London *Economist* been followed in 1965, he would have been Governor of the Bank of England as well.

But Nugget Coombs's true greatness was to be measured by his commitment to his aboriginal countrymen, which was steadfast throughout his life. As a young teacher, he had gone against the grain of local opinion by including Aborigines in his classes, and in his years as a public servant he became Chairman of the Australian Council for Aboriginal Affairs, with a particular resolve to make white Australians re-examine their attitudes to the native inhabitants. 'We all have a bad conscience about the Aborigines,' he once said; and 'I don't think any of us can fail to be ashamed by the history of Australia in relation to Aborigines.'[15] But much of his work took place behind the scenes, as in his years of patient devotion to the Pitjantjatjara people of South Australia and communities in the Top End of the continent, whose political, economic and social bargaining power he tried to improve while defending their most precious ancestral traditions. He could be intensely combative on behalf of the Aborigines, as when the mining industry launched an attack on aboriginal land rights, and a television producer loftily promised to consider a debate between some tribal elders and the Minister responsible, if the elders were prepared to appear live before the camera, speaking only English, which was a second or even third language to all of them. Nugget said a live debate was OK by him 'if the location of the debate is on aboriginal land in the desert west of Alice Springs and if the Minister will debate in the Warlpiri or the Arrerente language.'[16]

When Dr Coombs died, the Chairman of the Northern Land Council said, 'He was remarkable because he listened to aboriginal people rather than telling us what we should or shouldn't do....' Though he remained an agnostic to the end of his life, he was given a state funeral in St Mary's Cathedral, where the priest conducting it told everyone how Nugget had left instructions that there was to be 'Bach at the beginning, "Waltzing Matilda" at the end, and no God-bothering in between.'[17] The clergy didn't quite follow this injunction to the letter, because Nugget had even more wanted to please his widow, who was a Catholic. Ten Aborigines from Arnhem Land, in full tribal decoration, performed a leave-taking ceremony with smoke at the crossing of the nave; and afterwards left the cathedral immediately behind Lallie Coombs and the rest of the family, taking precedence over the Governor-General himself.

The symbolism of that event was important, but the aboriginal triumphs have, on the whole, been grudgingly allowed by white Australia. Not until 1967 were native Australians granted full citizenship and given the vote; not until 1975 were they allowed to own a bit of the country of which they had been dispossessed (most of the Wave Hill station, which was restored to the Gurindji people of the Northern Territory); and not until 1992 did the Australian High Court repudiate the two-hundred-year-old concept of *terra nullius*, the legalised fiction that Australia had been an empty land before the Europeans arrived. Nugget Coombs had much to do with the 1967 decision, and the other concessions were doubtless made at least partly in response to increasing aboriginal insistence on their rights. In 1972 some activists had set up a 'tent embassy' outside the Federal Parliament building in Canberra, from which flew a flag with a yellow disc upon a red and black ground, denoting the sun, the earth and the native people. This drew international attention to the aboriginal question for the first time, until the police moved in and dismantled the tents six months later; but, soon afterwards, the Sydney shops which stock repro aboriginal art were also selling enamelled versions of the flag on little badges for the lapel. There have been other protests since. Nothing has been more vivid than the march of some thirty thousand people (not all of them Aborigines) through the city centre on Australia Day 1988, to remind all the white patriots celebrating their Bicentenary whose Australia this originally was. And nothing has more sharply indicated a new and increasingly sophisticated mood among the Aborigines than the more recent establishment of an Indigenous Reference Group on Cultural and Intellectual Property. The title of this body may be a mouthful, but its purpose is very simple. It is lobbying hard to establish the aboriginal copyright in a number of fields where commercial profit has been made by white Australians (worse, by foreign investors) out of the aboriginal culture without so much as a by-your-leave to any Aborigine, much less a token royalty. The fields that IRGCIP has in mind include music, dance, song, ceremonies, symbols and designs, narratives and poetry, medicines, 'sustainable use of flora and fauna', human remains, sacred sites, burials 'and documentation of indigenous people's heritage on film, photographs, videotape, audiotape and all forms of media'.[18] A complete overhaul of the Australian Copyright Act would be necessary before Aborigines could establish their legal title to such matters, so that no one in future could freely reproduce the particular arrangement of dots in Western Desert art, say, or the crosshatched designs of Arnhem Land; but, in the changed climate of today, new legislation is not at all inconceivable.

For it was Nugget Coombs's crowning achievement that he did manage to prick white Australia's conscience before he died—well, most of it at least. The Aborigines acquired the vote and other manifestations of full citizenship in 1967 because 90 per cent of all Australians assented to the proposition in a referendum. Even more remarkable, perhaps, was the national Sorry Day on 26 May 1998. For weeks beforehand, something like books of condolence were displayed in the Sydney Museum, in the ever politically correct Body Shop and elsewhere in the metropolis, which all-comers were invited to sign, as they were in other cities across the land. And on the appointed day these books—in all, a thousand or so, it was said—were assembled in apology for the mistreatment of Aborigines across two centuries, while the Chief Justice of the Federal

Family Court called on the judiciary to do likewise, and other judges, civic and church leaders, police chiefs and even viceregal representatives all but prostrated themselves in contrition. The most conspicuous dissenter to this national catharsis was the Federal Prime Minister, John Howard, who, evidently unable to see that a gesture can sometimes be vastly more important than anything of greater substance, said he failed to understand why he should apologise for the actions of earlier administrations. By contrast, the Government of New South Wales announced that it proposed to change the name of the Botany Bay National Park to something more sympathetic to the aboriginal people; at which someone suggested that Gillingarie might be appropriate, as a Dharuk word meaning 'land that belongs to us all'.

Not that any of this has yet offered much in the way of redemption for Eveleigh Street. As she contemplates the dilapidated premises in which she and her neighbours live, the garbage outside their front doors, the police van just up the road, the increasing threat to their community from drug-pushers, the musty smell of decay and resignation, Joyce Ingram declares, 'There is a lot of heartache here.' A double-decker rattles past on its way into Sydney Central from Wollongong, and the house vibrates to the momentum of its passage. 'You know,' she adds, 'when you come down the slope from the station, you feel a depression coming on. Every time.' That is another measurement of what still hurts after forty thousand years, or whatever it is. And not a sign, just yet, of another Nugget Coombs.

CHAPTER THREE

❧

The Last Melting Pot

Tied up at a jetty outside the National Maritime Museum is a small craft which sits low in the water and does not look as if Darling Harbour is her natural habitat. Broad in the beam but shallow in her draught, she has a stubby mast amidships and a wheelhouse aft, and three other features make it clear that this vessel originated somewhere well outside Australian territorial waters. Just abaft the mast an awning is spread, but it is made of rattan instead of canvas; nowhere is there a safety rail to stop anyone tumbling into the sea; and the stem sweeps upwards, above the sharp prow, which gives it a distinctly oriental look. Oriental the fishing boat *Tu Do* most certainly is. The name means 'Freedom', and on this frail vessel thirty-nine Vietnamese boat people fled their country in 1977, following the fall of Saigon to Ho Chi Minh's troops.

Her story is not unique, but it is worth telling precisely because it typifies the epic journeys made in the past quarter of a century by thousands of migrants to Australia, who preferred not to live under South-east Asian communism. *Tu Do* was built by a wealthy man named Tan Thanh Lu, who owned a supermarket as well as a couple of fishing boats, and who decided to escape with friends and relatives because he assumed his wealth would be taken from him by the new regime in South Vietnam. On the night of 16 August 1977, they loaded the vessel with their possessions and their children, who had deliberately been made sleepy with cough mixture, and then, up to their waists in swamp water, they pushed her for over a mile out of the Mekong delta until they were far enough offshore to climb aboard and risk starting the engine. *Tu Do* was carrying almost four times as many people as she was licensed to hold as she headed for the open sea, together with enough food to last for five months, a small kerosene stove on which they could cook, 7,500 American dollars and a number of gold bars which were hidden around the hull. Her passengers were much better provided for than the majority of boat people who ran the same risks.

The first hazard was pirates, who were sighted in the Gulf of Thailand, but *Tu Do*'s diesel was more powerful than theirs and so she outran them. After two and a half days Mr Lu and his party made their first landfall, in Malaysia, but after being allowed to clean themselves they were told to move on; which they were more than willing to do because their hope was to finish up in the United States. They sailed further along the Malaysian coast before stopping again, and this time they were confined to the boat for a month while they awaited an interview with the American Embassy in Kuala Lumpur where, eventually, their application was turned down. That was when Mr Lu decided that Australia would be their goal.

Tu Do's next stop was Jakarta, where the Indonesian authorities gave the Vietnamese fresh water, more diesel fuel and some extra food, to encourage them to move along to somewhere else. Not that they had gone hungry on the voyage so far, fresh fish each day supplementing the provisions they had brought. But they lost a lot of their possessions and their cargo when they sailed through a storm in the Timor Sea, which caused the entire company, apart from those in the wheelhouse, to huddle together below deck. By the time the storm had blown itself out, they were coming up to an island where they found another refugee boat stuck fast in the shallows, and this they took in tow until they were close to the coast near Darwin. There Mr Lu and three other men swam ashore, asked a couple of passers-by to notify the police, and swam back to *Tu Do*, which was later escorted by a patrol boat into Darwin Harbour. It was 21 November, and the refugees had sailed well over three thousand miles, with nothing but a compass and a child's map to navigate by. Six months later, the Lu family were granted asylum, and lived for a while in Brisbane before settling down to run a restaurant in New South Wales.

The Vietnamese are simply the latest ingredient to be added to the last great social melting pot on earth. The British started taking refugees from continental Europe and other parts of the globe so long ago that their ancestral homelands have been largely forgotten—provided they or their descendants have a white skin— by everyone except those who are fascinated by names and their origins. The United States became the greatest host nation of all when it first opened its doors in the nineteenth century to Europe's tired, her poor, her huddled masses yearning to breathe free, on such a scale that a large proportion of Americans today have two very distinct (and often belligerent) loyalties: to the nation whose citizenship they craved and finally acquired, and to the land they left behind (but not emotionally) because of persecution and other hardships. And now, in this generation, Australia has become the last great host country in history, for it is impossible to see where else the processes of the second half of the twentieth century can ever be repeated again.

It is sometimes assumed that only Anglo-Saxons and Celts settled in Australia until Governor-General Sir William Slim, one of the few English generals who have ever been liked and respected by Australians, famously advised the nation to 'populate or perish' in the 1950s, bearing in mind that overcrowded Asia was all too aware that just to the south was a very empty continent. In fact, there has been a wider racial mixture from the earliest days of European settlement, if we start with the twenty-four Jewish convicts (including seven women and Jacob Messiah) who arrived in the First Fleet. These were forerunners of today's substantial Jewish community in Sydney, sixty thousand strong, whose religious focal point is the magnificently exotic Great Synagogue on Elizabeth Street. That initial handful were obviously British, and they were joined in 1821 by another compatriot, the first Jewish free settler, Barnett Levey, who built the Theatre Royal, Sydney's (and Australia's) first permanent playhouse. This did not, alas, long survive its founder, who died in 1837. Two years later, a drunken Irishman accidentally burned it down on St Patrick's Day. Jews from the European mainland didn't arrive until well into the nineteenth century, and many of them soon made a living in the rag trade, as did their siblings who at the same time were migrating to New York, to Manchester, to Leeds and to London's East End. They were fugitives from Czarist Russia or from hard times in Germany and Poland: Australia's most revered soldier, Sir John Monash, came from a family with its roots in Prussia. Monash, who made his reputation commanding troops on the Western Front in 1918, was from Melbourne, but Leonard Keysor, who had won one of the nine Australian Victoria Crosses at Gallipoli three years earlier, was a Sydneysider.

The Greeks were early arrivals, too, seven of them sailing into Port Jackson aboard the transport *Norfolk* in 1829, convicted of piracy in the Eastern Mediterranean, which sounds as if they were even luckier than William Redfern not to have hanged. They spent only a short time as servants around the town before a new Greek government persuaded London that the men had been engaged in a patriotic struggle against the Turks, not piracy; whereupon they were pardoned by Governor Ralph Darling and five of them lit out for home on the first available ship, leaving behind Andonis Manolis and Ghikas Boulgaris as Australia's first authentic Greek immigrants. Twenty years later these were joined by kinsmen who were attracted by the New South Welsh gold rush at Tambaroora and other diggings, including some sailors who had jumped ship in Sydney in order to share in the bonanza. By the end of the nineteenth century, nearly three hundred Greeks were settled in the city, enough to provide an Orthodox congregation for their Church of the Holy Trinity in Surry Hills, but not enough to sustain a Greek newspaper until 1915. They had by then entrenched themselves in the local catering industry, with fish shops (especially oyster saloons) along George Street and around Hyde Park, a tea and coffee business run by the brothers Andronicus on York Street, restaurants and fruit shops everywhere. It is reckoned that the milk-bar-complete-with-soda-fountain was popularised in Sydney by three Greeks who had learned their trade in New York, before seeing even greater opportunity in the Antipodes and launching their Anglo-American Company, which may have been responsible for the introduction of some American spellings to Australia, whose most common example appears in 'Labor Party'.*

As in every seaport on earth, there was always new blood trickling in from virtually anywhere at any time, as sailors jumped ship or dropped anchor after being paid off: Henry Lawson's name was an Anglicised version of Larsen, for his father was a Norwegian seaman who let his vessel sail without him, then went to dig for Australian gold. But Sydney's transformation from a quietly expanding seaport into a boom town, and the suddenly richer mixture of humanity than had been known here before, was a direct consequence of the gold rush. This began in New South Wales when Edward Hargraves, ex-Englishman, ex-fisherman, ex-squatter and always a chancer, found a four-ounce nugget near Bathurst in

---

*The spelling of Labo(u)r in Australian party politics was variable for many years, but the 'u' has long since been dropped; though not, interestingly, in the name of the Builders' Labourers' Federation.

1851, for which he was eventually given a reward of £10,000, topped up with a life pension so that he wouldn't go short. The reward was somewhat delayed because the first reaction in Sydney to Hargraves's strike was acute scepticism and even greater dismay. Unwholesome rumours had come from California, and Sydney's Catholic Archbishop Polding was so perturbed by them that members of his diocese were told they would be denounced from the pulpit if they were caught selling the Australian diggers sly grog. A newspaper editorial complained that 'Many persons are going to dig for gold who are wholly unfit for such work; men who would hesitate to walk the length of George Street in a shower of rain.... What can be the result of such reckless conduct, but that which happened in California—ruin, misery, disease, death.'[1]

The jeremiahs were paddling against the stream, even though Governor Sir Charles FitzRoy announced that no one could dig on the goldfields without a licence costing £1 10s per month, which was a tidy sum for a labourer or artisan to find. In spite of this impost, men of all trades and professions abandoned their jobs and scrambled out of town. As an observant bystander put it,

> Sydney assumed an entirely new aspect. The shop fronts put on quite new faces. Wares suited to the wants and tastes of general purchasers were thrust ignominiously out of sight and articles of outfit for goldmining only were displayed. Blue and red serge shirts, Californian hats, leathern belts, 'real gold-digging gloves', mining boots, blankets white and scarlet, became showgoods in the fashionable streets. The pavements were lumbered with picks, pans and pots; and the gold-washing machine or Virginian 'cradle', hitherto a stranger to our eyes, became in two days a familiar household utensil, for scores of them were paraded for purchase, 'from 25s to 40s'.[2]

The gold rush was what attracted the Chinese to Sydney in the first place. They began to arrive in 1853, on their way to what they called the Tsin Chin Shan, the new gold mountains, to distinguish these from the Chiu Chin Shan which had been opened up in California six years earlier, and where they had done much of the hard labour. A majority of them came from thirteen districts round Canton, so clannish that they would not have anything to do with fellow countrymen from other parts of China, who arrived in the city long after the gold rush had subsided. And although many Chinese communities on the goldfields of both New South Wales and Victoria dispersed after the diggings petered out, the populations in the big cities increased and prospered, with 3,800 in Sydney by 1901, getting on for twice as many as there were in Melbourne. Like the Greeks, the Chinese were soon selling food to their fellow citizens, but their commerce went beyond that, to include laundries and furniture factories; also less obtrusive premises where they gambled extravagantly and solaced themselves with opium. The city's Chinatown was born in those years, just down the hill beyond the Town Hall where, although its first boundaries have widened steadily, it is still centred on Haymarket, through which Sydney's sexy new tram glides quietly—its passengers almost all from out of town—*en route* to the amusements of Darling Harbour and the Casino.

The early Chinese were, of course, much disliked by many Australians, who voiced their hostility in the crude terms that are applied to the racially or tribally different in every country on earth. There had been riots against them on the goldfields; and in Sydney, where there was a noisy demonstration outside the Town Hall against Chinese immigrants in 1888, the local press agitated regularly against the Yellow Agony, as did the authors of various pamphlets. One of these suggested that the Chinese were 'an inferior race of foreigners, yellow skinned, plain looking, insanitary, opium using, gambling, immoral, cowardly, jabbering heathens who work for low wages ... and live on the smell of an oil rag'.[3] The man's target on this occasion, however, was perfectly capable of hitting back in much the same tone. Sydney published the only two Chinese-language newspapers in Australia at the start of the twentieth century and these, as well as invariably referring to 'foreign devils' and 'barbarians', consistently took the moral high ground when considering white Australia. Australians, they said, were 'inherently lazy. Their idleness is unsurpassed in the world' and their origins were 'sordid...all Australians' ancestors were convicts'. Australian women in particular were vilified, as sluts who were alternately vicious and domineering. As for the host country in general, 'The Chinese have higher moral standards than foreigners and can withstand the test of time....Foreigners, while enjoying political stability, cannot save themselves from moral degeneracy.'[4]

A number of the Chinese settled alongside the Greeks in Surry Hills in the late nineteenth century, whereas the Lebanese Christians who arrived in 1880 to escape from religious persecution by the Turks began to build their new lives in Redfern as well, where most of them earned a living as street hawkers and vendors. Italians, fleeing from Mediterranean poverty, came to Sydney in the 1890s, often to work as stonemasons and mosaic layers, and in other skilled crafts, though before the twentieth century was much advanced they had started selling fruit and vegetables more than doing any other job.* They settled at first in Redfern, Balmain and Glebe, but they later shifted to Leichhardt, which has remained Sydney's principal Little Italy ever since. They shared this with the Maltese, of whom there were about a thousand at the turn of the century, who also dabbled in greengrocery, from the market garden to the shop, though not as much as they sailed in and out of the Heads in a little fishing fleet of their own. From 1901, the Maltese were the only non-English-speaking migrants allowed into the country for several decades, because in that year the new Federal Government of Australia passed an Immigration Restriction Act which was chiefly aimed at the Chinese, though it covered every

---

*As always, there are exceptions to these generalities. The bronze replica of Il Porcellino outside Sydney Hospital commemorates a native of Tuscany, Thomas Henry Fiaschi, a surgeon who served at one time and another in both the Italian and the Australian army medical corps.

other kind of alien as well, an exception being made in the case of the Maltese because they were citizens of the Empire, after all. Naturally, anyone from Ireland or the British Isles constituted the biggest exception of the lot.

All this changed after the Second World War, and especially after Bill Slim wagged his paternal finger at Australia. Not only was such an underpopulated land considered vulnerable to aggression from a more assertive Asia, but the low birth rates that had existed between the two international conflicts—partly because sixty thousand young men had not come home in 1918, partly because the Depression caused surviving families to limit themselves—needed substantial reinforcement in order to revive the economy. So eager was Australia to replenish itself from proven stock that it quickly launched an assisted-passage scheme to attract as many Britons as possible, and these became known as the Ten Pound Poms, in a sometimes caustic reminder of how little they had forked out themselves in order to cross the world. The Australian Government's publicity apparatus in London and other cities shrewdly played on the most common post-war neuroses of the working-class British, with posters of a chubby infant under the slogan 'HIS FUTURE is in your hands. Take him to Australia'; and handouts which argued that 'Much as one may love Britain, one has to admit that these days it is becoming pretty crowded, while Australia still offers the attractions of space and opportunity'; and there was a tendentious reference to Sydney as 'the second white city of the Empire'.[5] Nearly a quarter of a million Poms travelled to Australia in response to this campaign between 1947 and 1982, when the assisted-passage scheme came to an end, but this was not nearly as many as the host country had hoped for (thousands more post-war British emigrants had opted for Canada instead, probably because it wasn't so far away, which would matter if they didn't settle well and decided to go home, this time at their own expense). It was because the Poms alone weren't solving Australia's problem that the net was cast wider from 1948, particularly when the 1950s got under way. At first, Displaced Persons (Reffoes in the local vernacular) from Germany and the Netherlands were invited in, to be followed by other Europeans whose lives had been disrupted almost as much by the war, and who could smell impending difficulties of a different kind: Croats, Serbs and Slovenes from Yugoslavia (Dallies)*, Poles, Russians, Byelorussians and Ukrainians from further away, Czechs and Hungarians, Latvians, Lithuanians and Estonians, who certainly didn't want what had just moved into their home territory. At this stage, with White Australia still a dominant article of the local faith, the Immigration authorities were pinning their hopes on the import of Aryans; or, at least, on those who could not be described as swarthy or even worse. But, with enclaves of exemplary Lebanese, Greek and Italian citizens by now well established in Sydney and Melbourne, there was no very good reason why they should not be joined by their compatriots; and so the door was opened to all Europeans and Levantines, whether they came from the Baltic or the Med or from points in between. By 1970, Australia had established immigration agreements with seventeen countries. There were over sixty-seven thousand Italians in Sydney by 1971, and thirty thousand Greeks. Two years later Nick Shehadie, son of an Orthodox Lebanese clergyman, and a distinguished rugby union international who started his own working life as a roof-tiler in Redfern, became Sydney's Lord Mayor, after serving for fourteen years on the City Council.

Coincidentally, White Australia was dismantled at the same time, and a points system for people under thirty-five years old, based on education and occupational skill, was adopted instead. In theory this meant that anyone who qualified would be admitted from anywhere on earth. A number of professional people from Hong Kong, India, Sri Lanka and Malaysia, plus some Armenians and Lebanese Muslims, did soon trickle in, no longer facing vari-

*Short for Dalmatia, though this is only one region of Yugoslavia, beside the Adriatic Sea.

ous obstructions to prevent the entry of anybody Immigration didn't like the look of, whatever it said on the applicant's CV. The most notorious of these was a random requirement to translate a passage of Gaelic into English, which would effectively defeat everyone except a small minority of Scottish Highlanders.* By the late 1970s, the door was fully open, and in poured all the displaced or threatened peoples of South-east Asia; between 1978 and 1988, thirty-five thousand refugees from the old Indo-China (Cambodians as well as Vietnamese) moved into Sydney alone, while in 1900–1 the city acquired fourteen thousand people from Hong Kong, as the date of the Chinese takeover began to loom over the colony. By then, almost two million of Sydney's 3,539,024 people were only first- or second-generation Australians.

The silent bungalows of the old Quarantine Station, which thousands of New Chums briefly inhabited, are Sydney's most poignant testimony to its long history of immigration, the nearest Australia ever came to an equivalent of New York's Ellis Island, but with a much more enchanting view; a stunning prospect up the bush-clad Harbour, with the skyscrapers just peeping above Bradleys Head. For well over a hundred years, after the convict transport *Bussorah Merchant* arrived with smallpox in 1828, vessels entering the Harbour had to pause just inside North Head until they were cleared by the port authorities, and those that carried infection were detained for much longer than their owners would have wished. At first, those unfortunates who might have contaminated Sydney had they been allowed to proceed were simply dumped on the beach with tents and provisions, their vessel being moored some distance away, until all danger had passed. Gradually,

---

*The test was most famously used against a Czech communist, Egon Kisch, who tried to enter the country in 1934: it was abandoned in 1958. Oddly enough, the annual report of the City Council for 1996–7 (when Sydney had a Deputy Lord Mayor who was born in China) noted that the Town Hall staff could speak a number of languages, including Italian, Greek, Maltese, Indonesian, German, French—and Gaelic!

clearings were made on the sloping ground above the beach, by ailing convicts at first, later by the labouring classes who had travelled Steerage; and buildings began to go up when the gold rush brought contamination on an unprecedented scale.

The last ship to unload infection here was the SS *Mooltan* in 1949, though the station remained open for several decades more, to quarantine people who had flown into Australia, as well as for larger emergencies (as when several hundred citizens of Darwin were accommodated after Cyclone Tracy had flattened their town in 1974) and for the detention of illegal immigrants. But since 1984 the long street of living quarters, which provided more than fifteen hundred beds, has been deserted except for its National Parks wardens and a few inquiring visitors, who are usually glad of the verandahs which shade them from the sun. The boxcar red bungalows are so well preserved that they could instantly be reopened were Sydney to be smitten by another bubonic plague, as it was in 1900, when hundreds of residents were tended here until they were out of danger. Here is a sick bay, with beds ranged against opposite walls, counterpanes tucked in and pillows all plumped up, and a bedpan (just in case) left thoughtfully inside the door. Here is a dining hall, where endlessly unappetising meals must have been consumed, with a copy of the Quarantine Act of 1908–12 tacked up at one end, so that everyone might take particular note of clause (i): 'No person in quarantine shall use any lavatory for purposes other than those for which it is provided.' And here is a kitchen with a vast institutional stove, which looks as if an eternity of elbow grease has been spent on keeping it spotlessly black.

Further down the slope from the main thoroughfare of what was, in effect, a small township are the shower blocks in which all-comers were disinfected as soon as they came ashore; and a tall chimney above the building where enormous autoclaves, whose armour plating would not have disgraced a battleship, were used to fumigate every last item in a passenger's luggage: Conrad Martens set up his easel on the North Shore in 1874 and painted a water-colour whose gum trees, dripping bark in the foreground, frame that chimney eructating smoke across the Harbour. Even closer to the water's edge are rocks on which bored and weary and anxious people chiselled mementoes of their presence across the best part of two centuries: RMS *Nigeria,* says one carving, which in its cryptic way commemorates the appalling influenza epidemic that killed millions all over the world in the wake of the Great War.

It was because there was a grave danger to public health if any infection slipped past this outpost that the measures taken at the station were as stringent as they became. Generally speaking, if a vessel came through the Heads with the quarantine flag at its truck, its passengers could go no further for the length of a disease's incubation, which was usually fourteen days. But some luck-less souls were stuck on this threshold of their promised land for up to three months, because if a new case appeared on the very last day of incubation, you had to start all over again. A number of stone posts standing every fifty yards or so in the bush below the living quarters is a grim reminder of how seriously all this was taken: they marked a boundary beyond which no one might venture, and guards patrolled this perimeter, with orders to shoot anyone who transgressed.

The shipowners regretted these procedures as much as any hapless passenger, because they had to foot the bill for everything that happened at the Quarantine Station while their vessel was held up there, apart from the medical services; and as passengers—especially the more prosperous ones—expected to be kept in the manner for which they had paid, up to the very moment when they disembarked, the station was run on exactly the same social lines as a Royal Mail steamer, or some pride of the P & O. There was First, Second and Third Class accommodation, dining rooms and shower blocks: First Class people had a bit of stained glass in some of their windows, and doors to maintain their privacy in the shower. This was simply a less elaborate form of the discrimination that everyone had been enjoying (or putting up with) during all those weeks on the high seas.

The hierarchy was firmly established aboard SS *Great Britain,* the biggest ship in the world when she was launched; also the first to be driven by a propeller, the first to be built with an iron hull. Her maiden Australian voyage took place in 1852, and in the next twenty-nine years she made thirty-two trips to Sydney and Melbourne, bringing twenty-five thousand passengers across the world, cramming six hundred or more souls aboard on every voyage. Cramming the majority of passengers, that is, for the few dozen First Class passengers enjoyed the space of single state rooms. And these grandees enjoyed twelve courses at dinner each night, with live chickens, sheep and cows penned on deck in order to ensure that the meat and dairy produce were always fresh. Back in Third Class and Steerage, where the passengers slept without privacy in tiers of bunks, the victualling ran to nothing more than salted meat and other food preserved in tubs and vats. No fundamental change to these arrangements occurred as long as Europeans travelled to Australia by sea. The majority of those sailing to Sydney aboard post-war immigrant ships were notoriously cramped when they played quoits and other deck games to while away the time it took to come from Tilbury Docks via Gibraltar, Suez, Aden and Bombay, about four and a half weeks. Their pastimes were invariably scrutinised by the First Class passengers, who had ample space on the deck overlooking theirs, and not much less when they retired for the night in well-ventilated quarters; whereas life in the six-berth cabins just above the waterline was usually so stuffy that their occupants resorted to home-made air-conditioning as they sailed through the tropics, scooping in the breeze by jamming cardboard boxes into the open portholes, with the inboard ends cut out.

Whether arriving in Sydney by sea or by air, however, this motley infusion of new blood has resulted in one of the two most cosmopolitan cities on earth, though Melbourne might (and frequently does) contest this suggestion, having staked its own considerable claim by spending several million dollars on transforming its old Customs House into an Immigration Museum and Hellenic Archaeological Museum 'to celebrate our cultural diversity and resulting Australian identity'. Certainly no Sydney newspaper takes note, as the *Melbourne Age* unfailingly does, of the daily Muslim prayer times; publishing these, what's more, in the transliterated Arabic usage for the day, the month and the year. Yet it is doubtful whether even New York contains greater variety than Sydney. The Greeks and the Italians have finally achieved parity here, with eighty-two thousand citizens apiece at the last count, while the Maltese are up to sixteen thousand now: there are twenty-two thousand Croats and thirteen thousand Serbs, fourteen thousand Poles and twelve thousand Russians, eleven thousand Indonesians and fifty thousand Vietnamese.* There are even said to be two and a half thousand Afghans roaming the streets of Sydney, and nearly five thousand Kurds.[6] The athletes will not want for patriotic support, wherever they have come from, when they turn up for the Olympic Games.

In the tradition of émigré communities everywhere, once a toehold was established in the new homeland by a vanguard of migrants from the old, others followed from the same region as the word got round, to settle in the district that the first brave souls had colonised. In Sydney, the earliest Italian migrants had invariably lived in Calabria and central Italy, while the Lebanese came without exception from a number of villages in the Bekaa Valley. Yet although, at first, both colonies were concentrated in the same two suburbs of Sydney—Redfern and Surry Hills—they steadily

---

*Apart from the figures quoted above, the languages other than English which are most commonly spoken in Sydney nowadays are as follows: aboriginal tongues by 10,269 people; Chinese 150,857; Dutch 6,274; French 12,032; German, 19,033; Hindi 17,688; Hungarian 8,296; Japanese 9,112; Korean 21,051; Macedonian 17,950; Spanish 41,806; Turkish 14,568; Portuguese 10,987; Tagalog (Philippines) 34,021. There are many more much smaller minorities, including a couple of Zulus somewhere, who converse with each other in Acholi. The figures include anyone over five years old, and are taken from the 1996 Census. They were displayed in the exhibition 'Tears, Fears and Cheers', which was mounted in the National Maritime Museum early in 1998.

spilled over into many other parts of the city, to establish a pattern that has been repeated by almost all the immigrant groups which have settled here since. With one exception, which we shall come to shortly, neither Sydney nor any other Australian city has ever produced the closely defined ghetto of this or that minority, and this sets them apart from the general custom in North America. The Lebanese are these days scattered across Bankstown, Punchbowl and Lakemba, where Sydney's first mosque arose in 1975, now attended by six thousand people for part of their social life as well as for their worship.* And, although Leichhardt and Drummoyne, facing each other across Iron Cove, may think of themselves as a bisected Little Italy, with their high concentration of trattorias, pizzerias and gelato bars, Italians are also to be found almost anywhere else, where their neighbours are quite likely to be Serbs, or Greeks or Balts, together with a fine tincture of old blood, whose pedigree goes right back to the convict ships.

A consequence of this dispersion and this propinquity with Old Chums is that, again unlike the tradition in North America, there are no ethnic bloc votes in politics yet, and to some extent this must be because the numbers are still too small for that: Sydney's sixty thousand Jews are as nothing compared with the two million in New York, and the eighty-two thousand Italians here must be measured against three-quarters of a million who inhabit Manhattan, Staten Island and the Bronx. The bloc vote cast for purely cultural motives may be something in store for Sydney, however, for recent years have seen Greeks and Italians elected to councils in Leichhardt and Marrickville, Yugoslavs in Rockdale and Fairfield, Lebanese in Canterbury (as well as that Lord Mayor in the Town Hall), Vietnamese in Cabramatta: oddly, none of these functionaries has remained in office for very long, a circumstance that nobody has been able to explain. And whatever animosities some of the groups may have felt in their earlier

---

*There were fifteen mosques in Sydney by 1995.

existences, they do not appear to have brought them to Australia. Serbs and Croats may behave disgustingly to each other in the Balkans, but they seem, at worst, to ignore each other's presence in Sydney. Greeks and Turks may be wary in view of their (to put it mildly) historic lack of a relationship, but no friction between them has yet been reported here. Lebanese Muslims and Christians have not re-enacted the terrible scenarios of Beirut in Bankstown or Lakemba; and, again, nobody can account for any of this.

Something in the quite recent climate of Australia may be responsible, since the official racism of the country was abandoned a generation ago. For although the White Australia policies were constructed to make life as difficult as possible for anyone who wasn't white, second-hand versions of them were always liable to spill over into other distinctive communities as well, before the Immigration Restriction Act of 1901 was repealed. During the Great War there were riots against the Greeks in Sydney because King Constantine, back home in Athens, was supposed to favour a German victory, and because a Greek was falsely alleged to have killed a soldier in Manly. For several years after this, no Greek dared speak his native tongue in public, for fear of being spat upon, and their young men were sometimes beaten up, invariably taunted with 'Dago!' As recently as 1955, a Sydney newspaper printed the headline 'Migrants by Air, Human Dregs' above an article which included the following quotation from an airline employee: 'I have travelled Europe extensively and I've never met a lower lot of people than some of these southern European migrants. These people are used to living in filth and squalor. The communities they will build up in Australia will be on the same lines. They are the dregs not only of Europe but of humanity.'[7] With prejudices such as these waiting to be loosed, it is maybe astonishing that Sydney has known very little anti-Semitism, certainly nothing on a European scale, though the Jewish community was clearly braced for it earlier in the century, when Rabbi Francis

Lionel Cohen, Chief Rabbi of the Great Synagogue, was one of the most vocal supporters of military conscription in 1916, just before a referendum was held on the subject. Together with other members of his community, he founded the Universal Service League, which worked for compulsory military service at home and overseas, to fight what he saw as an enemy that all Australians had in common.

At the opposite end of that particular spectrum were the Roman Catholic majority of Irish descent, who regarded the Great War as something the British had brought upon themselves, and took the view that Australians should have no part of it: the Protestant Irish, on the other hand, were as gung-ho about the war as any Australian with his antecedents in the Home Counties of England. The Catholic hostility was articulated most vehemently in Melbourne, whose Archbishop, Dr Daniel Mannix, remained a good hater of the British to the end of his days, seeing them as no less damnable than the Soviet Union, another topic on which he was slightly unbalanced. Over the years, the old grudges were worked out in Sydney as persistently as anywhere else but, whereas in Ireland itself, people moved away from extremes of religious bigotry only when they were driven closer together by the internecine atrocities that bigotry made possible, here they took a less brutal but still unpleasant form of Protestant v. Catholic hostility. 'Rockchoppers' was for generations a dirty word reserved for Catholics alone, even by those whose ancestors were also convict labourers. 'In Australia', an unmistakably balanced observer has written, 'anti-Catholicism was first cousin to anti-Semitism and just as covert. It was an attitude living feebly below the surface of consciousness, a residue of nineteenth-century sectarianism, the conscription debates of World War I, the subsequent polarisation of national life, Britain's trouble in Ireland and even post World War II dislike of non-British migrants.'[8] The hostility may at last have run its course Down Under, for the same voice was able to say, in 1994, 'Today it would be bizarre to suggest that Catholics

feel alienated from Australian society. Back then, however, alien-
ation was real, even though some denied its existence.'9 The beginning of a civilised relationship can possibly be dated to twenty
years earlier, when Cardinal Gilroy (Sir Norman, as he fancifully
became before his death) was invited into the pulpit of a Presby-
terian church on Macquarie Street. But the Protestants still had
their Masonic Lodges, the Catholics their Knights of the Southern Cross—secret societies both, that did not encourage ecumeni-
cal gestures.

So deeply did this fault line run through the life of Sydney that
it had even been known to produce enmity in the city's sporting
circles. When the Seventh Kangaroos, the 1948–9 Australian rugby
league team, were chosen to tour England and France, everyone
expected them to be led by the Newtown centre Len Smith, who
had already captained Sydney, New South Wales and Australia,
but Colin Maxwell of Western Suburbs was given the honour instead. It has been widely held ever since that this was because
Smith was a Catholic, and a majority of the ARL Board were
Protestants and Freemasons. So were most members of the Australian Cricket Board between the two world wars, which has
caused some people to wonder whether Don Bradman's notoriously easy access to this source of all patronage in the Australian
game had at least as much to do with his own Masonic background as with his cricketing genius. Another suspicion is that the
unconcealed friction between Bradman and his former team-mate
Jack Fingleton, which lasted as long as Fingleton lived, was at least
partly an expression of much older and more distant antipathies,
with Bradman's ancestry rooted in the Oliver Cromwell country of
East Anglia, Fingleton's devout Catholicism being inherited from
his grandparents, who emigrated from Ireland in the nineteenth
century and doubtless brought their long memories and unforgiv-
ing bitterness with them.

The Irish are the only people in Sydney who disrupt the city as
much as their siblings do in New York on the occasion of their

annual festivity. As St Patrick's Day approaches, students at the University's St John's College sing increasingly raucous and mostly tone-deaf versions of 'When Irish Eyes Are Smiling', dye their hair green, dress in appropriately stencilled shirts, and mow their lawn in the pattern of a shamrock. On the day itself, a daunting proportion of Sydney's population becomes purpose-fully inebriated (whether they have Irish connections or not) as they lurch from one celebration to another; and, while the grand parade is on, the city's transport system is inconveniently re-arranged so as to humour the marchers coming up George Street. Buses are rerouted from Central Station to reach the bottom of George and Circular Quay by circuitous ways and means, which caused one passenger to complain loudly during her 1998 circum-navigation of the city centre, especially when it turned out that the driver—from some distinctly non-Irish background, judging by his accent—had lost his way. 'I'm half-Irish meself,' barked this lady, 'but I've had St Pat's Day up to here. I'll tell yer somethin'. If it was the Chinese who were messin' the rest of us about like this, the Irish'd be the first people to say they oughta be deported!' Eventually she disembarked, still huffing and puffing against the iniquity of it all, while the driver slumped over his steering wheel, as bewildered as he was exhausted. 'Who was this St Pat?' he asked (quite seriously) the last passenger to get off his bus.

An exception to almost everything that has been written above about the distribution of Sydney's immigrants has to be logged in the case of those with their ancestral beginnings in the Orient, es-pecially those who have come to Australia impoverished. This rep-resents a rapidly growing proportion of the population, as anyone who has visited Sydney regularly over many years cannot fail to appreciate, without needing to pore over the relevant statistics. For not only has Australia turned to Asia as a new trading partner, while gradually loosening its commercial links with Europe in the past generation, but its principal city is actually *looking* more Asian almost annually. The stranger is most conscious of this downtown of the point at which Parramatta Road runs into George Street because, although the Chinese have spread themselves across the metropolitan suburbs like everybody else—in Ashfield and Strathfield, with a prosperous enclave in Chatswood on the North shore—the emotional heart of their community is still to be found in Chinatown.

And there, in a steadily expanding enclave which once was confined to the Haymarket side of George, but which now straddles Sydney's principal shopping thoroughfare, you can without much difficulty imagine yourself in Shanghai or Guangzhou; it lacks only some replicas of Hong Kong's celebrated tramcars to produce a very passable imitation of Central on the island of Victoria. Here are Chinese cinemas, the offices of Sydney's four Chinese newspapers, restaurants which specialise in the kind of dumpling they particularly relish in Beijing, others whose reputations depend upon arcane recipes for barbecued duck, food stores which sell everything from bok choy to abalone, by way of pork lung and dried fish, as well as a variety of crockery and woks and chopsticks and rice cookers and complicated appliances for serving up dim sum in Chinese restaurants, all trading in glorious assortment beside and between shops which specialise in infinite varieties of tea, and pharmacies whose stock includes a stimulating range of aphrodisiacs, some of which are clearly chemical, others which may be described (for want of a more obvious identity) as homeopathic remedies. This is where an even older civilisation than ours retreats from the West, when it feels in need of its own space. Here are mop-headed and immutably black-haired young men in denim jackets, who look as if they have just walked off a Bruce Lee film set, and little old ladies with the shuffling trot (and tiny feet) that speak not only of a different culture but of another age: they mingle and are at ease with dazzlingly delicate young women tricked out in expensive fittings by Gucci, Versace and Jean-Paul Gaultier; also with dapper businessmen who look as if they have just concluded—or are on their way to clinching—an immensely satisfying big deal (and there is great wealth in the Chinese community, with more than one multi-millionaire who arrived in Sydney with the proverbial five dollars in his pocket). At the start of Dixon Street, where lighting comes in the form of Chinese lanterns, there is an arch, a sort of Chinese lych-gate, with sturdy wooden posts and a pretty tiled roof, standard introduction to every Chinatown on earth.

An even more elaborate version of the same thing, with a highly ornate roofline, one sentiment gilded in English ('The world is for us to share as well as to respect'), another in an oriental script, and with two huge Chinese dragons at its base, stands at the entrance to Freedom Plaza in Cabramatta, another place of withdrawal and reflection on the past, this one on the south-western edge of the city, beside the Hume Highway, just before this plunges across the countryside towards the distant prospect of Melbourne. Still smouldering descendants of the convicts are apt to call the suburb Vietnamatta these days, in much the same tone of voice used by xenophobic Yorkshiremen who refer to Bradford scathingly as Karachi West. This is where virtually all the Sydney boat people have settled down, all the Cambodian refugees from the terrorism of Pol Pot, many of them no longer impoverished—though local unemployment has been running at between 20 and 30 per cent for many years—but as well content and safe as Mr Tan Thanh Lu.

And these people, together with the Chinese, are part of a strange and heart-warming irony in the life of this great cosmopolis. For although your next taxi may be leased to someone who started his working life in Accra, in Dubrovnik, in Istanbul or in Beirut, although your bus driver may be wearing the five necessities of a practising Sikh, although the chap sitting in front of you may be an ageing Ten Pound Pom who still follows Chelsea FC, but from the opposite side of the world for, ooh, nearly forty years now; although such people are voting and taxpaying Sydneysiders, too, and will never be anything else, they are not quite in the same category as the Chinese and the South-east Asian immigrants. Apart from a rabble-rousing chip-shop owner named Pauline Hanson up in Queensland (ever the most paranoid and racially prejudiced Australian state), nobody speaks (publicly, at any rate) of the Yellow Agony or the Yellow Peril any more. Instead, the people who were so long most vilified, most aggressively kept at arm's length lest they pollute and take over this land have been welcomed as New Chums, too, and have been incorporated into life here as generously as anyone else.

This clearly portends a number of interesting and occasionally disconcerting changes in the long-term future of Sydney, with hitherto steadfast traditions and loyalties no longer sure of safe-keeping. One of these is that, for a swelling proportion of citizens, the names of Luting, Dien Bien Phu and My Lai will always be much more evocative than those of Kokoda, Tobruk and Gallipoli.

CHAPTER FOUR

ॐ

Merinos, Shipping and Botany Bay

After 176 years, the Royal Easter Show returned to the outskirts of Parramatta, where the first Show was held in 1822. The move had nothing to do with sentiment, but was very hard-headed indeed, the old Showground in Moore Park having become so worn out that the next stage would have been downright dilapidation, followed by eventual collapse. So it was sold to Mr Murdoch, who, ever ready to expand his empire so long as the price is right, decided it would do very nicely as a site for his film studios. The move also commended itself to the Royal Agricultural Society of New South Wales, because it meant that certain facilities could be shared with the organisers of the Olympic Games, whose arenas and grandstands and accommodation and roadways and other necessities were beginning to take shape beside Homebush Bay, which was once celebrated chiefly for its colony of rare frogs, but had lately been touted as 'the new heart of Sydney', no less.

And there it was that, for sixteen days in April 1998, which were either swelteringly hot or as wet as any Indian monsoon (typical Sydney weather, in short), the citizens turned up in tens of thousands for their annual inspection of rural things, crossed with a form of open-air circus and a shopping binge. Shopping wasn't by any means the most important thing at the Easter Show, but for many it seemed to come mighty close, enough to make this the most obvious difference between the Royal Sydney and the big agricultural shows in what used to be referred to as the Old Country (and conceivably still is, by a handful of old identities in the farming community). Day after day, the longest queues stretched around, and the densest crowds were to be found inside, the enormous shed in which Showbags could be acquired. You could choose from a couple of hundred or more of these objects, all competing with each other in discounts and in variety of contents; between A Little Luxury, for example, valued at A$52.10 but yours for A$6, which included a Lady Mitchum Deodorant Towellette, a Civic Video Voucher, *New Woman* magazine (back issue) and twenty other largely feminine items; and the Monster 6 in 1 Bag, worth A$14.99 of anybody's money but absolutely given away for ten bucks, with its Wicked Chews Straw, its White Chocolate Mice, its Lag Fruity Sherbet Bombs and another forty toothsome indelicacies. Visiting the Showbag Hall at any time was a bit like fighting your way through Harrods on the opening day of the January Sales: if you didn't look out, you stood a reasonable chance of being trampled underfoot.

The amusements were more extensive than those generally laid on at the showgrounds of the northern hemisphere. There were Ferris wheels and all the other pleasures of the funfair, there were stunts by trapeze artistes and skydivers and paragliders and motorists driving cars at unlikely angles on only two wheels, and there were less spectacular diversions than these: ceremonial flagwavers who might have come from Siena but who actually hailed from Rome; a muscular competition to see which gang of tracklayers could put down a length of railway line faster than anyone else; and a fair dinkum bloke who handled snakes with aplomb, and persuaded children to overcome their fears and do likewise—also to distinguish between the reptiles they might safely cuddle and those they'd be well advised to leave alone. There were other happenings aimed at the same audience; a Farmyard Nursery, where small calves and other immature beasts could be approached with impunity; and a Maternity Ward, full of very pregnant ewes, which guaranteed visiting youngsters a glimpse of lambing several times every day.

That was where the entertainment drifted towards the essence of the Show. So was the demonstration of real horsepower, by half a dozen Clydesdales pulling a brewer's dray. And so, most especially, were the Chops, so popular an attraction that these had a little stadium all to themselves, and every seat occupied for every event. The Chops are a series of competitions to test a lumberjack's skill with an axe or a saw; a Tasmanian invention, it's said, but one widely practised nowadays in North America and New Zealand, as well as in Australia, whose woodmen tend to win all international contests because they are accustomed to hacking their way through hard eucalyptus trees, whereas the Yanks and the Kiwis have an easier time at home with their native softwood pines. Wherever they come from, these men wield axes that are not only heavy but sharp enough to shave with (and no Show is thought to be properly arranged unless someone demonstrates this particular aptitude without drawing blood). The normal course of events in 1998, however, was hair-raising enough as a dozen men, each immaculate in white singlets and trousers, cut their way to the top of fifteen-foot tree trunks and then shortened each by a slice which was removed with only a few blows; or, even more liable to raise goose pimples in the novice spectator, stood almost on the ground, legs balanced and only just apart on a bit of log, which they then bisected by cutting it precisely half-way between each foot. There were other tests of the woodman's craft and, whichever was going on in the ring, each man raised an arm when he had completed his task, so that the judges could spot the victor; but, to make quite sure they got it right, each log was wired to a device which clocked the competitors as accurately as a photo-finish out at Randwick or Canterbury Park. Tremendous applause all round the arena as each winner was announced, with his own band of supporters also punching the air, in the modern sporty fashion, for emphasis.

Things were much quieter where the Easter Show's essential purposes were displayed. The most pressing business of each day was over and done with before many of the customers had arrived, when cattle and horses, sheep and dogs, poultry and pigs, goats and cage birds, horticulture and grains were solemnly scrutinised and judged by expert men and women who were content to per-form before only a handful of dedicated and equally knowledge-able enthusiasts; graziers up from the rich sheep runs of the Riverina or down from the cattle country of the North-west for the week, cockies from more modest farmlands almost anywhere out of town. Ribbons and rosettes were then deployed, and you didn't need to read the names when these had been attached to the winning creature or display: their owners were the people who looked as pleased as could be for the rest of the day, as they loi-tered proudly, very open to questioning, beside their exhibits. Such care and attention they had spent since the last Easter Show, in nurturing and then sprucing up their charges for the most anx-ious moment of the year—as the following advice to Australian breeders of Jersey cows in 1928 makes clear:

> In summertime, rugging at night is beneficial, and when westerly winds are prevalent, it is as well to have cattle protected as the wind tends to harden the coat. Rugging keeps the coat sleek and soft. The teeth are easily cleaned by using salt on a large tooth brush. To polish the horns a fine rasp may be used to take the first roughness off. Then use a sheet of fine emery cloth torn in strips to remove any ridges. Just before entering the ring a little blacking should be rubbed into the animal's hoofs. The animal should be taught to lead with a smart and stylish appearance. The head should be kept nicely up.[1]

There are parents all over the world who don't take care of their children as well as that.

For the rest of the Show, the animals were on display in their various (and exceedingly well-appointed) quarters to anyone who might be interested enough to leave the jollifications behind, and savvy enough to grasp the point of being there. Stockmen in white coats, such as butchers wear, were continually washing and foddering colossal bulls, whose most crucial equipment was sometimes so awesome that it very nearly trailed along the ground. Shepherds in wide-brimmed Akubras and their best moleskin breeches stroked and brushed their Suffolks and their Dorsets, their Border Leicesters and their Southdowns so that these should still be seen to best advantage even though the trophies had already been won and lost; and magnificently brooding Merinos rested on ample beds of straw, their heavy fleeces palpitating in the heat and glistening with lanolin, whose oily smell hung comfortingly in the air, spiced here and there with the sharper tang of sheep dip. A gun shearer, said someone who knew what he was talking about, could clip three hundred of those beauties in a day, taking a fleece weighing seven kilos from every one of them—''Course, normally no one bothers to clip more than two hundred or so, because after that it's one for you and one for the bloody Government.'

There are a couple of famous paintings by Tom Roberts which show what cruel hard labour this was when only hand-clippers were used in the old shearing sheds; and back-breaking work it still is, even though the clippers are now on the end of a power-driven contraption which resembles an old-fashioned dentist's drill.* There is also a long tradition of Australian verse which celebrates the exclusive world of the sheep shearers. Henry Lawson composed on this subject, and so did other poets, like Geoffrey Dutton and R. A. Waters, and H. P. 'Duke' Tritton, who was a

---

*The paintings are *The Golden Fleece: Shearing at Newstead* (1894), which is in the Art Gallery of New South Wales; and *Shearing the Rams* (1890), which is in the National Gallery of Victoria.

shearer himself before he became a writer. Even more deeply embedded in the tradition are the anonymous ballads that most Australians—at least until recently—knew as well as they knew
anything written by Banjo Paterson or C. J. Dennis: 'Lachlan
Tigers' ('I have a pair of Ward and Paine's that are both bright and
new...'); and, most of all perhaps, 'Click Go the Shears' ('Click
go the shears, boys, Click! Click! Click! / Wide is his blow and his
hands move quick...').

The Royal Easter Show is Sydney's great annual reminder that
her hinterland—Australia, that is, narrowed down to New South
Wales—has depended on agriculture and husbandry for its survival from the outset. Of only one other country in the Western
world, Australia's next-door neighbour, can the same be said. And
you can track the steady development of this paramount industry
by following the growth of the Easter Show from its beginning,
when the colony was only thirty thousand people strong. The first
prizewinner was Jonas Bradley, who collected a silver tankard for
growing tobacco, and another winner was a former convict named
Samuel Terry, who had put his past far enough behind him to be
awarded a piece of silver plate for his three-year-old stallions,
while Maurice Rock went home £32 better off for having weaned
297 lambs from 316 ewes. A Mr Grose of Parramatta was suitably
rewarded for brewing a beer which was 'possessed of such strength
that many who drank it' found their 'betrayed reason dethroned
and madness and folly reigning in its stead'.[2] The wowser, like the
drunkard, made an early appearance in New South Wales.

Arthur Phillip had swiftly come to the conclusion that the only
future for his colony lay in the hands of farmers and anyone else
who, accustomed to hard manual labour, could live off land which
they themselves had cultivated. This was easier said than done
when the soil around Port Jackson was soon discovered to be thin
and almost sterile, though much richer land existed a bit further
inland; hence the early expansion to Rose Hill, which had been,
and would be again, known as Parramatta. In November 1789,

Phillip granted a cleared acre of land there, plus a tract of bush, to the ex-convict James Ruse, who had just completed a seven-year sentence, and who had been a Cornish farmer before he fell foul of the law. He was supplied with a hatchet, a tomahawk, two hoes, a spade and a shovel, together with the labour of a serving convict, and told to get on with it. He and his new wife (also an ex-convict, *née* Elizabeth Parry) continued to be fed and clothed by the Commissary until, only one harvest and fifteen months later, they declared themselves to be almost self-supporting, about to reap a dozen or more bushels of wheat from three bushels of seed, with a crop of maize expected later in 1791. And this is how Ruse did it:

> My land I prepared thus: having burnt the fallen timber off the ground, I dug in the ashes, and then hoed it up, never doing more than eight, or perhaps nine rods in a day, by which means, it was not like the government-farm, just scratched over, but properly done; then I clod-moulded it, and dug in the grass and the weeds—this I think almost equal to ploughing. I then let it lie as long as I could, exposed to air and sun; and just before I sowed my seed, turned it all up afresh. When I shall have reaped my crop, I purpose to hoe it again, and harrow it fine, and then sow it with turnip-seed, which will mellow and prepare it for next year.[3]

If that other ex-convict William Redfern can properly be called the father of Australian medicine, then James Ruse was assuredly the begetter of the nation's farming industry. Governor Phillip rewarded his diligence by giving him the second land-grant in the country's history, thirty acres at Parramatta, which became known as Experiment Farm; and by 1819 he was cultivating two hundred acres successfully.* Many other ex-convicts, and a sprinkling of free settlers, were working the land by then and agriculture was begin-

---

*But Ruse's story does not, alas, have the happiest ending. His luck eventually ran out, and he finished up working as a farm bailiff for somebody else. He did leave descendants who prospered, however, and a dozen of them are listed in the Sydney telephone book.

ning to blossom. Husbandry took a little longer to get to its feet, partly because the animals obdurately refused to breed at first in patterns which the colonists expected of them, partly because too many were lost to marauding natives, natural calamity or plain misadventure: some cattle broke out of their paddock one night and vanished without trace until they were found seven years later, ruminating placidly with their numerous offspring, in hitherto unexplored country close to the Great Dividing Range, which had stopped them from straying any further.

Replenishment of such losses obviously came from outside New South Wales, as when over a thousand pounds was sent to England in 1822 in order to acquire more livestock, with another hundred pounds for fresh seed and agricultural textbooks, money which was raised by the infant Agricultural Society. Three years later the fruits of this disbursement arrived at Port Jackson in the shape of three Durham heifers and a bull, five Devonshire heifers and a bull, forty-eight Merino ewes and five rams, all of them said to be breeding animals of guaranteed quality. Those Merinos were not the first of their bloodline to reach the continent, a distinction which belongs to four sheep which arrived in 1793 from San Francisco.

Originating in Spain—where it acquired its name from Berbers during the Moorish occupation in the thirteenth century—the Merino not only produces a big fleece of exceptionally fine wool, but in some of its varieties it can endure and even thrive in arid conditions which no other breed will survive. It is very striking that, if you drive from Sydney to Melbourne across a baked countryside which has gone far too long without rain, the Merinos appear to be in good shape even though pasture after pasture contains grass so withered that it is the same colour as the dusty earth. The ewes, moreover, can lamb more than once a year, which is uncommon among sheep. All these factors were to be the making of Australia economically.[4] This took time to achieve, however, and until the colony was almost half a century old the

exports that paid for almost all the imports were the oil, the bone
and the ambergris of whales, and the furry skins of seals; millions
of both creatures, it has been estimated, were killed in the bays
and on the beaches of Australia in the first decades of the settlement. But just as the supply of these commodities was fast dimin-
ishing, sheep farming was paying more and more of the colony's
bills, until it became easily the biggest earner. By the middle of the
nineteenth century, there were seven hundred sheep stations in
New South Wales alone. The annual wool clip is worth nearly
four billion dollars to this country today, which is not to be
sneezed at, even though other industries now produce more.

The man who is usually given all the credit for the early development of the Australian Merino is John Macarthur. There were
others who also did their bit, including the Rev Samuel Marsden,
Chaplain at Port Jackson from 1794 and part-time farmer at Parramatta, an unctuous and unpleasant humbug, assiduous in everything he did. Thirty years after his arrival in New South Wales, he
was running nine thousand sheep and five thousand cattle on his
property and he had presented George III with a suit made from
his Merino wool, thus securing useful publicity for what London
still thought of as merely a penal colony. Macarthur, however, not
only had the stamina for the long haul, but rather more imagination and only one flock requiring his attention, so he has therefore
been seen as the first truly professional Australian sheep breeder.

He was a draper's son from Devon, a lowly Army officer with a
great sense of his own importance, which was frustrated when the
American War of Independence came to an end before he had
time to take part in it and make his mark.* Recruiting was under
way for the New South Wales Corps, which was about to take
over garrison duties from the Marines, who had provided Arthur
Phillip with his first military presence, so Macarthur signed on as

---

*Macarthur was colourful enough not to need his life embroidered by rumour, but one of these
reckoned that he was an illegitimate son of George III.

a twenty-four-year-old lieutenant and set sail in the notorious Second Fleet with his wife, Elizabeth, and their infant son for what was to be an eventful life—with a couple of unavoidable absences—in Australia. The family arrived at Port Jackson in 1791 and within a few months they were living in Parramatta, where Macarthur had been appointed regimental paymaster. Shortly afterwards he was made inspector of public works as well and in February 1793 was granted a hundred acres of the best land that had yet been worked, which he had more than doubled (with the help of ample convict labour) before the year was out. His future and his fortune were assured after that, though there were a number of hiccups on the way.

Macarthur was arrogant and quarrelsome by nature; indeed, it is written all over his face, which is set in disdain above a bully's mouth in all the existing portraits. Before the *Neptune* had even weighed anchor in Plymouth, he was fighting a duel with her master, though neither man's aim was straight and so no one was hurt. He was reprimanded for headstrong conduct by Arthur Phillip almost as soon as he arrived, and his quarrels with every Governor who succeeded Phillip became legendary. John Hunter eventually decided that 'There is not a person in this colony whose opinions I hold in greater contempt than I do this busybody's....'[5] Phillip King discovered that Macarthur was behind a local racket in the sale of rum, and when Macarthur persuaded fellow officers to boycott the Governor, fighting and dangerously wounding one who refused to side with him, King had him packed off to England. Three years later Macarthur was back with the support of Lord Camden, Pitt's Secretary of State for the Colonies, who instructed King to grant Macarthur a further five thousand acres of land with a healthy herd of cattle on it. Emboldened by this patronage, Macarthur did not shrink from conflict when William Bligh succeeded King and concluded that he must curb this insolent fellow's activities. He did not know his man, and he particularly underestimated Macarthur's ability to whip up the animosity

of others towards anyone he nominated as an enemy. The upshot
was that Bligh was placed under house arrest by Macarthur's
cronies in the regiment—by now popularly known as the Rum
Corps—in the Rum Rebellion, which effectively finished Bligh's
Australian career. Its further outcome was Macarthur's second exile
in England, self-imposed this time, because New South Wales had
become just a bit too hot even for him. His wife stayed behind to
manage the farm, much against his wishes, until he returned eight
years later to find it in even better shape than when he left it.

At the bottom of all this friction was not only Macarthur's dis-
putatious nature, but greed: his own greed and that of virtually the
whole officer class in New South Wales. A limited amount of
commerce and landholding had begun while Arthur Phillip was in
charge, which that scrupulous man had kept in balance with the
public good, like everything else he did. But, when he left, Major
Grose, who had brought the Rum Corps out from England, took
charge for the three years before Governor Hunter arrived, and in
that time the colony underwent a form of moral collapse. Grose
wanted a quiet life above everything, and so he gave his officers
virtually anything they sought, which was a great deal more than
the hundred-acre plots of land London had authorised him to
allot. For a start they wanted the entire cargo of rum, 7,500 gallons
of it, that an American vessel brought to Sydney Cove in 1793,
which they secured and then proceeded to resell at a huge profit to
themselves. The regimental paymaster, name of Macarthur, was
the man who supervised this transaction. The people who paid, of
course, were much lowlier than the officers, more in need of
booze to relieve the pain of a hard and frequently miserable existence. They soon found themselves on the receiving end of other
extortions, as the officers quickly monopolised everything that
was imported into Sydney Cove. And when they couldn't meet
their bills, they surrendered for a pittance the bits and pieces of
land they were trying to farm, to the men who were already screw-
ing them. By 1799, the Rum Corps officers controlled 32 per cent

of all the cattle in New South Wales, 40 per cent of the goats, 59 per cent of the horses, 77 per cent of the sheep and a vast acreage of territory. John Macarthur was the driving force behind this rape of the colony, the one who made the biggest killing of the lot. He had arrived in Australia with debts of £500 and within ten years he was worth at least £20,000. Not even the East India Company Nabobs who were simultaneously despoiling India did much better than that. And yet...

In spite of this ugliness, there is something heroic in the story of John Macarthur, and it is the same order of heroism displayed time and time again in the opening up of America by men who were just as unscrupulous and nasty when it suited them. It is also something more than heroism, and again this has an American version: a form of dogged application and ingenuity, a vision of what is possible and a refusal to give this up, which cannot mitigate the avarice, but which in itself is distinctly admirable. Here is Macarthur, writing to his brother in England in 1794, when his prosperity was just beginning:

> I have a Farm containing nearly 250 Acres, of which upwards of 100 are under cultivation & the greater part of the remainder is cleared of the Timber which grows upon it. Of this years [*sic*] produce I have sold £400 worth & I have now remaining in my Granaries upwards of 1800 Bushels of Corn. I have at this moment 20 Acres of very fine wheat growing—& 80 Acres prepared for Indian Corn and Potatoes, with which it will be planted in less than a month. My stock consists of a Horse, two Mares, Two Cows, 130 Goats & upwards of 100 Hogs. Poultry of all kinds I have in the greatest abundance. I have received no stock from Government, but one Cow, the rest I have either purchased or bred. With the assistance of One Man & half a dozen greyhounds, which I keep, my Table is constantly supplied with Wild Ducks or Kangaroos.[6]

And he doesn't even mention sheep.

Three years after writing that letter, Macarthur acquired four

Merino ewes and two rams from South Africa and began to breed from them. In 1800 he sent eight fleeces to Sir Joseph Banks in England, and while most of them were cross-bred, one was pure Merino. Back came the word that if the colony could produce wool as good as that in quantity, then London would be glad to do business. The duel that almost killed Colonel Paterson came next, and with it Macarthur's banishment, which inevitably he turned to good account by talking wool wherever he went, talking up his own wool in particular, and evidently getting Lord Camden interested. On his return to New South Wales, authorised to acquire more land, he resigned his commission and began to farm in earnest. In London he had managed to acquire a licence to export ten Merinos from the King's own flock, and although four of the sheep died in transit to Australia, the survivors were soon adding to Macarthur's existing stock of lambs. When his quarrel with Bligh again interrupted these efforts, he spent his second exile profitably by studying agriculture in England, returning when he thought the dust had settled, to take up where he had left off.

By now he—and the devoted Elizabeth in his absence—was breeding Merinos prolifically and urging others to follow suit as enthusiastically as any other evangelist, though they were slow to imitate: in 1818 he lamented the fact that no more than ten sheep breeders were trying seriously to improve the quality of their flocks, with only half a dozen of them doing so sensibly. One of these was the Irishman Alexander Riley, who imported Saxony Merinos for cross-breeding from stock that Frederick the Great had brought to Prussia from Spain early in the eighteenth century, and which would now help to improve the Australian strain. Slowly the general climate changed, and by the time Macarthur was running more than two thousand pure Merinos on his properties, others had begun to pay attention, to buy his sheep and start breeding on their own account. Three hundred young rams were drafted to Tasmania, at about the time that Macarthur introduced a training scheme for new settlers on his principal holding out at Camden, which he had named after his most useful patron:

it had formerly been known as Cowpastures, and was the place where the errant cattle had finally been tracked down in 1795.

John Macarthur was an obviously flawed man and ultimately a tragic figure who in his final years swung from deep depressions to frantic activity, until he became so irrational that he was certified as a lunatic and thereafter rarely left his room at Camden Park. That was where he died in 1834, nursed to the end by the tireless and utterly admirable Elizabeth, who had supported him in every way possible throughout his turbulent life. By then he owned over twenty-four thousand acres, held mortgages on another thirteen thousand, possessed stock valued at £30,000 and various domestic items valued at £1,750. He had made too many enemies, had ridden roughshod over too many less forceful people to be liked or widely mourned at his death, and one of his farm pupils accurately identified his principal characteristics when he wrote that 'he is a very clever, shrewed [sic], calculating man, with an extraordinary degree of perseverance & foresight, but a man of the most violent passions, his friendship strong & his hatred invincible'.[7] Nevertheless, Australia can remember the name Macarthur, on the whole, with thankfulness.

So can anyone who sits on the verandah of Elizabeth Farm and listens to the drowsy buzz of insects in the garden, and the dripping of water through a sandstone bowl, which miraculously cools the liquid on the hottest of afternoons; for this was the home that convicts built for the Macarthurs and their children, still kept so beautifully by a trust that the family might have left it only yesterday. Romantics in thrall to the sea can also think benevolently of the Macarthurs when they roam over the *Cutty Sark* at her drydock in faraway Greenwich, and recall the saga of the wool clippers, which could run from Sydney to the estuary of the Thames in seventy-three days, *Cutty Sark*'s own record passage in 1885.*

**Cutty Sark started life carrying tea from China to England, but after only her eighth voyage the Suez Canal opened and made much shorter passages possible by steamship, though not by sail. The clippers thereafter turned to other cargoes, Australian wool being the most profitable.

Four years after Macarthur's death, Thomas Sutcliffe Mort arrived from England, another young man who was to become a key figure in Australia's prosperity. He reached Sydney from Lancashire when he was only twenty-two with no trade at his fingertips, but literate enough to find work at once as a clerk, and then a salesman. He was an altogether more agreeable fellow than Macarthur, and the only thing they seem to have had in common was an unusual amount of energy and determination to succeed. Within five years of his arrival, Mort had not only become part-owner of the Hunter River Navigation Company, but was also working as an auctioneer and a wool-broker. By the time he was thirty, he had founded the shipbuilders, Mort and Company, of Balmain, and from there he launched the largest ship made up to then in Australia, the *Governor Blackall.* Soon he was into all manner of other enterprises, without relinquishing anything he had started earlier: the Great Nugget Vein Mining Company (the first company formed to dig for gold), the Peak Downs Copper Mining Company in Queensland, the Waratah Coal Mining Company at Newcastle, and a farm with cattle spread across seventeen thousand acres. His reputation was always that of an exemplary employer, in whatever area his interests lay: among other things, he encouraged his workers to take shares in his various businesses. Yet he was not merely a businessman: he was first Chairman of the New South Wales Academy of Art when it was established in 1871; which, within a few years, had been translated into the Art Gallery of New South Wales and become one of Sydney's most precious possessions.

But, as a businessman, Mort concentrated more and more on the possibility of transporting meat over long distances—as far away, in fact, as England. In 1870, with his own slaughterhouses and freezing works flourishing at Lithgow, and an ice-making factory in Darling Harbour, he put up £60,000 of his own money and hustled another £20,000 from the graziers of New South Wales to back a Frenchman, Eugène Nicolle, who was experimenting with an ammonia machine that would refrigerate meat for weeks and possibly months. In 1877 the steamship *Northam* sailed from Sydney on a trial run to England with 170 tons of beef which had been frozen for months in Mort's factory, but the machinery broke down at sea and the cargo was lost. It was therefore another couple of years before the first Australian meat reached London via the Suez Canal, and a couple of Scots, Andrew McIlwraith and Malcolm McEacharn, were able to claim the credit for the SS *Strathleven*'s happier voyage, for they had modified Nicolle's machinery until it worked as intended. Thomas Mort missed this triumph by a few months, having died in 1878; but he had been for so many years the driving force behind the refrigeration experiments that the breakthrough would have been much delayed had he not done the preliminary spadework. Like John Macarthur, he was an Australian version of many American industrial and commercial pioneers.*

Within the lifetimes of those two men, Sydney was in every way transformed. The rudimentary settlement that awaited the Macarthur family on their arrival in the Second Fleet—which even ten years later 'had more the appearance of a camp than a town, mixed with stumps and dead trees'[8]—had become a thriving industrial city of nearly a quarter of a million people by the time Thomas Mort died. In that very year the first telephone was installed in Sydney, and the railway line was extended as far as Wagga Wagga. The streets had long been gas-lit, and Toohey's Brewery was also in full flow. Visitors could even buy souvenir postcards by then and the building of the new GPO in Martin Place—destined to be a great landmark for the best part of a century—was well under way. The era of the great department stores was about to begin, with David Jones already well established in

---

*In particular, his inexhaustible patience calls to mind the similar doggedness of the Boston shipowner Frederic Tudor, who spent twenty-eight years experimenting with various forms of insulation that would enable him to export ice from a frozen lake in Massachusetts to hot countries that craved cool drinks. He eventually found, in 1833, that sawdust did the trick.

small premises on George Street and Horderns's shop newly opened in the Haymarket, soon to be followed elsewhere by the Mark Foy Emporium and by Joseph Grace's drapery. The natural ellipse of old Sydney Cove had been modified by a need to accommodate bigger and longer vessels as the nineteenth century progressed, which meant berths constructed in straight lines, not curves: the head of the cove was scarcely a semi-circular quay any more, though the name stuck as the ferry-boats gradually monopolised it, and jetties were built at right angles so that they could all be fitted in. Down at the wharves of Darling Harbour, Woolloomooloo and Pyrmont—there would be eight miles of these by the end of the century—vessels lay stem to stern or alongside each other in a confusion of masts and funnels, while an endless rumbling of wagons brought the wool, the timber, the minerals and the other cargoes that would help this city to pay its way, or carried off to dockside warehouses the necessities and the luxuries that had arrived from the other side of the world and from places in between. The penal colony had become a respectable and increasingly prosperous outpost of Empire, a source of pride rather than shame to its citizens, but in one respect it hadn't changed at all. It was still a seaport, set within a magnificent harbour, through which the city and the country behind it were replenished and increasingly gave others sustenance.

As it remains, even today, though the rapid expansion of air freight has taken a little bit of the edge off maritime commerce, enabling the British, for example, to buy fresh Australian blueberries at their supermarkets in the depths of the northern winter. But the heavy stuff still has to travel by sea, as it always will, and that includes bulk cargoes of (quite frequently) bulky passengers. Interminably, between September and May, the cruise vessels steal up the Harbour with a quiet electrical hum, so many of them at times that while the luckiest one through the Heads will be able to nab the most favoured docking at Circular Quay, three others are obliged to berth round the corner and behind the Bridge, in line ahead opposite the Maritime Museum. Like all the most expensive ladies they are extremely conscious of their looks, and the most alluring at present are notable for being immaculately white from stem to stern, with sensational flare at the bows, as modern fashion in this particular kind of shipping dictates. This means that the dear old *QE II* ('an ikon of luxury leisure travel', according to a Sydney Ports brochure) is beginning to look a bit old hat, her only real concession to the modernist school of naval architecture being a tall and odd-looking funnel that doesn't seem to emit much smoke. But for real dowdiness there is nothing to compare with the occasional vessel flying the Russian flag, desperate for hard currency and a fresh lick of paint.

The cruise ships may be registered in almost any country with a seaboard of its own, but in common they are working the lucrative Pacific trade, picking up passengers from the American West Coast more than anywhere else, and touring them round various ports of call between Hawaii and Milford Sound NZ (where many may complain that there is nothing to do except gasp at some of the most thrilling scenery on earth). In Sydney, the passengers are usually on the town for a couple of days, inspecting the shops along George Street as much as anything, riding to the top of the Sydney Tower (the most certain attraction of all because until recently it was 'the tallest building in the southern hemisphere', from which you can see fifty-odd miles on a clear day), trying out the Harbourside café life, or plundering the nearby Rocks of its expensive trinkets and souvenirs. Not many of them are interested enough in Sydney's essence to wander round the uncommercial bit of the Rocks and Millers Point, where the oldest remaining houses in the city are to be found: terraces of tin-roofed buildings, with verandahs upheld by slender posts, and balconies decorated with intricate cast-iron, which go back to the days when John Macarthur was still alive.* And when these liners

---

*The very oldest building, Cadman's Cottage, which stands by itself overlooking Circular Quay, went up in 1816 as a small barracks for the crews of Governor Macquarie's personal flotilla.

set sail again, their departures are not the emotional upheaval, either aboard or ashore, that was the case well within living memory, with people seeing relatives off for years and (who knows?) for ever perhaps, with streamers binding ship to shore until the great hull began to edge away from its berth and the ribbons snapped, one after another, until the last of them broke and all contact was gone. Few citizens bid farewell to the industrial tourists of today, and the visitors themselves have usually abandoned the deck long before the Bridge and the Opera House are out of sight: down in their cabins they are by then, showing each other the objects they think they acquired at bargain prices, and consulting the ship's timetable to see how long before the next meal.

Workaday shipping trudges in through the Heads, day in and day out, all the year round; and while most of it, too, is remarkably spick and span even in the case of the unabashed tramps, now and then a bedraggled veteran of the high seas comes up the shipping channel 'with smears of rust like the red gum of the eucalyptus tree' down her sides, as Kenneth Slessor once observed.[9] Ships arrive with superstructures rising abruptly in umpteen storeys like an apartment block; ships with the bulbous bow that became fashionable again after being out of favour for the best part of a century; ships so top-heavy with containers that they resemble a railway marshalling yard, and you wonder why they haven't turned turtle in the latest storm; ships that are nothing more than boxes on keels, so unspeakably ugly that whoever drew up the blueprints must have thought they were being asked to design a septic tank; ships that have become floating advertisements with their owner's name flashed ostentatiously along the side—an unthinkable vulgarity not so long ago—STOLT TANKERS, LINEA MEXICO, CONTSHIP, WILHELMSEN LINES, MAERSK, HAPAG LLOYD and many more. A huge tanker, so far down to her marks that her squat red hull seems much, much wider than its height, comes upstream ahead of a newly risen sun with an attendance of tugs, which gently bully her fore and aft until she reaches her berth at Gore

Bay with an exhausted puff of smoke. Other vessels will follow her—sometimes only a couple at the weekend, when the wharfies may not be there to empty them, more frequently a dozen or so at regular intervals—to deliver cement, or soda ash, or sugar at Glebe Island, or to swap cargoes in any number of commodities at the still practical bit of Darling Harbour.

But, just as the Port of London had to give way to Tilbury Docks because of market forces and other obfuscations, so Sydney Harbour has had to yield to the (in a sense) upstart Botany Bay. Not a great deal had happened around the bay after Arthur Phillip gave it the thumbs down, until Sydney's municipal aerodrome was started on its northern shore just after the Great War. Steadily, the airport expanded, as these things always do, becoming an international terminus under the name of Mascot (an adjacent suburb) at first, then under that of Charles Kingsford Smith, the local aviator who made the first crossing of the Pacific and a number of other heroic flights. And that was that until ships became generally much bigger than ever before and stowing cargoes in enormous boxes, below and on deck, was the increasingly profitable thing to do. The wharves that had served the city so well for more than a century and a half were thought to be just a bit too cramped for the new maritime calculations, and so the very obvious thing was done: they built a new port in the nearest safe anchorage with lots of yet unoccupied space, which today handles almost three-quarters of Sydney's total seaborne trade. One half of the bay is now either runways or docks, with all the industrial detritus that they invariably attract, oil tanks and suchlike, which gleam smugly in the sun. The long wharves with their endless rows of containers and their vast rectangular gantries for dropping big boxes on to ships look from afar as though some child has got his Lego and his Meccano sets mixed up.

One way and another, Botany Bay is becoming an environmental disaster, already so dreadful a mess that even a local mayor has been moved to describe it, with a very Australian sense of propriety, as 'the anus of Sydney'.[10] It is almost as if, in sparing the Harbour from the worst excesses of our progressive world, Someone In Authority had decided to compensate by taking it out on this poor neglected reminder of what might have been. The disaster is not simply the erosion of the shoreline because sixty million tons of sand have been dredged to produce enough depth of water for very big ships, or because a considerable oyster fishery in the Georges River estuary has been wiped out by pollution, or because Authority is so heedless of what it has already done that it is planning to double the number of ships entering the docks, and plotting an electricity-generating plant that will pour endless torrents of chlorinated water into the bay, at ten degrees warmer than the natural temperature. The disaster is not even—though it is very much also—because some people happen to have lived a long time inside the northern arm of the bay at La Pérouse but, being aboriginal, they were not consulted about any of this. The disaster is as much as any of these things to do with a defilement of Australia's history, with the very beginning of European settlement on this continent.

For just across the bay, facing this unlovely spectacle, is the place where James Cook landed and knew for certain that he had at last discovered the fabulous Unknown Southern Land. The shore is the same one he stepped on to in 1770, strangely puckered rock that holds little cups of water at low tide. Above this is a strand of minutely pulverised shells and above that a long slope of grass fringed with trees, which conceal a very decent information centre run by the national park. In it you can see a superb replica of the barque *Endeavour*, a sturdy three-master whose builders in Whitby could never have dreamed what was in store for her when she went down the slips into the North Sea, destined, so they thought, for nothing more adventurous than the coal trade along England's east coast.* A commemorative obelisk has been erected

---

*HMS *Endeavour* was launched as the *Earl of Pembroke*, 368 tons, and acquired her more famous name when the Royal Navy bought her for Cook's great enterprise.

just above the shore, and near by is a boulder which notes that this was where, in Cook's phrase, 'fresh water . . . came trickling down',[11] though it is little more than a ditch now. Poor Forby Sutherland's grave is marked by another stone. There is nothing else at Botany Bay from the time of Cook, though there might have been had the city fathers been more alert three-quarters of a century ago; but, for some unaccountable reason, Sydney allowed itself to be bested by the other place in 1934, when Cook's cottage on the outskirts of Middlesbrough—within hailing distance of the engineering firm that built Sydney Harbour Bridge—was dismantled stone by stone and shipped out to the Fitzroy Gardens in Melbourne, where it has been a popular tourist attraction ever since.

If ever a European heirloom in Australia ought to have been preserved from all forms of pollution, this was the one. Cook's Landing, under the exemplary management of the New South Wales national parks authorities, could have been a place for quiet reflection about many things in Australia's past, not least on the relationship between the two peoples who have a particular attachment to Botany Bay. Instead there is violent noise, as the Jumbos come thundering down the runways at Kingsford Smith, scarcely airborne when they climb above that obelisk.* There is endlessly irritating noise, as the speedboat drivers and the water-skiers zip past the beach, with not a thought in their heads except having a ball and making waves. There is the filth that careless or villainous shipmasters rid their vessels of by pouring it into the bay. There is even an encroachment of tradesmen who have set up their ostentatious little businesses as close to the national park boundary as they dare (from the landing you can read the name on the side of

---

*This noise does, at least, abate between ten o'clock at night and the following breakfast time, a notable triumph for the inhabitants of Mascot, Sutherland and other southern suburbs. But this causes problems for the captains of aircraft which are flying behind schedule along the international routes: they have to judge, long before they get there, whether they can make it to Kingsford Smith before it closes for the night. Many are the disgruntled passengers who have been required to kill time for several unwanted hours at Brisbane's airport instead.

the 'EZE by the Bay' fast-food joint). The coming and going of ships may be in harmony with what happened here in the past, but the incubus that feeds off them looms ominously, enlarging itself year after year. The skyscrapers of downtown Sydney are a sympathetic distance away, their tips visible above the horizon, but this unwholesome sprawl is revoltingly near.

Botany Bay, handled with imagination, might have been an unspoilt sanctuary, a healing place where two races could have been clearly and gratefully and generously reconciled. As things are, it is difficult to avoid the conclusion that the people who thought up the port extension, and those who want both it and the airport to be even bigger than they already are, have spat upon their own past, and upon all Australian ancestry.

CHAPTER FIVE

※

A Haven, a Battle and Endless Suburbs

Sydney's most healing place lies beside the Harbour, as you might expect; and, as with the Harbour, there cannot be anything else to match it anywhere in the world. Neither Hyde Park in London, nor Central Park in New York, nor the Giardino Borghese in Rome, nor the Jardin des Tuileries in Paris are remotely in the same class, and even Golden Gate Park in San Francisco doesn't pass muster because, although it is a blessed corridor between that city and the Pacific Ocean, it is too self-consciously a place for having fun—you can play baseball or throw horseshoes or have your dog trained there—in which you frequently can't see the flora for the stream of people relentlessly jogging past. None of these afflictions are visited upon the Royal Botanic Gardens, which are nothing less than a miracle of tranquillity only a few hundred yards from some of Sydney's busiest streets. This was part of the ambience Anthony Trollope found so enchanting that he scarcely knew how to express it for posterity.

The Gardens were, in the first place, one of Arthur Phillip's brainwaves, for it was he who ordained that the area immediately to the east of his new Government House should remain in the

public domain for ever, an uncontaminated reserve which would
be secured by the Crown for the refreshment of the citizens, a
concept that was subsequently to be adopted throughout the Antipodes. The Domain it has remained to this day, though only
part of the original reserve still carries that title, an expanse of
trees and turf that Sydneysiders make for in their thousands when
they feel strongly enough about politics or economics to demonstrate *en masse* that they're not at all happy with the way things are
going. But most of the area, about seventy-five acres running down
to an inlet in the Harbour between Circular Quay and the naval
base at Woolloomooloo, is the Botanic Gardens. Because this was
where the very first, and fruitless, attempt at agriculture took
place, the colonists spoke of it as Farm Cove. To the Aborigines it
had always been known as Wuganmagulya, the place where they
held initiation ceremonies on the shore, and there performed their
Kangaroo and Dog Dance.

John Macarthur and the Rum Corps officers predictably ignored both the letter and the spirit of Phillip's announcement as
soon as he was out of the way, and tried to annex the Domain for
their own purposes. They were seen off by William Bligh, who
happened to be a keen gardener as well as a disciplinarian, characteristics that may both have weighed with the Admiralty when
they chose him to go looking for breadfruit plants aboard HMS
Bounty in 1787. But it was Lachlan Macquarie who took the steps
that eventually led to the Gardens as we know them today, by
building walls to safeguard the boundaries of this public property,
by creating a road round the cove so that his wife could more easily reach her favourite vantage point on a rocky knoll high above
the water, and by appointing Charles Fraser, of the 46th Regiment, Superintendent of the Botanic Gardens in 1816 (within the
year he was Colonial Botanist as well). And it would be a strangely
blank soul who, sitting on the ledge known as Mrs Macquarie's
Chair, with one of the best of all views up and down the Harbour,
and this glorious acreage of natural history at his back, did not

feel at least a small spasm of gratitude at the end of the twentieth century for three of those much maligned early Governors.

There are several sides to the character of the Gardens, and they harmonise wonderfully. Much of it is like a great parkland, with trees that take your breath away by their size, their shape, their foliage, their flowers, set in a tremendous grassy amphitheatre, with long and spacious slopes of green between each, so that a balance is held perfectly between effulgent light and soothing shade. Such trees they are, upstanding and gnarled, straight-limbed and bent, with barks that invite you to place your open hands across their smoothnesses or draw your fingers down the furrows and the ridges of their roughnesses, before stooping to pick up the cones, the nuts and the other fruits which in season lie in such profusion upon the ground that you crunch them underfoot and occasionally trip over a root concealed by them—and some of the roots extend for twenty yards or more; shaped, in the case of the banyan tree, in great flanges which hint at some structural role in the belly of an oceangoing ship. It would be no surprise to discover that every subspecies of fig tree on earth (and there are reckoned to be two thousand of them) grows here, and so many of them do that presently you tire of inspecting the information attached to each, to see in what subtle way this *ficus* differs from the Moreton Bay specimen just over there, which is said to be 140 years old. The same goes for the gum trees, with their upright spindly bodies and their mottled, flaking skins, and their so peculiarly Australian nature that they can make the heart lurch when you are too far away to stroke them or rub the smell out of their leaves, yet remember them perfectly.

A lot of Australian natives are here, quite apart from an enormous spread of those eucalypts: Queensland bottle trees, firewheel trees, scrub beefwood, bush nuts, Oliver's sassafras, soapberries, coachwoods (some of them do sound as though they ought to be yielding drinkable wine in the Hunter Valley), snow woods, swamp she-oaks, cheese trees. And then there is the plant collection, deployed in lush plots and borders protected by shrubbery, which between them produce dazzling colour somewhere in the Gardens at every time of the year: there are supposed to be twenty-five thousand different kinds of plant life in Australia, and well over a quarter of them are growing here. As you potter along the pathways with vivid beds on either side, misty with the spray of gentle irrigation, it occurs to you that some people have ruined their health, lost their lives, in trying to add to this display. Charles Fraser's immediate successor, Richard Cunningham, was speared to death in 1835 after wandering too far off the beaten track to look for specimens along the Bogan River. His brother Allan, who became the third Superintendent, was paralysed by some infection which he picked up on a field trip in New Zealand, and died a few weeks later at his cottage in the Gardens. John Bidwill, the first man to be given the title Director of the Botanic Gardens, died of exposure in 1853 when his zeal outran his prudence in a remote part of Queensland.

They were, of course, animated by the same spirit of scientific inquiry that sends people to the moon, and the spirit lives on in the herbarium, where botanists pore over bracts and sepals and ligules and the distichous parts of a stem, until identification has been made beyond all doubt, and the specimen has been carefully filed and preserved if it's out of the ordinary—which was not always the case in the past. The rarest palm trees in the world must be the two examples of *Pritchardia maideniana* which the Botanic gardeners tend lovingly, because they have never been rediscovered in the wild since they were acquired by Sydney from somewhere or other that everyone has long since forgotten: and, unfortunately, no record was kept of where that was.* But part of Sir Joseph

---

*The other great rarity in the Gardens is the Wollemi Pine, which has been successfully propagated away from its natural habitat and is now a sapling cosseted under a special awning to protect it from the sun. Belonging to the conifer family *Araucariaceae,* it was unheard of until a national parks warden, David Noble, discovered a small stand of these trees in August 1994 in a deep and damp gorge in the Wollemi National Park, about 120 miles north-west of the city. It has many botanical features in common with fossils belonging to the Cretaceous and early Tertiary periods—that is, about 65 million years ago.

Banks's collection, dating back to the voyage of the *Endeavour*, is cherished between the heavy covers of pressing books, and there are other remembrances of those times, scattered here and there. Many of the gum trees are descended through regeneration from eucalypts that were standing here when the First Fleet sailed in. And to remind us that this was a hard place to farm in those early days, a comparatively woebegone plot has been kept open on the original site, with its rhubarb and its brassicas looking a bit sorry for themselves in the heat of the day, especially when everything else in sight has had the benefit of nearly two hundred years of generous composting.

The Gardens are bursting with wild creatures as well as vegetation. Cockatoos swoop endlessly from tree to tree in brilliantly white and crested covens, and ibises pick their mannered way across the softer ground, prodding it with long curved beaks for grubs and other tasty things. Most of the birds are colourful Australian natives but, because nostalgic Englishmen in the nineteenth-century Acclimatisation Society wanted reminders of home, their house sparrow, their starling, their blackbird, their thrush and their pigeon are here, too; also the mynah, which they had become attached to in India (their homesickness could have taken a more ill-advised form, like bringing the blackberry to fertile New Zealand, where it has plagued the farmers ever since). Ducks paddle around the ponds, keeping an eye lifted for the eels who are a menace to the youngest birds. Possums amble about at night, but they're no danger to anything except insects and foliage. And then there is a peculiar Botanic Gardens sound, which gives away the presence of some other local fauna on a soporific afternoon. On first hearing this, you wonder if it might be something to do with an oriental wedding, for the Gardens are very popular with Japanese and Korean couples, who are said to find it cheaper to fly in from Tokyo or Seoul to hold their nuptials alfresco here instead of more traditionally at home; besides, there's only one place where you can take photographs after the ceremony in front of the Opera House. But the noise, which sounds as if half a dozen dustbin lids are being clashed together, is made by gardeners trying to disturb the flying-foxes which are having a post-prandial nap after gorging themselves on the Botanic Gardens figs. Often mistaken for huge bats, these are one of Sydney's great natural curiosities. They mostly roost on the wooded slopes north of the Harbour, and fly across the water in their thousands at dusk, to feed throughout the night in the Gardens and in Centennial Park before taking off for home again at dawn; but occasionally they outstay their welcome to the unacceptable detriment of the trees.

The marvel of the Botanic Gardens is not only its prolific beauty and its heavenly stillness and quiet (distinguishing it, again, from the great urban parks of the northern hemisphere, where there is always a muted roar of traffic in the background), but the fact that it is so close to the restless energy of Circular Quay and the city's main streets. One of its gates is beside the Opera House, another overlooks the Cahill Expressway, which an appalling misjudgement by planners and City Council just after the Second World War allowed to be driven through a cutting which now separates much of the Domain from its natural companion. The error was compounded by a further violation of the Domain with the construction of a car park and its slip roads. More happily, you can walk into the Gardens straight off Macquarie Street, which is lined on one side by some of the most handsome and historic public buildings in Sydney. Within the grounds are two notably castellated buildings, one of them the Conservatorium of Music, which used to be the stables for the adjacent Government House, both structures designed with a bob in the direction of distant Inverary Castle; which, intentionally or not, would have pleased the Governor who ordered them, for his father was chief of the Clan Macquarrie (*sic*), whose tribal lands lay just offshore of the Campbell headquarters at Inverary. Along this side the Garden Palace was built to house the International Exhibition of 1878 and, judging by photographs—for it was burned to the ground within a few years—it looks as if its architect had been inspired by both the Crystal Palace in London and something a maharajah might have owned.

How long these will remain the *Royal* Botanic Gardens is anybody's guess, and the honorific is surprisingly recent, not con-
ferred until the Queen Mother came visiting in 1958. Royalty has
certainly been mindful of a need to keep its memory green out
here, periodically dropping by to plant another tree and take the
salutes. The first arrival was one of Queen Victoria's sons, Prince
Alfred, who planted *Martiusella imperialis* (from Brazil) in 1868, followed thirteen years later by his brothers George and Albert Victor, who put down *Melaleuca quinquenervia* and *Livistona australis*
(on the lawn north-east of bed 49). The twentieth century had
scarcely begun before the Duchess of York, later to be the gracious and almost kleptomaniac Queen Mary, came out and installed *Araucaria columnaris* bang in the middle of lawn 53 (and very
likely dropped a heavy hint that the silver spade used on that occasion would look very nice in her own garden shed). After that,
there was a long pause in these visitations until George VI's widow
arrived and then, in the self-perpetuating manner of all monar-
chies, her grandson Prince Charles turned up in 1981 to plant a
Red Cedar marking the centenary of the two trees his great-
grand-uncles had dug in: and, as always, a tremendous fuss was
made of the royal visitor.

Even now, Sydney may not have made up its collective mind
about the royal connection, in spite of rearing one of Australia's
most vociferous republicans in Tom Keneally, and others who
make careful distinctions between the 'royal anthem' and the 'national anthem' (but why, oh why, did they not have the courage to
go for 'Waltzing Matilda' instead of the conventional thing?). Not
that such dissidents are a recent phenomenon: Henry Lawson
composed a withering ballad about the Duchess of York's visit in
1901, and the sycophancy it attracted ('There'll be royal times in
Sydney for the Cuff and Collar Push... But the men who made
the land will not be there').* Plenty of memorials already well past
may still be detected in this town. On Cumberland Street, in the

---

*From Lawson's ballad, 'The Men Who Made Australia'.

Rocks, they may by now have completed a brand-new King George V Recreational Centre from the proceeds of a fund set up in 1936 'throughout what was then the British Empire, to provide playgrounds for children in memory of the King' (it said on the hoarding which enclosed the building site). There is a large oil painting of George V and his queen in the lobby of the New South Wales Legislative Assembly on Macquarie Street; while, a few hundred yards away, outside the Hyde Park Barracks where convicts were housed and which one of them designed, a statue on a very large plinth is inscribed 'The People of New South Wales to Albert the Good, Prince Consort of Queen Victoria 1866.'*

Victoria herself is to be found at her grandest on George Street, just below the Town Hall, complete with orb and sceptre and dimpled chin in ample bronze, which Dublin happily passed on to Sydney when the statue was no longer thought appropriate to its position outside the Irish Parliament, after the republic there became a reality in 1937. This now stands by a side entrance to the splendid Queen Victoria Building, which is one of Sydney's greatest architectural glories, though its existence has been a very close-run thing more than once. The city fathers were extremely brave to have commissioned it in 1893, when Sydney's development was faltering after the failure of several banks across the country. They nevertheless gave the go-ahead for their new Queen Victoria Markets, where fresh produce could be bought and sold, though the revitalised successor has gone just a bit upmarket from its original self. After hovering between Gothic and Renaissance styles, the architect George McRae, who had just finished part of the Town Hall, opted for something he described as American Romanesque, which in this case turned out to be a rum but gorgeous mixture of

---

*Much worse has come out of Melbourne. If anyone wishes to embarrass an Australian, simply recall the time when Prime Minister Robert Menzies recited a mawkish sixteenth-century verse which ends, 'I did but see her passing by, / And yet I love her till I die.' This not only referred to, but was actually uttered in the presence of, the young Queen Elizabeth.

Italianate domes, Mughal cupolas, and tracery that owes something to the Early English school of thirteenth-century ecclesiastical architecture. The inside was, and is, galleried in several tiers,
just like the GUM department store in Moscow, though a big difference is that in Sydney you can make your purchases from all the
assorted goodies of the West—from Body Shop, Bally, Canterbury Woollens, Ralph Lauren, Versace and their peers—while
People Who Are Going Places wander past with mobile phones
jammed in their ears, and expressions of fulfilment or expectation,
but never of resignation, which is the very particular caste mark of
the poor. In the main concourse, well-to-do Sydney sips its *caffé
latté*, munches its pastries with a restrained form of gusto, periodically consults its Filofax, and exchanges gossip with others who are
on the way up or disconcertingly starting to slide, but who are
never, never standing still. Yet this wonderfully stimulating rendezvous was very nearly demolished in 1959 to make way for a municipal car park; being saved only because a Malaysian company,
with more money than it knew what else to do with, eventually
stepped in to finance the construction of the car park underground instead, and to refurbish the tired old building until the
QVB became by a long chalk the most distinguished commercial
property in town.

Not many developers in Sydney have emerged with as much
credit, and that goes for, as much as anyone, the elected vandals
who cut the monstrous ravine of the expressway straight through
the Domain, when they might at least have covered all, instead of
only part, of it to restore the landscape when the engineering was
done.* Other treasures in this city have periodically been threatened by the avaricious, the ruthless and the simply heedless, ever
since John Macarthur cast his acquisitive eye on public property,

---

*Perhaps someone had learned a lesson from this by 1988, when it was decided that the Harbour
Bridge should be augmented by a tunnel—which was opened four years later—instead of another bridge.

and little was done to frustrate them until the public began to hit back on its own account in what has already been enshrined in civic history as the Battle of Woolloomooloo.

This was a conflict that had been waiting to happen for the best part of a century, ever since the first proposal for a railway extension to be run straight through this part of the inner city to the eastern suburbs, followed by a 1909 development plan which wanted to dig tunnels and widen roads there for other purposes. The railway wasn't completed for another seventy years, the trains eventually emerging from a hole under the Domain and the Art Gallery, before bounding away to King's Cross and Bondi Junction across the middle of the 'Loo, where a great swath of property had been mown down in the late 1960s to make way for it. By the time that happened the great battle was imminent, but it was to be fought over other issues as well. On one side were big businessmen and their political placemen, whose eyes had caught the glint of the hard cash that would accrue if they bulldozed the 'Loo and started all over again with expensive developments. On the other was a medley of residents, of liberals from various backgrounds, and of trade unionists, all of them outraged by this added threat to Sydney's oldest suburb, where square riggers used to berth, where a fishing community still hung its nets out to dry, and which retained much of its old atmosphere (in spite of those high-tech warships parked alongside Cowper Wharf Road), because its deeply unfashionable streets accommodated some of the city's most precious old terrace housing, complete with that very local style of cast-iron embellishment which is known as Sydney lace. Run-down in so many ways, on the slide since the end of the war, Woolloomooloo was nevertheless as comforting to its inhabitants as an old slipper with holes. Some families had lived on those streets for generations and a few owned their own properties: but it was the impecunious majority renting their homes who were the most vulnerable.

The planning applications had started coming into the Town Hall in the mid-1950s and, when the council at first rejected them, the landlords who hoped to make a killing turned nasty, deliberately damaging or failing to repair occupied premises, and cutting off services with specious excuses, until the homes were so tumbledown that the council gave them the permissions they sought. Not all the villains in this piece were Australian (a South African company bought a row of houses, which it wanted to demolish for an apartment block, and a London firm had nefarious plans for a pair of skyscrapers), but the two principal bogeymen were the local property tycoons Frank Theeman and Sidney Londish. Theeman will reappear much more ominously in a later chapter of this book; for now, it is enough to note that both he and Londish began buying up dwellings whose owners, expecting their investments to decline in value with the arrival of the railway extension and the expressway distributor, were ready to sell up and get out while the going was good. Two other things appeared to settle the hash of the local community. One was legislation passed in 1957 to nullify a much earlier statute which prohibited any building in Sydney higher than 150 feet; the other was a subsequent announcement by the State Planning Authority, which could if need be override the City Council, that it favoured a high-rise future for Woolloomooloo. What the authority appeared to have in mind was a revamping of the waterfront there until it was the gateway for cruise liners, which would attract 'tourist shops, hotels and convention centres ... a sports stadium and exhibition buildings were to attract Sydneysiders. . . . Piccadilly Circus in London was often mentioned in the planning papers as a model to be emulated.'[1] God knows why, when it is a good half-mile from the nearest water, as Woolloomooloo is not. The City Council, whose members were not always disinterested when they contemplated the profit that development might extract from the 'Loo, became collectively very confused indeed as it wondered what on earth to do. Sidney Londish, who knew exactly what he wanted, simply continued methodically to acquire real estate until, by 1971, he had become the largest landowner in the area.

Shortly after this, the residents started to fight back. Action groups had already been formed in other parts of the city a year or two earlier, to combat infringements of their living space, both by official bodies and by private developers: protests had occurred in Balmain and South Sydney, among other places, and had met with some success. So, one Sunday in October 1972, about a hundred people gathered on a sunny street and founded the Woolloomooloo Resident Action Group. Most of them lived just round the corner, and some of them were local councillors and aldermen, but they welcomed anyone who wanted to give a hand, including a priest from St Mary's Cathedral who only went along because he thought he had a duty to stand with them, and whom they elected secretary and treasurer almost on the spot, because he had literary as well as theological credentials. He put both of them to use forthwith, writing to the Lord Mayor of Sydney that very night, telling him of their existence, their moral position and their aim, which was to see that any further developments in the 'Loo should be confined to medium-density housing. Placards went up on walls and stickers appeared on car bumpers ('Let's live in the 'Loo. We love the 'Loo'), and stories about this unrest began to win space in the Sydney newspapers, as well as time on television. Picket lines were set up and, after one of them, somebody rang the cathedral to complain about the priest's presence there, which he hadn't expected to subsidise in his donations to the Church.

By this time, Sidney Londish had secured official approval to develop his land, and was ready to start wholesale demolition. On the brink of catastrophe, the action group approached the Builders' Labourers' Federation and asked if there was anything it could do to help. The federation was led at the time by a principled communist named Jack Mundey, whose interests were not confined to getting the top dollar for his members; he had already demonstrated his willingness in the Rocks and elsewhere to call his men out of contracted work in any circumstances where local residents requested it. These were the famous 'green bans', so called because the blokes first downed tools to save a small woodland from destruction out at Kelly's Bush when some nice middle-class ladies asked them to. They exemplified, in a particularly attractive form, the long Australian tradition of mateship, and they came to the rescue again when the beleaguered people of the 'Loo turned to them. Many union leaders were sceptical of the green bans, having hardbitten beliefs that trade unions had been invented to get better pay and conditions for their members, and nothing else. But Mundey won a few of them over and, before long, the Federated Engine Drivers and the Firemen's Association had been recruited into the battle for the 'Loo as well; and presently the projected demolitions and the existing building sites were abandoned, and the developers began to wring their hands.

One of them was foolish enough (and gutsy enough) to confront a meeting of the action group, and the result was memorable, as Fr Campion has recorded:

> The people of Woolloomooloo howled and howled and howled. I have never forgotten the howling rage of the people that afternoon. The sullen, dull anger at life in Woolloomooloo, so rarely displayed, now boiled over.... Face to face with one of their oppressors, they could only rage. It cannot have been a welcome experience for the developer. Yet he could not have known, what seemed clear to me, that this boil-over was not really directed at him personally. It was rage against all that he represented: money, power, political connections, planners, experts, advisers. It was a protest against bad housing and poor food and no jobs and bleak futures and skimped schooling and few doctors ... all the hard things that life had done to them, just because they were poor.[2]

So much pressure was applied on authorities who were bound to have the last word that these cobbled together a new plan for low-cost housing in the 'Loo; and it was fairly typical of much that had gone on for years secretly, out of the public eye, that a new Lord Mayor, who a few years earlier had backed Sidney Londish, now switched horses and appeared in a more sympathetic guise. Londish was denied what he wanted and, owing a great deal in taxes without enough money to pay them, went into receivership, like many others who had expected to become immensely rich on the pickings from Woolloomooloo. But the residents didn't get all they wanted either, didn't even manage completely to prevent high-rise buildings invading their territory, having to be satisfied with a modified version of their ambitions: a development of public housing, some of it new, some of it in restored old terraces, a new shopping centre, a recreational centre in a refurbished old warehouse, and decent landscaping. There are worse places to live in Sydney than the 'Loo nowadays. And all achieved, in the end, by a community coming together, articulating its grievances intelligently, and fighting for its needs. 'The battle for Woolloomooloo', according to one highly qualified onlooker, 'was waged using the language of morality and of "rights", but the real weapon was power. What was significant was not the moral rights of this or that group but the fact that so many citizens had come to understand that they did have power, where previously they had believed they did not.'[3]

There has never been any need to fight such a battle further down the eastern suburbs of the Harbourside, where much of the big money resides in this town. True, there are plenty of salubrious dwellings on the northern shore, and not many of the people living over there need to count their pennies before they spend, though this was not always the case. At the beginning of the twentieth century North Sydney was a distinctly working-class area, a majority of its population labouring in various brickworks, in a quarry, in an asphalt factory and in all the small ancillary industries that kept the city's ferry-boats shipshape. They might still have earned their bread and butter from the by-products of whaling, but years earlier people living around Mosman Bay had complained about the smell of blubber being reduced to oil, and the try-pots there became a thing of the past. They could have been coal miners, too, if it had seemed a better idea to work the local seam from Cremorne rather than from its southern end across the water in Birchgrove. However they kept afloat, their lives were to be transformed from the moment in 1923 when work began on creating the approaches for the Harbour Bridge, more than five hundred of their homes being demolished for a start, with another three hundred knocked down on the city side. On North Sydney's Hill Street these included a 'tiny tumbledown structure sited directly on the street [which] was proudly named "Pozières". Presumably the Digger who lived there survived the horrors of France in 1917, only to have his house demolished ten years later.'4 None of the dispossessed families received any compensation for this.

There had been thoughts of a bridge as far back as the middle of the nineteenth century and tenders were actually invited in 1900, ignoring suggestions that a tunnel might be a better idea. Nothing was done until the English firm of Dorman Long was given the contract in the face of stiff international competition, and despite the indignation of rural New South Wales, whose representatives lobbied hard for the funds to be spent on a better railway service across the countryside instead. But for the next seven years the building of this unforgettable structure gave employment to some fifteen hundred workmen, and cost no more than sixteen lives (one way and another, the Brooklyn Bridge had killed 139). It did just a little to take the weight off the Depression that hit Sydney as the work was being finished in 1931 by, at least, being some sort of assurance that better times would come. They came instantly for the souvenir industry, which has fed well off the Bridge ever since, with everything from ashtrays to pencil sharpeners and totally impractical and usually tacky mementoes, all selling in perverse quantities year after year. More substantial and more widespread benefits took a little longer to arrange, but one thing was abundantly clear from the moment vehicles and trains (and trams, until 1959) began to pour from one side of the Harbour to the other: that North Sydney was going to be transformed.

Business rapidly followed transport, as the local journals published special Bridge Supplements loaded with advertising. 'The most pointed comment came from *Smith's Weekly,* whose cartoon entitled "School of Real Estate Agents Crossing the Bridge to Spawn" accurately depicted the coalition of interests of property owners, real estate agents and would-be north shore dwellers.'[5] The transformation has accelerated since the 1970s. The precipitous office blocks now clustered around the northern end of the Bridge approach, whose flickering neon signs at night challenge the downtown skyscrapers across that floodlit arc of steel, mean that North Sydney is into business in a big way on its own account, to the extent that it is now hailed as Australia's third most important commercial centre, after 'Sydney' and Melbourne. The office blocks, inevitably, have been accompanied by apartment towers, which give way further along and behind the northern Harbourside to spacious bungalows and houses standing in their own gardens. Cremorne Point, where coal miners might have dwelt, has become known as the Peninsula of Gentility. Average incomes are so high in Mosman, Northbridge and Balmoral that only three of the eastern suburbs better them.

Things are generally a bit more opulent on the other side of the water, and from there householders get better views of the Harbour on the whole because they are facing the much more natural shore, whose bush-clad slopes still camouflage to a gratifying extent the northern dormitories: besides, more of them have the classic spectacle of Bridge and Opera House in their window frames. It is also true that when the eastern suburbanites dwell in apartment blocks, as many of them do, these tend to be a bit more modish than the ones belonging to the people opposite. Just as many inhabit well-landed homes bearing names that speak of other habitats, Del Rio, Arinca, Casa del Sol and even (surprisingly) Darnley Hall, each with its highly polished brass doorbell, each with its deliberately obvious burglar alarm. They are set in winding streets which faithfully follow the outlines of the Harbour, where scarlet and green parrots and other brilliant birds squabble and dart among the frangipani, the bougainvillaea and the bottlebrush trees, and so give many parts of Sydney between

Elizabeth Bay and South Head a distinctly Mediterranean air, with exotic additions that belong only here.

The most exclusive properties, of course, are the ones standing on the headlands, surrounded by trees, this cluster separated from that one by a bay dappled with jaunty craft awaiting their owners' pleasure. They have been set at careful angles by the builders, not only to have the best view of everything, but to catch the north-easter coming off the sea, which refreshes these parts in the heat of summer, but brings only humidity to the inner city and has worn itself out long before it can do anything at all for the western suburbs. And so famously exclusive they are, as tourists discover when they take the standard Harbour boat trip, and the man with the mike points out that that's where Kevin Costner now has a pad on Darling Point, with Tom Cruise and Nicole Kidman just over here, and that building over there on Point Piper, ladies and gentlemen, has just been sold for twenty million dollars or so. You can follow all these levels of celebrity and their exorbitant transactions in the Saturday edition of the *Sydney Morning Herald*, which now rivals the *New York Times* in its fifty full pages of real estate dealing and news. That's where you learn that the residence 'of Coonanbarra Café owners Rod and Robin Maclure has been listed for March 26 auction through L. J. Hooker Pymble agent David Johnson. More than $1.6 million is expected for the Howard Joseland-designed residence'; and that 'Crookwell-bound Murdoch Magazines' ad executive Linsey Hackforth, who sold her Artarmon house for $625,000 last August, paid $430,000 midweek for a two-bedroom Tamarama apartment...'; and so on, almost *ad infinitum* and certainly *ad nauseam*.[6] Moreover, what the estate agents call premier apartments have been going up in virtually every part of the inner city as well in recent times—Darling Harbour, Balmain, Surry Hills, Pyrmont and even poor old Ultimo all have their share—and there seems to be nothing that won't set you back at least a quarter of a million bucks for a place with only one bedroom and not a lot more.

But the vast majority of the citizens live in something a bit less prestigious, standing well back from the expensive Harbour view. From a couple of stops out of Central Station and all the way to Penrith—which is forty miles to the west and within cooee of the Blue Mountains—Sydney provides a perfect and continuous illustration of what is meant by that unloved expression suburbia. Through Haberfield and Ashfield and Strathfield and Lidcombe and Granville and Wentworthville and Claremont Meadows and Kingswood (just read their names and know them for what they are), the neat but featureless blocks of housing follow each other in numbing continuity, as do their equivalents in other directions out of town: in Marrickville, Earlwood and beyond to the south-west, in Chatswood, Roseville and most stations to Hornsby in the north. They are a memorial to the expansion of the railways before the Great War, and to the rush of people from an increasingly expensive or dilapidated inner city in search of decent but low-cost housing in the years that followed it. The principal figure in the shaping of this migration was the estate agent Richard Stanton, who hoped to raise the status of his profession by founding the Real Estate Auctioneers' and Agents' Association of New South Wales in 1910. More important, he visualised a form of Utopia for the working population, and his business was prosperous enough to start experimenting on what was known as the Dobroyd Estate, because it was close to Dobroyd Point on an arm of the Parramatta River. What he was doing there, in fact, was trying to create an Australian version of an English vision which Ebenezer Howard had lately propounded in his book *Garden Cities of Tomorrow* and had started to practise in Hertfordshire.

Stanton's own vision at Haberfield has been summarised like this:

Wide streets (66 feet) with enough room for two-way traffic and the parking of cars or buggies.... A 'nature strip' dividing the roadway from the footpath. One residence per block of land with a street tree in front of each. Blocks of land at least 45 by 150 feet although the norm became 50 by 150 feet—enough room for the laying-out of a good-sized garden. Separate zones for residential and commercial areas with no encroachment by secondary industry. Buildings designed in harmony with each other yet distinct in detail.[7]

The most important clause in that prescription was the separation of home and industry, and after it, the emphasis on greenery: whereas the norm had been to house working people as close as possible to their factories; as had always been the case in Europe, too. There is a photograph showing the Vicars Woollen Mills in Marrickville surrounded by housing, and it could have been taken almost anywhere in the north of England but for one thing; the dwellings do not have an upstairs and a downstairs, and they are not arranged in the stone or brick terraces of the Industrial Revolution, but in individual bungalows.[8] This was not to happen again, if Richard Stanton had his way; and he did, and was increasingly imitated as Sydney spread outwards from its beginnings. He it was, too, who introduced the house design which has been most frequently followed in these suburbs, the prefabricated Californian style of bungalow, with a shallow roof and a low verandah and wooden walls set on brick foundations, and roofs that were no longer of corrugated iron. Popular domestic architecture before this had gone through various styles, but always it had included a steeper pitch of tin roof, and a hallway that went straight ahead from the front door to the back, instead of turning right or left almost at once and much more interestingly.

These suburbs, because they are so extensive now, may be thought a little depressing in their uninterrupted sameness, even a trifle boring after you have driven past block after unrelieved block of them for the past hour or so. But the fact is that they represent Everyman's dream come true, the craving for a home of his own on his own piece of land, with space between his family and the next-door neighbours: this is irrefutable, even when it is mocked as a sentimentality. No one on the other side of the world, lucky enough to have made it in this modest way and knowing that they do not have it in them to go further in life or prosperity, would trade such a dwelling for a picturesque tenement on the Bay of Naples, or a serviced apartment on the West Side of Manhattan, or a prettily thatched but tied cottage in Piddletrenthide. Yet Richard Stanton's expectations haven't always been realised out here, where some of the inhabitants have found life as much of a struggle as anybody living on the Block in Redfern.

Poverty and Sydney, in fact, have not been associated with each other much except in the Antipodes, where most people have been in the know, well aware that the one has always been a disfigurement of the other. The image of Sydney circulated round the northern hemisphere is of a sparkling city full of boundless opportunity and a heartwarming sense of community that would never let anyone down, much less exploit them cruelly in the well-known manner of Europe and America. Yet there have always been hard times for some in this city, which has its bottom of the pile like everywhere else. Some of Sydney's indigents have been famous, like Henry Lawson, who struggled to write his short stories and his ballads in the face of perpetual adversity, which wore him down till he died at the age of fifty-five. Some of the outcasts have been memorably eccentric, none more than Bea Miles, who was the inspiration for a good novel by Kate Grenville. Bea had been a brilliant student at university before something went seriously wrong in her head when she was twenty-one, which caused her to spend the next three years in a mental hospital. After that, in a sense, she never looked back, in and out of the courts for a variety of offences, from breaking taxi doors after not paying the fare, to assaulting policemen who lost patience and arrested her yet again. Mysteriously not always short of funds—she once hired a cab to take her all the way to Perth to collect (she said) rare plants for the Botanic Gardens—she simply refused to conform, and paid the penalty in advancing decrepitude. She never had a proper dwelling in her life and finished up in an old people's home—the only one in the city that would take her—run by some nuns who had rescued her from a large drainpipe in Rushcutter's Bay, where she had been encamped for several months.

And then there was Arthur Stace, who was born into a Balmain family that didn't have a lot going for it, most of them being perpetual drunks, some of them running brothels in Surry Hills. He made his own way in the world by acting as a look-out for illegal gambling dens or for burglars, and by fetching and carrying liquor for the brothel-keepers. He signed up for the Great War and returned from it gassed and half blind; and soon became a regular drunk himself, with one appearance after another in front of the beaks, which presently changed his life. A magistrate berated him one day in biblical terms, pointing out over and over again that he had the power (almost) of life and death over Stace; who, as a result, became obsessed with a need to find the power that would release him from the booze. He found it one day in a Baptist church in Darlinghurst, where the preacher hectored his congregation about the need to 'shout eternity in the streets of Sydney'. That did it for Arthur Stace. For the rest of his life he became known to an increasing number of citizens as the little old man who wrote the word 'Eternity' with a piece of chalk on every surface he could find that would display the word prominently. He spent every morning doing this, becoming so celebrated that, when he died in 1967, an aluminium plaque was set into a wall next to the Town Hall, with Arthur's dates and the word 'Eternity' in his own perfect copperplate.

Behind such famously poor has always loomed the larger shadow of Sydney's anonymous poor. If anyone wants to know what it was like for most of its people once upon a not too distant time, *The Harp in the South* is still the greatest source of enlightenment, a novel in which Ruth Park captured the reality of life in Number Twelve-and-a-Half, Plymouth Street, so truly that it has not been out of print in the fifty years since it was written. And Sydney still has its Darcy families, living from hand to mouth, only they are not as obvious these days as they were in Surry Hills then. The once downtrodden Glebe may now be a base of the chattering classes, and even parts of poor Redfern are becoming gentrified, but the most obviously deprived people have simply moved from the increasingly expensive inner city and rearranged themselves in its western suburbs, where almost half the total population lives. These are the Westies, the local equivalent of 'the bridge and tunnel crowd', as Manhattan's snooty elite refer to the helots who pour on to the island from the Bronx, Brooklyn and Queens each day. Places like Campbelltown and Minto, where there are no jobs, little public transport and no other services to speak of, no prospect of anything to relieve the bleak pattern of every day, all now have unemployment figures well above the Sydney average, and health statistics that tell of a people becoming seriously weakened and at risk. Worse still, there are reckoned to be twenty thousand homeless adults in Sydney, and another twelve thousand 'street kids' between the ages of twelve and twenty-one: this is a Federal Government computation.[9]

If you know where to look, you can detect traces of this misery much closer to Circular Quay and the expensive Harbourside properties. Since the beginning of 1997, there has been an Australian edition of the *Big Issue*, that very good idea from London whose intention has been to give a bit of dignity and some sort of income to those who would otherwise have to make ends meet humiliatingly from state handouts, or sink into a slough of despond by begging for a crust. As in the cities of the United Kingdom, the deal is that the vendor is licensed to sell the magazine for a fixed price, a proportion of which he keeps, and there is a lad who stands on George Street, across the road from Martin Place, doing just that. He doesn't, alas, seem to attract the same guilty acknowledgement that young men and women in Britain have earned, or the same trifling generosities:

'Thank you. Here's your change?'—subtle and crucial question mark.

'No, that's OK.'

'Thank you very much indeed. Have a nice day.'

Perhaps this is because thrusting Sydney, hurrying past with its mobile phone clamped to its ear, really does think it has more important things to do, or simply regards him as an irritating abnormality in a land which has not generally known desperately hard times since before the last war. Nor does he quite fit the image the rest of the world has of Australia as a whole. But he's there, on George Street, most days of the week.

CHAPTER SIX

✦

Have Fun, Sport!

Having so much water on so many of its doorsteps, both in-side and outside the Harbour, it is scarcely surprising that Sydney has always taken to it as eagerly as it does, in a boat, on a surfboard, or just happily splashing about. You can feel the pulse of this city best when it is enjoying itself, and enjoyment does not come any higher than in its passionate love affair with boats, which are cherished and pampered and proudly displayed almost continuously all the way from the Parramatta weir to Manly Wharf, and up the Middle Harbour as well. There won't be a single bay or inlet, not one cove or backwater—anywhere that gives a little shelter from a sudden squall—in that long stretch of navigation without something at anchor; and usually there are dozens of craft companionably tugging at their cables in any haven, while they wait for their masters to come aboard. They can be a dickens of a nuisance to the ferry skippers, because small-boat owners, especially the ones who rely on engines alone, are not al-ways as seamanlike as they should be in such a busy waterway as this, but they give this city such a buoyantly optimistic air that their misdeeds are generally forgotten as soon as the last cussword has carried away downwind.

Sydney's heart never pumps more strongly than when the wind is set fair and the sailing boats are out. On some days there will be scores, possibly hundreds, of them racing up and down the Harbour, or tacking from one side to the other in their own sweet time, or venturing bravely out into the Tasman Sea, where the long, low swell takes them in its mighty hand and indulgently lets them play with it for a little while. On a brilliantly sky-blue Saturday, the hours are told by the regular boom of the starting gun on an official boat moored just below the Quarantine Station, when yet another line of dinghies gets under way on what is probably the finest small-boat water in the world. You can well imagine the first sporting yachtsman to enter the Heads, whenever that was, taking a deep and satisfied breath and saying to himself, 'Yes, this is the place.'

Just messing about in boats is not quite enough for most of these sailors, because competition has always mattered enormously here. People have been racing each other on water since Governor Macquarie's time, when his Harbourmaster, Captain John Piper, picked a crew in 1818 to match the best oarsmen that could be put out against them by three vessels then in port, and his men got to Sydney Cove fifteen minutes ahead of the runner-up, after pulling their heavy whaler all the way from Bradleys Head. Towards the end of the nineteenth century, in fact, rowing rather than sailing was the most popular pastime, with regattas that attracted masses of spectators, who followed the fragile racing boats down the water aboard paddle steamers and anything else that would serve. The successors of those oarsmen do not attract the same attention now, and these are the one sort of craft never seen below the Bridge for obvious reasons; but most days of the week the fours and the eights and the solitary shells will be out on the Parramatta River, blades dipping in perfect unison, backs bending as one, coxswains keeping a sharp lookout for the next coming of the Rivercat and its boisterous, jet-propelled wake. One of the most thrivingly comfortable clubs in town belongs to oarsmen whose headquarters and rendezvous it is on a bend in the river at Abbotsford; from which, if you glance through its enormous windows, you will almost always catch sight of at least some lusty young fellow fluently sculling himself along.

Its social superior—and there are such peculiarities in this generally democratic society based, as in America, on wealth rather than breeding in the tiresome old European way—is the Royal Sydney Yacht Squadron's establishment just above Kirribilli Point, with its mainmast planted firmly in the middle of its lawn, and some very expensive craft drawn up on the hard for painting or caulking or draining or some other form of marine overhaul. In every sense, the squadron represents the big league of Sydney boatmanship, and its members still rejoice at the memory of what happened here in 1987, just after Australians had lost the America's Cup (won four years earlier from a very grudging New York Yacht Club) in home waters off Fremantle. The victorious Dennis Connor, hoping to underline his superiority in Sydney, challenged *Kookaburra III* to a race round the Harbour—which he might well have won had he not tried to take a smart short cut off Shark Island. Unfortunately, he didn't know the water as well as the Australians who, giving a notorious shoal a wide berth, romped home in style this time, while *Stars and Stripes* remained stuck until the next high tide, to considerable mirth aboard every ferry that passed her for several hours.

The height of the year for the big yachtsmen comes every Boxing Day, when one of the world's great ocean-going races begins, with scores of boats setting off for Tasmania from Rushcutters Bay. The first Sydney–Hobart classic was the notion of a Royal Navy engineer, Captain John Illingworth, who was stationed in Sydney in 1945 and put it up to the locals as a more stimulating alternative to their annual Christmas cruise. He had a new thirty-four-footer, *Rani*, and he entered this in competition with eight other craft, all of them bigger than his; and it was the Tasmanian cutter *Winston Churchill* which led the little fleet out through the Heads. What followed was nothing less than an epic, and very rough, tutorial for the Australian novices:

Before they had gone eighty miles, they began to learn a lot about ocean racing. As the seas built up, untested gear began to carry away, poorly trained hands began to make those horrible gurgling noises that indicate they would sooner die than eat, decks and hulls, under unaccustomed strains, began to behave like badly constructed colanders. To top off this unhappy situation, there came a bouncing southerly gale sweeping up eagerly from the Antarctic to show them just how welcome they were.[1]

One boat ran for shelter as the gale built up, but the others stuck it out, to the increasing consternation of weather-watchers ashore. An RAAF plane was sent looking for them as soon as the storm eased, and reported that all the yachts except one seemed to be still afloat, but that *Rani* was nowhere to be seen. In fact, she was so distantly ahead of the rest that the plane had not flown far enough south to spot her in the course of its search. Listed as missing, the English boat became a topic of front-page news across the nation and editorial commiserations for the families of her crew, until she appeared out of the mist off Tasman Head one morning and reached the finishing line after six days, fourteen hours and twenty-two minutes at sea, which was a good seventeen hours before *Winston Churchill* sailed in.*

Yet, for all its undoubtedly heroic scale, the Sydney–Hobart cannot compare as a spectacle with a form of racing that the Australians themselves invented a hundred years ago (and even more boring were the America's Cup contests until television made it possible to see what all those rich people were playing at out there on the horizon). A little way above the RSYS headquarters, snugly at the head of the cove that shelters them both, is the base

---

Winston Churchill went down with three of her crew in the disastrous Sydney–Hobart race of 1998. A storm hit the fleet as it rounded the south-east corner of Australia and sailed towards the Bass Strait. This cost a total of six lives and half a dozen boats, with fifty sailors rescued from abandoned or sinking craft, and with 70 out of 115 yachts failing to complete the course. Even so, this was not as catastrophic as the Fastnet race of 1979, when fifteen yachtsmen drowned.

of the Sydney Flying Squadron—and if ever a phrase taken from its natural context was placed faultlessly in another one, then that is it, for the boats the squadron sails do everything across the water but actually take off and stay in the air. They are eighteen-foot dinghies and they are the world's fastest single-hulled craft of their size, which is why they are known as the Flying Eighteens; or, to their enthusiasts, the Formula One boats of the sailing world. If that suggests yet another very expensive toy beyond the reach of all but the local plutocracy, it is a misleading description, for all manner of Sydneysiders crew these things, three daringly agile souls to every boat. True, the craft was invented at the end of the nineteenth century by the department-store boss Mark Foy, who wanted something a bit livelier than the cumbersome boats that raced before; but anyone at all was welcome aboard from the start, sometimes as many as fifteen hands in those days, most of them regarded as mere ballast to stop the dinghy capsizing as it picked up speed. One of the most celebrated skippers before and just after the Great War was Wee Georgie Robinson, a shipwright at Cockatoo Island, who played the working man's form of rugby in winter, and in summer sailed with a crew of family and team-mates aboard his *Britannia,* which for twenty-six years was virtually unbeatable.

That tradition has been maintained, while the crews have been much reduced and the boats have become leaner with the passing of the years. The Eighteens are easily identified even by the veriest landlubber, because light metal frames project as a sort of outrigger from either beam, and on these trapezes (that's what the boys call them, and you quickly see why) the crew balance and splay them-selves to get as much weight on the wind'ard side as possible and so prevent the dinghy being turned upside down when every stitch of sail has been set and the hull is planing along; they even rig little bos'n's chairs from wires fixed high up the mast, so they can lie even further outboard and increase the leverage. And the Eigh-teens make a thrilling sight as they beat down the Harbour, with their gaudy sponsorships printed on their sails, their spinnakers so voluptuously full that your instinct is to caress them, their hulls almost leaving the water as they lunge and cant through the spray, their crews pumping the adrenaline as at few other moments in their lives.

The same goes for their mates who flock to the beaches with their surfboards and their kneeboards and their boogie boards, to ride the great, long glassy tubes of water that the South Pacific rolls incessantly at the shore. There are something like seventy beaches within using distance of Sydney, from Palm Beach, which is almost as far north as the Hawkesbury River estuary, down to Maroubra, which is getting close to Botany Bay. All of them attract their quota of sun-worshippers and paddlers and swimmers, who pleasure themselves on these sands without let or hindrance, because every beach is dogmatically *public* property in this country, the place, as many have remarked, where Australian democracy visibly functions most effectively. That inviolate principle apart, most beaches are esteemed and evaluated for their surfing properties above all, each having its own distinctive characteristics, its place in a pecking order of excellence, and attracting its own tribal loyalty, which has even been known to result in a spot of stoush if its reputation is thought to have been impugned by surfers with a rival preference. Maroubra is reckoned to be the one where tempers are most likely to flare at the drop of a board, and is also the beach where conditions as often as not are as rough as it gets for safe surfing. North Narrabeen is regarded as a corker, but you have to be a top-class performer to master its subtle and wayward characteristics. Bondi, where Australia's first surf club was founded in 1906, is the most familiar to the rest of the world, the choice of new arrivals in town precisely because people who couldn't name another Sydney beach to save their lives have heard of it (though its international reputation has never disclosed the fact that it has always been the beach most likely to be fouled by sewage slopping back and forth on every tide). In the first decade of the twentieth century, when surfing was very young and usually referred to as 'surf bathing', commercial optimists thought they saw the makings of another Coney Island at Bondi Beach, which never quite happened, though the waterfront, with its long curve of fast-food eateries and its atmosphere of sandy neglect, does have something in common with New York's bedraggled playground nowadays.

Manly Beach, on the other hand, is reached after getting off the ferry and strolling along a rather chic boulevard—known as the Corso, even though it feels more French than Italian. This was part of an 1850s development by a banker, H. G. Smith, who was newly arrived from Sussex with another Brighton in mind, though Manly in time became more attractive than that, even without the Pavilion and all the other Regency elegance. Its seafront is fringed with a long line of Norfolk Island pines, and its sands stretch so far between the two headlands protecting them that they never seem to be crowded even on a holiday weekend. Wet-suited young people—more boys than girls, though the balance has been shifting in recent years—with their flippers in one hand and a board tucked under the other arm, are likely to arrive on any day of the week, but they come in great numbers when they have heard an encouraging weather forecast: a low off the Queensland coast will usually produce a good north swell, the same thing in the Tasman brings a surge from the south, and Manly is served best by a sea running straight in from the east, which gives it the finest surf in all Sydney, so it's said.

Slowly the kids paddle themselves out from the shore, until they are so far away that they are only just visible as a scatter of bobbing heads. There they rest and watch the water gather its strength, talking to each other in an argot that has evolved with their cult, in which cornering means surfing sideways across a wave and a Goofy Foot rides with his right leg in front of his left: until someone breaks off, climbs on to the board as a swell picks it up and, crouching low with arms outspread, balances miraculously upon this precarious thing, cornering and side-slipping and (most spectacular feat of all) sometimes riding the inside wall of a curl, until the wave tumbles apart in a shattering of foam; and the gasping surfer blows the saltwater out of his nose, shakes his head like a dog, reaches for the board that has been carefully tethered to a foot, then turns and paddles back for more of the same, on a swell that seems to breathe in long movements under him. And you remember something written forty years ago, by someone who came to know this city well and was more perceptive than most. 'The boys who sail their little boats out beyond the Heads in Sydney Harbour, or dare the great Pacific rollers on the surfing beaches, make brave soldiers when they grow up, as two world wars have proved.'[2]

They are brave because the hazards they face so nonchalantly are well known to them and so very obvious to everybody else. And Sydney has plenty of hazards, one way and another: there are bush fires which in recent years have reached the metropolitan outskirts more than once, and might have destroyed much more than they did had the wind not changed when the flames seemed unstoppable; there is the funnel-web spider, more poisonous than any other in the world and particularly prevalent on Sydney's North Shore; there are several snakes whose venom can kill that you wouldn't want to come across in the surrounding bush; but there is nothing on land quite as dangerous as the hazards that await anyone who goes out in a boat here, or simply takes to the surf.

There is, first and above all, the danger from the sea itself, which caused an association of lifesavers to be formed the year after the Bondi Surf Club was born. (The very first person saved was a boy named Charles Kingsford Smith, who grew up to be the great aviator.) These guardians of the beaches became one of the Australian images most familiar to the rest of the world, together with the Digger's slouch hat, mobs of sheep being mustered by horsemen, Sydney Harbour Bridge, Don Bradman and Chips Rafferty. They were often seen on the newsreels in British cinemas when the Australian Government was trying to attract Ten Pound

Poms, doubtless to persuade us that we, too, could have bodies like these if only we would emigrate. We saw them parading at the surf carnivals, with their quaint bathing caps, their oddly stamping march as if they were in a Levantine military review, each platoon carrying a reel of long line with a harness attached: there would always be a shot, too, of these wonderfully muscular men riding the surf in leaping long boats with a massive sweep instead of a rudder at the stern. When a bather was thought to be in difficulties, the strongest swimmer in the team, already harnessed to the line, would go to the rescue, and the pair of them would be reeled in like fishes by the lifesavers ashore. That was the custom on the Sydney beaches until twenty years ago, when the reels and lines were superseded by fast, inflated rescue boats with outboard motors. A lot of people had already been saved in the old-fashioned way. There was a Black Sunday in 1938, when eighty lifesavers at Bondi rescued all but eight of three hundred people who had been swept out to sea by three freak waves. Off the same beach in 1996, the inflatable brought back a hundred people who were seriously out of their depth.

And then there are the dangers that lurk in the water, which include a sea snake whose venom is much more toxic than a cobra's, stingrays that can kill with a lash of the tail, the small blue-ringed octopus, which can paralyse its victim in a few minutes, and the highly unpleasant Portuguese man-o'-war jellyfish, which can sometimes be so plentiful that beaches have to be closed until the shoal has drifted away again. Above all, of course, there is the presence of the shark, which comes in many varieties, some of them up to twenty feet long, others weighing as much as seven tons.* To see much smaller specimens than these swimming around you on the other side of plate glass in the Sydney Aquarium is to be im-

---

*These are not casual estimates, but two examples which have occurred off New South Wales in recent years. The first was a great white shark killed at Twofold Bay, near the Victorian border, the second a whale shark washed ashore at Anna Bay, just north of Newcastle.

pressed enough by the blank and lethal menace of these creatures, to be aware how much they are in their element, as human beings never can be, and to wonder why it is that every Sydneysider who is ever likely to be at some risk from them is strangely dismissive of the threat they pose. Water-policemen, surfers, small-boat sailors, experts of one kind and another, all tend to take the line that 'I've been doing this for X number of years and I've never had trouble with a shark yet.' They then go on to point out that there hasn't been a fatality inside the Heads since 1963, when an actress named Marcia Hathaway, standing in water that didn't even come up to her waist, was mauled by a nine-footer in the Middle Harbour. A schoolboy had been killed in the same bay three years earlier, a couple of dogs only the week before. Miss Hathaway was savaged one January afternoon; and people who keep track of these things have concluded that most shark attacks occur between Christmas Day and 14 February, that if you want to avoid a more dangerous moment than any other in the day, keep clear of five-fifteen with the sun past its peak.

There may have been no deaths in thirty-odd years, but the threat remains, and it is well recognised. Two women were attacked inside the Harbour as recently as 1997, one off Darling Point, the other above the Bridge, and both were lucky that boats were close enough for them to be rescued unharmed. Several beaches inside the Harbour are netted so that people can swim safely there. During holidays, when thousands take to the surf, spotting planes fly up and down the adjacent coast, looking for ominous shadows in the water: on Australia Day a few years ago, a three-hour flight along the northern beaches revealed sixty-six sharks cruising just offshore, so eight of the beaches were closed for several hours. No one who has been around when the alarm goes up ever forgets what happens next. John Pilger, recalling his youth at Bondi in the 1950s, remembered 'the sight of thousands of bathers beating their personal best whenever the shark bell rang...'.[3] Yet those same scared swimmers, a week later over a beer, probably asserted that sharks were nothing much to worry about.

Water is an almost natural habitat for nearly all Australians, which produces their endless success in international swimming competitions and follows from the fact that the majority of them live by the seaside of an extremely arid continent. This city is probably addicted to the sea more than any other, but its hedonistic appetites have never been satisfied by it alone. You can pretty well name your sport and be sure that it is played in Sydney with great enthusiasm, tremendous application and much more than moderate skill (curling may be an exception, but it wouldn't be wise to bet on it). There are floodlit tennis courts in every suburb, public and private golf courses galore, bowling greens, basketball arenas, swimming baths, cricket ovals and football pitches within reach of everyone. As for Sydney's great spectator sports, these are so deeply embedded in the local psyche, so inescapable a feature of almost everyone's life here *as spectator sports,* that it is possible to overlook the fact that they are essentially expressions of urban tribalism within the metropolitan area.

If you forget about racing (we shall come to that shortly, though it essentially represents something other than sport), the most popular athletic activities in Sydney have traditionally been cricket and rugby league football. In a sense, the second of these is the more interesting phenomenon and raises the more interesting questions: 'a working-class Christian Brothers sort of game.'[4] It began as a protest by working men against the rugby union authorities at the start of the twentieth century, which followed exactly the pattern traced a few years earlier in England, and was to do with payment for playing the game, which until then had been run by a leisured class who didn't need to take time off work (and thereby lose income) in order to enjoy sport; they had the time and the means to afford whatever pastime they preferred, as working men did not. The two versions of rugby football went their separate ways with slightly different playing conditions but identical animosities, though the demarcation lines have become blurred in recent years, as the union players (the rah-rahs, to their old adversaries) have become professionals, too. But what's always been true and particularly intriguing about league is why in Australia it never attracted working-class sportsmen outside New South Wales and Queensland, just as in England it has never become popular outside three or four northern counties. Why have Victoria and South Australia always preferred Australian Rules to league or any other variety of football? Why has Melbourne always been potty about Rules and disdainful of league, with Sydney taking exactly the opposite tack.* No one has ever explained these peculiarities convincingly.

Top-class league and cricket in Sydney have always had clearly defined territorial boundaries in the city, and because of the exceptional ability of the local turf to recover from one season and be used for the other almost at once, the local clubs have frequently shared the same facilities, which would be impossible in the northern hemisphere. Cricket preceded any form of football in Australia by a quarter of a century, the first properly regulated match being played on Hyde Park in 1803, the first game of football not being arranged until 1829, again in Sydney (and rugby was not exported from England until thirty years after that). A result of this chronology is that most of the playing areas shared by the two sports are ovals rather than rectangles, and are generally referred to as such, because cricket got there first. And certainly, when you watch a league match at, say, North Sydney Oval, with the forwards taking the ball upfield in a series of battering rushes (just like American footballers, but without being over-dressed), the place seems to be waiting for the summer game to begin, with its palms and its fig trees casting shadows across one touchline,

---

*These boundaries are not quite as hard and fast as they were until two or three years ago. League teams have lately been established, with varying degrees of support, in Perth, Adelaide and Melbourne, while Rules has made an increasingly popular pitch in Sydney.

with its white picket fence separating the field of play from the spectators, and with its lovely period Bob Stand, which was tenderly rescued some years ago from the authorised vandalism of the Sydney Cricket Ground.

Winter or summer, whichever game is being played on that oval, the honour of North Sydney and its people is at stake to a degree that no one to whom all sport is a crashing bore can possibly understand. It would be unthinkable for them to follow another side just because their team was having little success (and North Sydney league supporters have endured that as staunchly as anyone over the years). 'By and large Norths fans...regard exchanging allegiance to their football team as no more possible than swapping their mother. As one supporter explained in 1987, "Being a North supporter is like asthma—if you catch it as a teenager, you've got it for life."'[5] The same goes for people in Canterbury, in Cronulla, in Balmain and in the other league strongholds of this town, as a recent experience of the Balmain team illustrates. The league bosses found it expedient to shunt the side to Parramatta, twenty miles away, under another name which would dissociate it from its origins, but the experiment failed because virtually no one out there wanted to watch this displaced hybrid play, and soon Balmain was back where it belonged at Leichhardt Oval, magnetically recovered by local loyalties. These are so strong that it is known for an all-rounder to play for his local club at two different sports, as Ray Lindwall did. He was one of the greatest and most honourable fast bowlers of all time, who once memorably said that he wouldn't have thought himself fit to wear an Australian sweater if he had ever bowled a bouncer at any batsman below No. 8. He played for St George at both cricket and league, so good a full-back in the winter game (he starred in the 1946 Grand Final, among other big matches) that, if he had not decided to concentrate on his cricket at the highest level and leave football alone, he would probably have won a Test cap in rugby league too.

It is typical of what can be quite an argumentative and exceedingly stubborn city, with tempers running high and feelings very deep, that both its cricket and rugby league have damaged themselves by schisms in this generation; and in both cases the rift was caused by the manipulations of television magnates, whose motives had nothing at all to do with sport. Cricket in Australia—and by extension in the rest of the world—was changed for ever after 1977, when the World Series Cricket competition was launched as a rival to the established form of the game. Behind it was the Sydney billionaire Kerry Packer, who wanted to monopolise first-class cricket in Australia in order to boost his Channel 9 ratings, and who was driven to buying sixty-six of the world's best players when the Australian Cricket Board refused to co-operate. The players signed up because Packer offered them much better money than they had ever known before, and for a couple of years there were two different forms of the game in Australia, with feelings increasingly bitter between the rebels and the loyalists, until both parties to the dispute had spent so many millions of dollars—on lawyers as much as on anything—that they decided to call it a day and make some sort of peace.

By then the damage, some would say, had been done. In order to attract maximum audiences, both at the cricket grounds and in front of the television set, Packer and his henchmen had deliberately jazzed up the game, modelling it on American major league baseball. The very title of WSC gave it away, but that wasn't all: there were night games under floodlights (unheard of in cricket before), coloured uniforms (instead of the traditional white flannels and shirt), white balls and black sightscreens (better at night than a red ball coming at the batsman against a white background), and changes to some of the rules, together with a new and largely artificial culture to jazz things up. Endlessly, Packer's channel played a noisy jingle during the commercial breaks ('C'mon, Aussies, c'mon!') and, whenever a batsman failed to score, had a Walt Disney duck waddling sorrowfully across the screen. Some of this has stuck and been exported overseas, in spite of the Australian rapprochement. 'Pyjama cricket' under floodlights, or even in daylit competitions, is now regarded as an alternative form of the game. International one-day events occur so frequently that the players reasonably complain they are overused, but their extra workload is necessary to generate the income that everyone has become accustomed to and doesn't want to lose. Worse than anything, however, has been the effect all this has had on traditional cricket. The great new audience of young Australians who were attracted by Packer's version as they never had been by anything before are simply not interested in matches that last more than a few hours. Inter-state Sheffield Shield cricket in Sydney and the five other capitals, when each match lasts four days, now tend to be watched only by the proverbial man and his dog. Yet Shield cricket is where Australians grow into (more often than not) the finest Test cricketers in the world.*

The crisis in rugby league didn't happen until 1995, when the naturalised American media baron Rupert Murdoch (a Melbourne man by birth and upbringing, who renounced his nationality in order to secure various franchises he coveted in the United States) dangled money in front of footballers and officials, just as Packer had done with the cricketers, as part of a strategy to boost his television interests. Again, there was a bitter rift between those who took the money, and those who wouldn't associate with Murdoch for anything; and although the playing of rugby league in Sydney was not changed to anything like the same extent as cricket, there were two seasons when the local teams played in two different competitions which would have nothing whatsoever to do with each other. The visible changes were small, and largely to do with reinventing the image, from its traditional working-class

---

*Even traditionalists agree that one good thing emerged from this great upheaval in the game, however: fielding became more thrilling than ever before and, again, we have American baseball to thank for that.

background, to something that, again, imitated the big stuff in America: North Sydney, which had always been known as Norths to its supporters, now became the Bears, Balmain's nickname of Tigers was suddenly made part of its official identity too, Eastern Suburbs were translated into Sydney City, and so on. But there was serious damage, quite apart from broken friendships which weren't always mended when the two competitions merged again. Crowd loyalties were affected too, and some people took to watching the newly professional rah-rah game instead (Strewth!), while others were attracted to Rules, which hadn't gained a professional footing in the city until 1982, when the South Melbourne club was transmogrified into the Sydney Swans. Attendances were not much to write home about until rugby league started to fall apart, but from that moment they began to build up until the Swans were perfectly capable of filling the Sydney Cricket Ground for every home match.

The SCG, as it is known all over the world, has always been at this city's sporting heart, recognised as such even by people who have never entered it. It stands in the middle of a spacious public park, with some of Sydney's most attractive old houses just on the other side of the trees, not far from the Victoria Barracks, whose soldiers, in 1852, marked out the first pitch.* For most of the twentieth century it was the place where the biggest fixtures in both cricket and rugby league were played, Test matches in both games, rugby Grand Finals as well. The greatest players from all over the world performed here at one time or another and some of their feats are legendary, their names still remembered like a litany by all who follow their sports. This was where Ron Roberts, his green and gold jersey slutched up with mud, scored a try in front of the Sheridan Stand in 1950 that wrested the rugby league Ashes

---

*Since 1988, SCG has shared Moore Park with the new and stylish Sydney Football Stadium, which is in some ways an improvement on what its neighbour has become, but lacks the atmosphere the old Cricket Ground generated.

from the Poms for the first time in thirty years. And this was where Don Bradman, the greatest batsman cricket has ever seen, hit 452 not out for New South Wales against Queensland in 1930, which is still the highest score an Australian cricketer has made, surpassed only twice in the entire annals of the game by a mere handful of runs scored in the first instance by a Pakistani, and then by a West Indian. Apart from the skill involved in Bradman's innings, it was a feat of great stamina, for it meant being at the crease for nearly seven hours. 'Everything else in this game', it was noted in the following season's *Wisden Almanack*, 'paled before the phenomenal performance of Bradman who... displaying a wider range of strokes than usual... batted without a trace of error during his long stay and hit no fewer than forty-nine 4's.'[6] Queensland may be said to have got its own back after a fashion thirty years later, when the unprecedented finale of a famously tied Test match was played between Australia and West Indies, not at the SCG, but up at the 'Gabba in Brisbane.

Yet the SCG was always more than a place pickled in a past that was re-enacted every time a traditional fixture came round to remind the crowd of things that had happened ages before, and these were not always the most stunning athletic feats in two great games; sometimes they were incidental to the match itself.* The SCG gripped everyone's imagination, too, because of the way it had always looked, with its delicately constructed and aesthetically pleasing stands, with its marvellously comprehensive scoreboard (which the English inexplicably chose never to imitate), and with its celebrated—many would say notorious—Hill, where some of the most knowledgeable cricket watchers in

---

*There is, for instance, a panoramic photograph from the illustrious Melba Studios, taken before a rugby league Test between England and Australia kicked off in 1946, with the footballers already deployed in their playing positions across the field, standing to attention while a brass band performs in a corner of the ground (at a curve in the almost perfect circle, to be geometrically precise). It is playing the national anthem, the same one for both countries in those days; which makes that photograph something of a collector's piece.

the whole world would gather and offer their opinions loudly to all and sundry, especially to the players. The most famous barracker was Stephen Harold Gascoigne, more widely known as Yabba, who between the World Wars sold rabbits from a handcart to the housewives of South Sydney and Balmain, but made for the SCG whenever a big match was on, especially if it was a Test match between Australia and their oldest enemy. He had a reputation for endlessly impromptu and vivid quips, and the following example was typical. During a drinks interval on a very hot day, with Bradman (almost inevitably) at the crease, one of the English players considerately offered him a glass of orange juice, though these were really meant for the fielding side. As the batsman gratefully reached out to take it, this fourteen-stone voice carried right round the ground: 'For Gawd's sake be careful, Don. Make sure the bugger tries it first!'

Much of this priceless heritage has disappeared in a redevelopment of buildings and a rearrangement of the SCG's soul. The old Bob Stand was rescued by North Sydney Oval, but many of its fellows have simply been destroyed, and anyone who last saw the ground thirty years ago would scarcely recognise it now. Apart from the handsome Members' and Ladies' Stands, everything has been replaced by a universal sports architecture of luxurious executive suites and featureless caverns where large quantities of people can sit on cramped plastic seats. The floodlighting shines down from crushingly thick columns and illuminates not only the playing area but the night sky as far away as Manly. The Hill and its traditional population have disappeared, because the witty barracking there was superseded by the foul mouthings of drunken slobs who had been newly attracted to pyjama cricket by Mr Packer & Co., and something smarter was thought to be a solution of sorts to their offensiveness. The old scoreboard still stands, but it has been effectively hidden behind an electronic device, which tells you no more than the previous appliance did, but does it with microchips, so we must have one of those. You can't see the familiar old Grandstand, either, where the Royal Easter Show's patrons sat on the other side of the SCG's wall, but as that's become merely another of Mr Murdoch's toys, perhaps it's just as well. If there was a moment when traditionalists at the SCG—the heirs of Yabba and Don Bradman's other worshippers—took the hint that things could never be the same again, it was probably in November 1981, when twenty-seven thousand frequently drink-sodden people turned up for a one-day international against the West Indies—in front of an almost empty Members' Stand.

Even cricket may not go back quite as far as horse racing in Sydney, however. A stallion, three mares and three colts, as we know, arrived with the First Fleet, and some kind of racing was held early on along the road to Parramatta, which was made before Arthur Phillip went home. The first formal race meeting occurred in 1810 on Hyde Park, when Captain Richie's grey gelding Chase won the purse of fifty guineas donated by the ladies of the colony. Within little more than a decade, there were three racecourses in the area, one of them on land now occupied by Sydney University. By then, the rich man's sport with its enormous following of labourers and artisans was as much of an obsession in New South Wales as it had been for centuries in the northern hemisphere. Today, there are eleven different tracks between Penrith and the sea, and the obsession with what goes on there has not diminished. There are people in this city to whom it is bitter gall that Australia's principal horse race takes place on the first Tuesday in November five hundred miles to the west, at Flemington Racecourse, but a high proportion of them could almost certainly rattle off the names of every Melbourne Cup winner since Archer was first past the post in 1861. Not even the big spring meeting at Randwick brings the nation to a standstill for five minutes, as the great event at the other place does, year after year, but in every other respect Sydney gives way to nobody. The racing supplements in the local papers may be more comprehensive than any other on earth, as they supply endless information about each forthcoming race, and provide tips from a bewildering number of experts, past form of both horses and jockeys, information on which horses will be wearing blinkers and which will race with their tongues tied, and what are the latest bloodstock prices. Even this exhausting coverage isn't enough for some people, who need an additional fix from a local radio station dedicated wholly to the turf.

The racing supplements also offer information and advice about the odds and the money recently made in betting on a variety of other sports; and in Sydney you can lay bets on, among other things, horses, greyhounds, Australian Rules, rugby league and rugby union, American football and English soccer. This is, in short, a city full of obsessive gamblers, who spend more money on their passion each year, it's said, than anyone else in the world except Tasmanians. If nothing else is available, there's always two-up, the simplest and most idiosyncratically local form of gambling, which probably dates from very early in Australia's history, though its popularity increased after the Anzacs returned from the Great War, when there had been nothing more entertaining for them to do in the trenches of Flanders.* In the heyday of the two-up schools, as many as a hundred men at a time would play in basements whose walls were padded to muffle the sound of their feverish gambling. Until thirty years ago one of the most famous schools was Thommo's, which moved from place to place in Surry Hills and Darlinghurst to avoid being raided by the police, and employed a man nicknamed Cockatoo to keep a look-out for the constabulary. The one moment of the year when the police turn a blind eye to two-up (for it is still illegal outside casinos) is after the Anzac Day parade, when all the old sweats keep up another part of their tradition, squatting on their hunkers in shady corners of Hyde Park and elsewhere, to the regular cry of 'Come in, spinner!'

Sydney's Star City Casino didn't open until 1998, its major

---

*Two coins are tossed in the air, and the bet is on whether they both land heads or tails or one of each.

shareholder being a company based in Nevada. Much patronised every day of the week by, it is fair to say, a complete cross-section of the community, it has devised a very crafty way of separating Vietnamese immigrants in particular from their money. It runs a shuttle bus service to Cabramatta, where most of them live, sixteen hours a day, seven days a week, and charges them only A$12 for the round trip, a complimentary drink on arrival, and A$10-worth of chips with which they can start gambling. It's believed that these poor suckers lose an average of A$100 every time they're bamboozled into the casino, 'and ride the bus back in despair to the commercial kitchens, backyard garment factories, the housing commission estates or social welfare queues whence they came'.[7]

But racing has always soaked up most of the cash, nowadays followed by lotteries and poker machines, without which it would be difficult for a pub to attract customers. At every hospitality club in the city, the most obvious thing to the casual visitor apart from the generally expensive furnishings and an air of confident prosperity is the great bank of 'pokies' (scores of them as often as not) that lie in ambush for anyone coming through the front door, before he can reach the other club facilities, their innards burbling tunelessly, their lights flashing convulsively, their digestive systems just occasionally regurgitating. The machines explain the opulence of the premises, for the money they make is staggering. The social club attached to the Penrith Panthers rugby league team, it was disclosed in 1997, made A$40 million in clear profit the previous year.[8] That was the season in which the Sydney cricketer Steve Waugh, batting for New South Wales against Western Australia, earned himself and his team-mates A$140,000 for hitting the match sponsor's sign with a drive that in Don Bradman's day would have been worth only six runs.

The danger to a society which surrenders as completely to physical pleasure as Sydney always has done is that it has little energy or inclination to cultivate anything else at leisure that might do something for its finer sensibilities or help to explain its singularity to itself, to shed light on its darknesses and its perplexities; and it is true that the arts in this city have always lagged behind her sports in impetus and in vigour. Theatricals may have been a feature of life from the outset, and Sydney has never been short of painters, from the days of the convict Thomas Watling onwards; but the fact is that, by the time Barnett Levey built that first permanent theatre, the cricketers had been well served for almost twenty years and there were already three racecourses; while the nucleus of a municipal art collection had to await the foundation in 1871 of the New South Wales Academy of Art, which a few years later was reconstituted as the Art Gallery of New South Wales. What's more, although there was a subscription library in Sydney as early as 1826, its terms of business excluded everyone but the colonial gentry, and this whole metropolis as late as 1947 contained only eight places where anyone could consult and borrow books at the public expense.

Like the Botanic Gardens which it overlooks, the Art Gallery is one of this city's great glories, though some of its early policies were more fashionable than they might have been in an establishment whose purpose is partly to educate. Up to 1890 it concentrated on buying European works when, perversely, a considerable exhibition of Australian paintings was being put together for private showing in London. Although it subsequently began to acquire local work it remained for many years a British provincial gallery rather than a distinctively Australian one, but between the two world wars the Gallery became so aware of its Australian heritage (like everybody else after Gallipoli) that it paid scant attention to the artistic revolution then taking place in Europe; to the extent that when a travelling exhibition of modern paintings closed in 1940, and international hostilities made it impossible to return the contents to where they belonged, these were carefully packed and stored in the Gallery's cellars, instead of being left hanging on its walls. They included works by Picasso, Matisse,

Braque, Modigliani and Dalí, and the Gallery's Trustees may have decided to duck below the parapet after the violent reaction they provoked in many of Sydney's connoisseurs, up to and including a book by the energetic and highly influential Lionel Lindsay, who 'set out to prove that Picasso, Matisse and the surrealists were pawns in a vast Jewish conspiracy'.[9]

Things are much more tranquil in local art circles nowadays, and the school parties that daily enjoy tutorials in the Gallery are treated to as fine and eclectic a collection as any city of this size could be expected to house in one building, which has been periodically extended to accommodate more and more imaginative ideas, like the room devoted to the arts of Asia.* Europe is now represented by anything from Italian Old Masters to Kandinsky and Henry Moore, from Rembrandt to Picasso and Edvard Munch. The Yiribana Gallery is the place above all others on this continent to see the art and artefacts of the Aborigines and the Torres Strait Islanders. The other Australian collection stretches comprehensively from the earliest days (when the artists, not yet acclimatised to the southern light and much else, thought they saw gum trees resembling the European elm) through Tom Roberts (*The Golden Fleece* is here) and Arthur Streeton to Sidney Nolan, Russell Drysdale and the latest upcoming school—but if you want your fill of Brett Whiteley, it's best to make for his old house in Surry Hills, which the Art Gallery also runs as a museum.

The Gallery is complemented, across the Botanic Gardens, by the State Library of New South Wales, which everyone tends to think of more cryptically as 'the Mitchell', because David Scott Mitchell was responsible for laying the foundations of its unrivalled collection of Australian history. The son of cultivated par-

---

*The city is generally well served with imaginative touches of this kind. In the Town Hall a marvellously detailed model of central Sydney is permanently displayed, with new buildings added to it as they go up on the streets. The Sydney Museum has made the best of its restricted space by housing most of its collection in a series of stainless-steel chests with many illuminated drawers, which open and shut noiselessly.

ents whose wealth derived partly from medicine but mostly from extensive coal and railway interests, Mitchell began collecting books while still a boy, before becoming one of Sydney University's first graduates. Although he was qualified to practise law from 1858, he never needed to work for a living, and in fact became a recluse from the age of thirty-five until he died in 1907 when he was seventy-one, emerging from his bleak house on Darlinghurst Street only once a week in order to visit bookshops. He did not neglect the classics of English literature, but his particular genius was to recognise that his own country was developing a culture of its own, and that the growing documentation of this still tender plant needed safeguarding. 'The main thing', he once said, 'is to get the records. We're too near to our own past to view it properly, but in a few generations the convict system will take its proper place in our perspective, and our historians will pay better attention to the pioneers.'[10] To this end, he once bought ten thousand items in one lot, so that he could acquire Sir Joseph Banks's journal, several letters from Arthur Phillip to Banks, and many rare documents about Pacific exploration.

It was Sydney's second great stroke of luck that, no sooner had David Mitchell bequeathed his entire and massive collection to the Public Library of New South Wales, which was descended from that first Australian Subscription Library, than Sir William Dixson took over from where Mitchell had left off. Tobacco was the basis of his family's fortune but, although he didn't need to, Dixson worked for many years in Sydney as an engineer for a company specialising in dock design and refrigeration. In common with Mitchell he stayed single all his life, but he was a sociable bachelor who enjoyed travel, golf, gardening, photography—and collecting things he came across in foreign countries. Gradually this mania narrowed itself down to an obsessive desire to amass only things of Australian or Pacific provenance, which differed from Mitchell's passion in so far as it meant, rather more than books and other documents, acquiring pictures and compiling great indices of arcane Australiana. Strangely, although Dixson was in his thirties before Mitchell died (and went on to live until 1952), the two men never actually met. But between them they left a priceless legacy to Australia, to Sydney above any other part of it, which has been well described in the following terms: 'It is no slight to other major Australian collections, such as the La Trobe Library in Melbourne, the Allport Library, Hobart, and the National Library in Canberra, to say that what is preserved in the Mitchell and Dixson archives constitutes one of the world's absolutely indispensable repositories of knowledge about a single nation or state: they are to us what the National Library of Congress is to America.'[11]

Yet Sydney's own literary bent has tended above all towards poetry, rather than history, belles-lettres, drama or even fiction, from the time of Michael Massey Robinson.* He was an Oxford graduate who had been transported for attempted blackmail and was then rescued by Governor Macquarie, who made him the colony's laureate, with a regular duty to compose odes celebrating notable occasions, just as John Dryden and his successors had been doing in England since the seventeenth century. Rolf Boldrewood or Henry Kingsley may be considered the first novelists influenced by this city (you take your pick, especially as both were born in early-nineteenth-century England), and Patrick White (b. London 1912) was easily the most tortured, but for every respectable writer of fiction here you can name two or three who have made reputations in verse. Many critics still think Kenneth Slessor was the finest poet Australia has yet produced, though he virtually stopped composing verse during the Second World

---

*Taking the twentieth century as a whole, that is. Poetry, in fact, has lost ground in Sydney in recent years, with fiction coming on more strongly than ever before. Thomas Keneally and Kate Grenville have long had international reputations, of course, but others are coming up on the rails fast, Peter Corris, Marele Day, Susan Geason, Dave Warner among them. The increasing vitality of literature in the city may be measured as clearly as anywhere in the Sydney Writers' Festival, which was launched in 1998 and seemed set fair to more than hold its own at the turn of the new century with competitors already well established in Adelaide and Melbourne.

War, and concentrated on journalism for the rest of his life. Christopher Brennan was a commanding figure from the generation before Slessor's, but he exhausted himself and his talent on alcohol and a tempestuous domestic life. If two more of the locals tend to be remembered for something they did more than for what they wrote, that is unfair but understandable, because they were perpetrators of the greatest literary hoax of all time. And though the story is well enough known, it bears repetition in a book about Sydney because it is the classic example of our lot giving Melbourne one in the eye.

In 1944 the Melbourne poet Max Harris was editing a magazine named *Angry Penguins*, which did its best to encourage rising new talents by publishing their work, but was thought by some people to be a bit too precious in its literary attitudes. He received a letter from an Ethel Malley, which enclosed a couple of poems by her brother Ern, and asked whether they had any literary worth. Ern, she said, had died the year before, after a short but creative life as a Melbourne tram-driver; and Harris was so intrigued by all this that he requested Miss Malley to forward whatever else the poetic Ern had left behind. There was quite a lot of it; enough, indeed, to fill a whole issue of *Angry Penguins*, where the *oeuvre* duly appeared within covers that were illustrated by Sidney Nolan.

Ern Malley had not, in fact, died; he hadn't even been born, and the loyal Ethel was a concoction as well. The letters and the poems were the work of James McAuley, of Lakemba, and Harold Stewart, of Drummoyne, who disliked the modernist movement in poetry so much that they had decided to see if its adherents could tell the real thing from the spurious. They called this 'a serious literary experiment.... We opened books at random, choosing a word or a phrase haphazardly. We made lists of these and wove them into nonsensical sentences. We misquoted and made false allusions. We deliberately perpetrated bad verse, and selected rhymes from a *Ripman's Rhyming Dictionary*. The alleged quotation from Lenin in one of the poems "the emotions are not skilled workers" is quite phoney.'[12]

It says a great deal about the cultural values of the day that the police became involved, though not because of the hoax itself. They charged Max Harris with having published indecent material, including seven poems by Ern. Only one person appeared for the prosecution, Detective Vogelsang of the South Australian constabulary, and one of his objections was to a Malley poem entitled 'Night Piece', which seems to be set in a park at dusk and whose most suggestive moment is 'And you lay sobbing then / Upon my trembling intuitive arm.' The good but ponderous detective objected to this poem because 'They were going there for some disapproved motive. Because of the disapproval and the nature of the time they went there, and the disapproval of the iron birds make me say it is immoral. I have found that people who go into parks at night go there for immoral purposes. My experience as a police officer might, under certain circumstances, tinge my appreciation of poetry.'[13] If there was laughter in court, it went unrecorded, and the upshot was that an unhappy Max Harris was found guilty and fined £5, with the option of twelve weeks' imprisonment.

No such pranks and follies have ever beset music in Sydney, whose particular pain has been to produce generation after generation of fine singers and instrumentalists and then watch them leave the city in order to earn a living overseas. Until the Town Hall was built, musical life here was restricted to singing and to chamber concerts, such as those given regularly by Mr Paling's quartet at the French Club in Wynyard Square; and even the Town Hall had its limitations. It was a terrible place for echoes, external noise and general discomfort, and was in some danger of its ornate plaster ceiling collapsing on the audience whenever the organ—added to the building as an afterthought—descended to a thunderous basso profundo from its sixty-four-foot lower-C pipe. This was a possibility only during organ recitals at first, because the instrument had been tuned to a philharmonic pitch which became almost at once universally redundant, and half a century passed before the organ was retuned and could play in harmony with an orchestra.* Not until 1903 did Sydney hear a symphony concert, in fact, and then it was a performance by amateurs who disbanded shortly afterwards. Five years later a group of professionals formed the Sydney Symphony Orchestra and this, too, had a fairly short life, which ended after the musicians demanded fees for rehearsals and other performances that were considered exorbitant. After the Great War, yet another attempt was made to give the city some musical backbone, with the formation of a New South Wales State Orchestra (it lasted until 1922) and, more important, with the foundation in 1916 of the Conservatorium of Music on the edge of the Botanic Gardens.

This has been producing first-class singers and musicians ever since, though most of them have still found it necessary to emigrate afterwards, to the great benefit of the British among others. Some have been world class, and if the other place can still bask (just about) in the reflected glory of Nellie Melba, Sydney can comfortably reply that this is where Joan Sutherland began. Yet the Conservatorium has never produced anyone more remarkable than Joan Hammond, who was not only a very considerable singer of opera and oratorio, in recital or in concert, but someone with an exceptional range of other accomplishments. She studied the violin as well as singing, and her first musical job was to play in the Sydney Philharmonic Orchestra for three years before giving her first public recital as a soprano in 1929. Like every other Australian of her generation, she went to Europe for further study as

---

*The old philharmonic pitch had gradually risen in Britain and elsewhere during the nineteenth century to 452.5 vibrations per second in the key of A, but most European musicians thought this too high. Shortly after Sydney Town Hall's organ was installed, a revised pitch of 435 vibrations per second was adopted by the French, and then imitated by everyone. Sydney's difficulty was that retuning an organ is much more complicated, and vastly more expensive, than altering the pitch of any other instrument.

soon as it was realised that her exceptional voice was her greatest asset; and it was in Vienna that she made her operatic debut (singing Nedda in *Pagliacci*) on the eve of the Second World War, having sung her first *Messiah* in London the year before. After the war, no soprano in the world was in more demand for twenty years, and there was no concert hall or opera house of any significance where she did not repeatedly sing. Whenever there was a big *Messiah* she was always the one the impresarios sought above all, and year after year she brought the house down with her 'Rule Britannia' on the last night of the London Proms; but her repertoire also spanned all the great operatic roles, which she sang on five continents. And that was only Joan Hammond's musical life. She had another existence as well. While she was studying her art, she kept herself afloat by working as a journalist for the *Sydney Daily Telegraph*; during the war, she served as an ambulance driver in the London Blitz; and in her youth she was an uncommonly gifted sportswoman. Twice she won the junior golf championship of New South Wales, thrice she won the state Ladies title, once she was runner-up in the Australian Open, and in 1935 she was a member of the first Australian Ladies team to play against Great Britain. She was also a runner-up in the NSW state squash championship, and for many years she was an active member of the Royal Sydney Yacht Squadron. We shall not, almost certainly, see Dame Joan Hammond's like again.

Nor is it likely that the world will ever know another saga like the one which eventually produced the Sydney Opera House; and which, for a start, was a measurement of the general public's indifference to the fine arts in this city, even though there had been calls for such a building from teachers at the Conservatorium for forty years before it became a fact. The Opera House eventually cost A$102 million (over fourteen times the original estimate), most of which was paid by the state government, with one-quarter coming from the sale of lottery tickets, but with Sydneysiders otherwise giving less than a million dollars to an Opera House fund.* It is no exaggeration to say that it would probably never have been built had it not been for the powerful advocacy of the Sydney Symphony Orchestra's conductor, Sir Eugene Goossens, the political ambitions of the state Premier, the Labor leader Joe Cahill, and the instant recognition of genius when the Danish Joern Utzon submitted his design to an international competition. Goossens had built up the orchestra until it was one of the best in the world, which gave him the clout that commanded attention. Cahill had a forthcoming election on his mind and wanted something dramatically memorable to impress the voters and secure a further term of office. Utzon certainly had genius, but it eluded the selection committee until the great Eero Saarinen, turning up late for the final meeting and being unimpressed by the shortlisted designs awaiting him, looked through the pile of rejects and told his colleagues that they were out of their minds, that this daring arrangement of elliptical paraboloids was the only entry that merited the prize money. The saga, of course, ran for years after that, with strikes, sulks, recriminations, preposterously escalating costs, structural misjudgements and an eventual walk-out by Utzon, who has still not visited the building that was essentially his baby, though Sydney offered him the symbolic keys of the city to commemorate his eightieth birthday. In spite of all the difficulties, the baby was eventually born, and on 17 December 1972 it heard its first music, which began with the *Merry Wives of Windsor* overture and finished with the *Polovetsian Dances*, with bits and pieces of Mozart, Beethoven, Ravel, Sculthorpe and Hamilton Harty in

---

*The fund-raisers tried many ways of attracting cash, one of which was the sale of celebrity kisses. Joern Utzon paid $100 to kiss the flautist Elaine Shaffer, while his partner in the original design team for the Opera House, Erik Andersson, paid a similar amount to kiss Joan Hammond. There was a tragic sequel to the lottery, however. The winner was a commercial traveller from Bondi, whose son was kidnapped for ransom shortly afterwards, the first case of its kind in Australian history. In fact, the child was already dead when the demand was made. His murderer was sentenced to life imprisonment and, while in gaol, he passed the grade 3 test of the Australian Music Examination Board.

between. This was a complimentary and exclusive performance given by the Sydney Symphony Orchestra for the Governor of New South Wales, the state Premier and a handful of other bigshots, plus two thousand site workers, their wives and their girlfriends. And it is probably true that such a thing could have happened only in Australia.

There it stands, one of the great architectural wonders of the modern world (in spite of periodic complaints—usually by people who have a professional interest in the building, rather than the general public—that it has functional limitations), on a tip of land whose first building went up when Governor Phillip had a little hut made for his protégé Bennelong. Subsequently Fort Macquarie was raised here as part of the Harbour's defences until it was superseded by a castellated tram shed and terminus in the city's transport system. Now we have this place of sheer delight, with its glowing russety-brown floors of brush boxwood, its deep-purple carpets, and its vast expanses of glass which allow the opera-goers and the concert-goers and the balletomanes and the straight theatre audiences to connect—before a performance and during the intervals, and afterwards, as well, if they're not in too much of a hurry to get off home—the beauty of whichever art is to their taste to the beauty of the Harbour and its endlessly stimulating activity.

The famous exterior has been compared to many things: to an airways terminal, to an albino tropical plant rootbound from too small a pot, to something that has crawled out of the sea and is up to no good, to the hindquarters of a giant crayfish. Witty such observations sometimes are, but perhaps they are also a little contrived when those billowing roofs seem so obviously to be a ceramic reflection of spinnakers swollen with wind, which is one of the great images of this Harbour.* No matter; they are beauti-

---

*It was Joan Sutherland who likened the Opera House to an airport terminal. She probably had in mind the TWA terminal at J. F. Kennedy Airport in New York, which can be seen as its progenitor, and which Eero Saarinen designed. Utzon himself said, 'If you think of a Gothic

ful and they are part of something about Sydney that is quite incomparable. Where else in the world, on a Friday night in June,
could you choose between a first-class match of rugby football full
of blood and thunder at a very modern stadium and a dazzling
(and mostly home-grown) production of *Fidelio* in such a brilliantly vivacious building as this? And afterwards enjoy rock oysters and a local Chardonnay beside one of the loveliest waters on
earth, twinkling with light and movement, and breathing an assurance that all things in the end shall be well?

---

church, you are close to what I have been aiming at. Looking at a Gothic church, you never get
tired. You will never finish looking at it. When you pass around it, or see it against the sky, it is
as if something new goes on all the time. This is important—with the sun, the light and clouds,
it makes a living thing.' Quoted by Yeomans, p. 43.

CHAPTER SEVEN

❧

Mardi Gras and Tall Poppies

The twentieth Gay and Lesbian Mardi Gras parade began on a sultry evening at the beginning of March with two hundred women, in motorcycling leathers and astride powerful machines, zooming away down the route from Hyde Park to huge applause from a vast crowd. It ended some time the following day when even the most ardent homosexual in town was exhausted by all the exhibitionism, the dancing and the partying, desperately trying to cure a hangover with a hair of the dog or copious quantities of Coke and Powerade. In between the send-off from the Dykes on Bikes, and a bleary-eyed return to business as usual, Sydney had wallowed in an extravaganza that bore some resemblance to both the Rio and the Notting Hill Carnivals, with a nod or two in the general direction of the Munich Oktoberfest.

Yet it was inimitably of this city, not least because it commemorated a black day in the local history, when police—having first removed the individual identification numbers from their epaulettes—had viciously attacked a crowd of people taking part in the first International Homosexual Solidarity Day march, which was itself saluting events that had happened in New York in 1969.* Things had changed so much in Sydney since then that a platoon of New South Wales police were given permission to march with all the other homosexuals in the 1998 parade, which they did with great precision, drill-perfect and in their uniforms, behind a banner announcing, 'We're Here Because We Care'; for which they were applauded as much as anybody else during that long and sticky night. They were, by a long way, the most conservatively dressed people on show as the gaudy sequence of floats and other exotica wound its way from Hyde Park to its climactic demonstration along Oxford Street and in Taylor Square, which were gained after over two hours of passing fancy and frequently startling eye-openers.

There were chaps sitting back to back on a lorry with their mouths gagged in what could have been almost straight bondage or maybe something subtler. There were other men posturing with immense phallic bananas, behind chums who exposed their buttocks like offensive European soccer players. There were marching boys in G-strings, baseball caps and nothing else, and there were some almost naked males groping each other for the especial benefit of the prurient television cameras. There was a float of Christians dressed like somebody's idea of angels, complete with haloes, and there were lesbians looking as belligerent as the Valkyries. A gaggle of self-proclaimed Leather and Fetishists went by, clad in nothing but jockstraps as wickedly spiked as anything devised by the Inquisition. There were luridly dyed feathers galore, garlands and garlands of flowers, outrageous things to put on your head—and legs that would have been wiser not to have exposed themselves so visibly in fishnets. You half expected to see Terence Stamp somewhere in there, wearing that gorgeous outfit from the

---

*Police had raided the Stonewall Bar in Greenwich Village and beaten up some of the customers, which caused the New York homosexual community to organise and assert themselves for the first time. This was the beginning of the Gay Rights movement in the USA.

big dance scene in *Priscilla.* Some of the groups carried banners: 'Lust for Life', said one, 'Homophobia. What Are You Scared Of?', asked another (and it's a good question to put to anyone). Not all these exhibitionists were Australians. The locals marched and rode in concert with the Miss Tonga Galaxy, the Exotic Blossoms of Fiji, the Filipino Queens and, inevitably, the San Francisco Gay Men's Chorus, who particularly wished to draw attention to the late Harvey Milk, sometime politician in that city, who was bumped off by a deranged cop many years ago, thereby becoming America's first homosexual martyr.

It needed much courage, still, for some people to be in the parade: those police officers, for a start, and a party of very happy-looking people whose banner identified them as 'Parents, Families and Friends of Gay and Lesbian Children', because not everybody in Sydney is yet reconciled to what has happened in this city since 1978. A droll little man supplied the evening's one touchingly funny moment, by walking all alone with a placard which said 'Genitals Are Rude'; but much more baleful figures than he were to be seen on the sidelines. The Rev Fred Nile of the Uniting Church, a man notoriously unwilling to unite with anything reprehensible (which is a strange inhibition in a paid-up Christian), had brought along thirty like-minded citizens who prayed and sang hymns and brandished a billboard that said 'God Forgive Sydney', but nothing at all to indicate that fifteen clergymen were somewhere in the parade. The Reverend was, in a manner of speaking, taken care of shortly afterwards, when the Sisters of Perpetual Indulgence pranced past (all bearded, all wearing nuns' habits) bearing a papier-mâché version of his head on a platter; and other effigies thus publicly mocked ranged from that of the Federal Prime Minister down in Canberra to the ineluctable Pauline Hanson up in Queensland.

Tens of thousands watched the parade, and it was said that this long spectacular was simultaneously seen in eighteen countries. If these were sharing the Australian coverage, they would have heard a pair of simpering television presenters saying things like, 'We've got a lot of queer Irish people here,' and participants in the parade declaring, 'I've had my hair set rock hard,' with a giggle and a smirk, just in case anyone hadn't taken the point. Excited marchers, interviewed on the hoof, congratulated each other with such remarks as 'She's one of the most talented and creative lesbians in Sydney,' while others said over and over again that this evening was a dream come true, it really was. As everyone could see for themselves, especially at the moment when the homosexual police officers marched past and were given a big hand from the crowd. For not only was the entire event orderly in a raucously undisciplined way, but not a hint of violence was anywhere to be seen. Only one suspect was arrested in the course of the evening, a young man from Ermington, who was subsequently charged with having two grams of cannabis concealed in his underpants.

Fred Nile may very well be the last representative of an essentially cruel tradition in the history of Sydney, in which the persecution of homosexuals was certainly not confined to the constabulary. When that savage reaction to the Solidarity March occurred near King's Cross police station in 1978, fifty-three people were arrested and subsequently charged with a variety of catch-all indictments, ranging from 'failing to cease taking part in an unauthorised procession' to 'using unseemly words'. Next day, the *Sydney Morning Herald* published the names and addresses of everyone accused, as a result of which many of them lost their jobs, and some even received death threats through the post. Fourteen homosexuals were, in fact, murdered in New South Wales between 1989 and 1993, and all but one of these crimes were committed in Sydney. At the same time, if it is true that judicial punishments reflect the attitudes of society as a whole, then most Australians until relatively recently were happy to see men put behind bars for fourteen years after being found guilty of homosexual intercourse.

That tradition goes back to the very earliest days of the Australian settlement, when homosexual relations were a norm among many convicts, especially among those unfortunate enough to be incarcerated offshore on Norfolk Island. 'How can anything else be expected?' a realistic magistrate asked his superiors. 'Here are 800 men immured from 6 o'clock in the evening until sunrise... without lights, without visitation by the officers. Atrocities of the most shocking, odious character are there perpetrated, and that unnatural crime is indulged to excess; the young have no chance of escaping from abuse, and even forcible violation is resorted to.'[1] The magistrate's report was censored before publication, omitting all references to convict homosexuality, but, as Robert Hughes has suggested, 'it is hardly possible that news and rumours of such doings on Norfolk Island and other penal stations, over the years, did not leak out into the colony and contribute to the atmosphere of nameless evil, of unutterable degradation.... There could have been no better breeding ground for the ferocious bigotry with which Australians of all classes, long after the abandonment of Norfolk Island and of the System itself, perceived the homosexual.'[2]

In recent times, homophobia was at its height during the Cold War, when Australia officially marched in step with Senator Joseph McCarthy, who was then running the show in Washington, denouncing homosexuals as one of the principal risks to national security. In Sydney, the number of prosecutions markedly increased and legislation enacted in 1951 tightened existing laws, a codicil introduced in 1955 actually creating new categories of homosexual crime. The temper of the time was plain in the columns of the *Sydney Daily Telegraph*, where it was observed that 'the increasing number of sex perverts in Sydney... is causing grave concern not only to the public at large, but also to the judges who are charged with the responsibility of administering justice'.[3] Not long before that was written, the local Vice Squad had raided an extremely respectable art gallery, where the Contemporary Art Society was exhibiting a painting by Donald Friend, which included male nudes, and which the police thought obscene. As recently as 1976, the Roman Catholic hierarchy tried to stop a Royal Commission on human relationships from considering homosexuality in Australia.

But Sydney's homosexuals were never the only targets of popular and legal prejudice, as Sir Eugene Goossens discovered in 1956. He came from a famous Belgian family of professional musicians (his brother was an oboist, his two sisters both played the harp), but his career as a conductor and composer was based in England and then in America until, in 1947, he was asked to take over the revived Sydney Symphony Orchestra and to become Director of the Conservatorium.* The orchestra was not highly regarded outside Australia when Goossens arrived, but within a few years he had transformed it into one of the ten best in the world; and some said it was one of the best half-dozen. It was this remarkable feat of earning Sydney music an international reputation at last, and quickly, that gave Goossens the authority to be heard with respect when he argued that the city must next have an opera house that would hold at least three thousand people and attract the best singers in the world, to replace a Town Hall which was used for everything from orchestral concerts to the Sydney Grammar School speech day, and could barely accommodate two thousand.† The orchestra's reputation was so high that Goossens was knighted in acknowledgement of its, and his, new eminence. After receiving the knighthood from the Governor-General, he went to Europe on leave towards the end of 1955 and returned the following March, expecting to conduct his orchestra a few days later in the first of the new season's subscription concerts.

The Sydney Vice Squad was awaiting him when he flew into Mascot and, together with Customs officers, the detectives went through the great man's baggage. They interviewed Goossens for

---

*Another Belgian, Henri Verbrugghen, had preceded Goossens in 1915, as conductor of the first SSO and then its successor, the NSW State Orchestra, a post he held until leaving for America in 1922.

†The Opera House, in fact, finished up with a principal auditorium holding 2,690 people, an 'opera theatre' with 1,547 seats, and two other theatres which were smaller still.

more than six hours and later issued a statement that they had recovered over one thousand photographs, some 9mm film, three books, four rubber masks and 'a quantity of incense ... of the type used for burning at rituals'.[4] Then they let Goossens go, but reporters who pursued him as soon as the story broke found that the gates of his home in Wahroonga had been tied with rope, that its resident, his wife and his daughter had gone to stay with friends. Two days later it was announced that he had been temporarily relieved of his musical duties through ill-health, at his own request, and that his assistant Joseph Post would conduct the first concerts instead.

The Vice Squad's actions did not go unchallenged. The newspapers began to get telephone calls from all over the world, 'mostly [from] very important persons', asking what the hell was going on, and the police themselves were 'inundated yesterday with calls from prominent local citizens'.[5] Letters to the Editor also began to pour in, pointing out what Goossens had done for the life of this city, and one of them came from someone who (cautiously perhaps) signed himself W. Wagner of Edgecliff. Within a week of his return to Sydney, Goossens appeared at the Court of Petty Sessions in Martin Place, charged with importing prohibited goods, for which the maximum penalty under Section 233 of the Customs Act 1901–54 was £100, the amount Sir Eugene was duly fined, after pleading guilty to the charge. But not before the Vice Squad had told the magistrate that their inquiries had been going on for six months (that is, since before Goossens had left for Europe, presumably because he had been informed upon in Sydney); and not before Mr J. D. Holmes QC had declared that it was 'difficult to imagine a worse case.... The exhibits speak for themselves and I do not propose to use any adjectives to describe them.'[6] The General Manager of the Australian Broadcasting Commission, Charles Moses, said that Sir Eugene's appointment was one of the most fortunate things that had ever happened to Australia, that he was a very timid, nervous and diffident man away from the podium or the master class, that he had never tried to change his contract with the ABC, although the cost of living had risen considerably. Mr J. W. Shand QC, for the defence, suggested that the vast quantity of items found in the conductor's baggage could only mean that they were part of some pornographic trade, and that Goossens had brought them into the country under some sort of threat.

Within a month, it was announced that Goossens had relinquished his musical positions in Sydney, the very day that in the Federal Parliament in Canberra, a Mr E. J. Ward (Labor, NSW) asked Sir Arthur Fadden, the Deputy Prime Minister, whether it was the Government's intention 'to recommend to the Queen cancellation of an award in the case of a well-known personality in musical circles who was recently convicted of a very grave breach of Australian Customs law'. He further wished to know whether Sir Arthur would ask for more police reports 'with a view to ascertaining whether there was any basis for rumours involving other top persons in conduct of a reprehensible character'. Fadden, to his credit, sat silently until the moment had passed. After reporting this, the *Sydney Morning Herald* added the following editorial comment:

> With the possible exception of Mr Ward, whose question yesterday was a disgrace to Parliament, everyone in New South Wales will read of Sir Eugene Goossens's resignation with profound sadness. The end of his career has been pitiful beyond measure. Yet it will be of some consolation to him to know that, long after the nature of his offence has been forgotten, he will be remembered as the man who re-created the Sydney Symphony Orchestra and, with the help of the Australian Broadcasting Commission, brought great music to millions for the first time in Australia. Sydney, which has so long heard 'his voice in all her music' will not forget its debt.[7]

But the irreparable damage had been done. Sir Eugene Goossens had already returned to Europe, where he occasionally appeared as a guest conductor but nothing more, a badly broken man who died flying home from Switzerland to London in 1962.

A senior figure in Mr Ward's party at the time was Arthur Calwell, who a few years later would become Leader of the Opposition in that Parliament. He had earlier made something of a reputation as Minister for Immigration in a Labor government, whose policies were succinctly summarised in something he said in 1947: 'We have 25 years at most to populate this country before the yellow races are down upon us.'[8] He could be just as blunt in his observations on domestic affairs, where he regarded intellectuals as 'people who always want to go their own way', which limited their usefulness in Arthur Calwell's ambitions for Australia. He saw a need to 'cut down the tall poppies' wherever they appeared in his field of vision; and he was not the only man, in and out of politics, who looked at society in this way.[9] He was a very typical Australian of a certain rough and ready kind, and a majority of his fellow citizens—certainly a majority of Labor Party supporters—saw things in the same light in those days.*

They were deeply suspicious of any nonconformity, they resented anyone who wanted to be something more than just another good bloke, and they could be pathologically stubborn in their refusal to countenance all forms of change that did not have anything to do with economic improvement. After twenty-odd years of Mardi Gras festivals, it will be hard for young Sydney to believe that when Arthur Calwell and his cobbers were alive, as

---

*The reflex has never been confined to the Australian working class, as the case of Walter and Marion Burley Griffin illustrates. They were hugely gifted American architects and planners who had worked with Frank Lloyd Wright, and they came to Australia in 1913 when Walter was enlisted to plan the new Federal Government reserve in Canberra. They later moved to Sydney to set up in private practice, but were effectively run out of town and out of the country (to India, where Walter designed a library in Lucknow) by the ostracism and destructive criticism of much smaller local talents. Apart from Canberra, their memorial is what remains of an imaginative housing scheme at Castlecrag, up the Middle Harbour in Sydney.

they were for many years after the Second World War, this was one of the most repressed societies in the Western world, whose various prejudices dominated local life—sometimes brutally— along a wide range of issues, from sexual behaviour to the consumption of alcohol. You could only be absolutely certain that she'll be right if you drank with the boys and took up surfing or constructed your life round some other sport. Sydney and the rest of the country lost many major talents in all the arts, not only because painters, designers, writers and musicians lacked an adequate audience here, but because they felt threatened and stifled by the prevailing philosophy. Those who stayed usually did so because they could not bear to exile themselves from a homeland that was the irreplaceable inspiration of their work. But many of these, like the painter William Dobell, lived in a constant state of anxiety lest their private lives should be revealed and denounced; in which case public humiliation and other punishments would surely follow.

Even now, the overbearing cast of mind can still be encountered in Australia, and every stranger gets a whiff of it before he even arrives if he flies here by Qantas. While the plane is making the usual circumnavigation of Heathrow before takeoff, the passengers are asked to watch the demonstration of safety procedures, as they are when travelling by everybody else's Jumbos. What sets Qantas uniquely apart from the rest, however, is the dogmatic tone of the man's voice (and it is never a woman's voice) coming out of the sound system: 'Ladies and gentlemen, I must *insist* on having your complete attention.' No other airline is as adamant as that, though perhaps they ought to be. And when the stranger arrives at his destination, Sydney can still provide examples of authoritarian heaviness that are all its own.

Until Mr Murdoch got his hands on rugby league football, the game was controlled throughout Australia by the New South Wales authorities, whose headquarters are on Phillip Street. Like many sports administrators everywhere, they have been much beholden for many years to a tobacco company, in their case to the makers of Winfield cigarettes, who have put vast sums of money into the game in exchange for the endless trumpeting of their product. This was hampered somewhat in 1987 when the North Sydney Council banned tobacco advertising at the local oval as a matter of public health policy, newly adopted on that side of the Harbour. Even more alarming to the people in Phillip Street was the appointment in 1990 of the Australian Broadcasting Corporation's chairman, David Hill, as president of the North Sydney club, because Hill was a highly articulate critic of the tobacco industry, who had consistently condemned rugby league's reliance on Winfield's sponsorship. The outraged, and extremely worried, authorities decided to intimidate the club into replacing Hill, and one way of doing this was to get the other fifteen clubs in the Sydney competition to declare at the NSW League's annual meeting in December 1991 that they would not play North Sydney in 1993 if David Hill remained president. At the same time, they voted another North Sydney official off the League's policy committee to underline the point. As someone remarked at the time, this was 'a classic Australian low-life gang bang'.[10] And a successful one: David Hill gave up his presidency in 1992, and was replaced by a much safer company director.

The Church can be caught bullying too, even when it does not necessarily share the Rev Fred Nile's particular obsessions, and the local Anglicans provide a case in point. The history of their Church in Sydney is to some extent a re-run of ancient Irish animosities at yet a further remove; it is the old Australian Catholic v. Protestant enmity in microcosm. The Protestant Ascendancy was nowhere stronger than in this city, probably because the first Roman Catholics deposited here were despised Irish convicts, because virtually everyone in authority subscribed to the tenets of the established Church of England, and because the Irish (often Ulster) Protestants who began to come after the early settlement did so as respectable free men with the same distinct social, political and economic advantages as the existing colonial gentry. The chronology of colonisation ensured that, in this as in other respects, matters had become deeply entrenched in Sydney when they were only just taking root in other parts of the continent. The enmity was, as elsewhere in Australia, most marked between Roman Catholics and Protestants in general, but the Anglicans here had their own private war going on at the same time.

The Sydney diocese is famously the most evangelical in the country, and this is largely because towards the end of the nineteenth century its patronage was seized and then monopolised by people whose ancestry lay in the Church of Ireland.* (It is also said to be the wealthiest diocese in the Anglican world, and certainly the diocesan offices behind St Andrew's Cathedral are of an opulence normally encountered at the headquarters of international corporations.) That patronage has never been relaxed. A typical member of the Anglican establishment in Sydney was the Rev Thomas Chatterton Hammond, who in 1935 was appointed Principal of the Moore Park Theological College, which meant that he could ensure that a whole generation of ordinands would follow the evangelical line of scriptural fundamentalism, rather than emphasise the primacy of the sacraments and the continuity of Anglo-Catholicism from before the Reformation. Hammond was a Cork man who came to Sydney from Dublin, where he was well accustomed to—and doubtless relished—perpetual conflict with the Roman Catholics. 'Hammond had been shot at, blacklisted,

---

*Nothing is more confusing than the terminology of what, in its country of origin, is known as the Church of England, which is part of the worldwide Anglican Communion. Other branches of this organism are the Episcopal Church in the USA, the Church of Ireland and the Anglican Church of Australia. In all of them there is a much greater variety of emphasis and ritual than exists in any other Christian denomination. Anglicans can thus be extremely Protestant (evangelicals, Low Church) or almost indistinguishable from Roman Catholics (Anglo-Catholics, High Church) or something that lies between the two (Broad Church). Usually baffling to the outsider and often to the insider, these traditional differences have been both a strength and a weakness of Anglicans.

mobbed and put under police protection. He continually held open-air meetings in the face of rowdy hecklers and brass bands. He came from a polarised religious environment in which controversy and politics were the order of the day.'[11] Only a little less obdurate in his Low Churchmanship was John Charles Wright, who had arrived from England in 1909 to be installed as Archbishop of Sydney.

Most Anglican churches in the diocese conformed to the notions of ecclesiastical propriety that these men at different times shared, but there were some exceptions. On the Archbishop's very own doorstep, at the top of George Street, stood Christ Church St Laurence, which was, and still is, the sort of place that sends Anglo-Catholics into raptures as a foretaste of heaven, and gives most evangelicals apoplexy because it seems to have gone much more than half-way to Rome: its rituals are wreathed in incense and punctuated with genuflexions, and its priests wear sumptuous vestments whose colours change with the liturgical seasons (it also has what may well be the finest choir in the entire Anglican Communion, a band of men and women who sing everything in the classical repertoire, from Gregorian chant, through Tallis and Monteverdi, to Stanford, Duruflé and Herbert Howells, week in and week out, with a tonic brilliance that not even an English cathedral or an Oxbridge college chapel could improve upon).

It was the vestments that offended Archbishop Wright most of all, and especially the wearing of the chasuble, a richly decorated garment which is loaded with theological (and particularly Catholic) significance. He had already extirpated this piece of papistry from St James's, the church that Francis Greenway designed, by refusing to install a new parish priest unless he agreed to forswear the chasuble. Now he turned his attention to Christ Church St Laurence and had a special Vestments Ordinance passed, which forbade the wearing of eucharistic garments there, again with the threat of having no new priest appointed—which would effectively have meant the church closing down. The ban has remained in force ever since—though such vestments are often worn in every other Australian diocese—and successive prelates in Sydney, a self-perpetuating hierarchy, have indicated that as far as they are concerned it will always be thus: this accounts for the fact that Christ Church St Laurence, in its dutiful obedience, pointedly keeps its chasuble in a glass case at the bottom of the north aisle, where everyone can see it and ponder the small-minded ways of Christian authority.

As repressive as anything for forty years were the Australian liquor laws, which were imposed upon the nation because of a drunken riot in Sydney during the Great War. This had always been a hard-drinking country—unavoidably, given the part that spirits played in forming society here from the beginning. From the time that John Macarthur and the other officers of the New South Wales Corps got their hands on that cargo of American rum, and effectively held to ransom everyone who fancied a drop, liquor was for many years the most important currency in Sydney. It was generally referred to as rum, though the word covered every kind of home-made hooch as well, and the real thing was available only by shipping it in expensively from Jamaica and Bengal. As long as convicts were brought out here, and assigned to settlers or ex-convicts as cheap labour, such payment as they received was very often in rum, invariably because they preferred it to any other reward: hard liquor, after all, was the best anaesthetic a man could reach for when life was becoming too painful to bear. Governor Bligh, who had more cause than most to rue the influence of alcohol on his bailiwick, disliked the trade not only because it gave the Rum Corps the power that eventually put him mortifyingly under lock and key, but because of the damaging effect it was having upon His Majesty's other subjects. Settlers from the countryside would neglect their fields while they made a four-day journey to Sydney and back, simply to buy at inflated prices a gallon of liquor. Their thirst for spirits, said Bligh, 'was so very strong that [they] sacrificed everything to the purchase of them, and the prices were raised by that monopoly to so high a degree that it was the ruin of many of those poor people'.[12] So important was this commodity in the local economy that Governor Macquarie later built Sydney's first infirmary from the profits on forty-five thousand gallons, which caused it to be known as the Rum Hospital.

Beer had been available, too, almost from the start, after John Boston and Thomas Palmer brewed Australia's first pint in 1796, which they did after consulting the only encyclopaedia in the colony. That same year saw Governor Hunter issuing licences to ten public houses in New South Wales, which worked out at one for every 344 people, and they naturally adopted names that were familiar to the inhabitants from their previous existences—The Wheatsheaf, Dog and Duck, Black Swan, Woolpack and so on. Booze was so vital to morale, and Australians became so heavily addicted to it, that it is surprising to find that Sydney's two most celebrated breweries were not established until well into the nineteenth century. John Tooth arrived from the hoplands of Kent in 1835, and thirty-five more years passed before James Toohey came out from Limerick and set up a rival business.

It was probably beer, rather than the hard stuff, that produced the riot in 1916 which led to the draconian drinking laws. The appalling news from Gallipoli had begun to sink in, and young soldiers were not quite so eager to go off to the war as the first Australian volunteers had been two years earlier. Men under training at Liverpool rebelled against the harsh conditions there, broke camp and raided a local hotel, drank themselves daft and boarded trains to Sydney. The vanguard disembarked at Central Station and headed into town, where they began to smash windows and overturn the fruitsellers' carts, but a mob of five hundred recruits, arriving soon afterwards, found an armed military picket awaiting them when they staggered off the train. 'It was about 11 p.m.,' according to an eyewitness. 'The grille on the eastern end of the assembly platform was closed. The military police ... called upon the soldiers to halt. The soldiers turned a hose on them. A few pressed forward. Rifle shots rang out. A soldier of the 6th Light Horse fell dead on the platform, shot through the eye. A number were wounded. That was the end of the riot. Bullet holes in the roof, and one in the ticket office wall, provided reminders of the Battle of Central for years.'[13]

As a result, the Government ordered that all pubs (except, curiously, in Queensland and Western Australia) should close at 6 p.m. for the duration of the war. The restriction remained in force long afterwards because the politicians could always rely on the wowser vote to back them up on this and, in truth, they cynically pandered to it: there were a lot of narrow people in all the Churches, after all, but there were enough expansively God-fearing souls as well to block an attempt at complete prohibition, when this was put to a referendum in New South Wales in 1928. As it was, all citizens, especially the sober ones, had to endure the legendary 'six o'clock swill', when men dashed to the pub straight from work to get in an hour's steady drinking on empty stomachs, with predictable results. The early evening streets of Sydney even after the Second World War were habitually awash with swaying figures who, already well sluiced, generally clutched a brown paper bag which concealed a couple of large bottles for further consumption at home, the ones who were already too far gone to see the way properly being propelled in the right direction by their long-suffering wives. Yet an overwhelming majority of people in New South Wales in 1947 voted for 'continuance' of the existing law. And this was the way of the world until a royal commission was set up in 1951 to investigate various scandals that were lurking in and around the liquor trade. In the course of his investigations, Mr Justice Maxwell came to the conclusion that 'there are evils associated with six o'clock closing which ought not to be tolerated in a civilised community'.[14] In 1954 another referendum was held, and this time a narrow majority of voters caused closing time to revert to 10 p.m., which is what it had been before 1916; but it was not until 1963 that an obligation to shut for an inconvenient hour between 6.30 p.m. and 7.30 p.m. was removed.

Things are all so very different now. You can drink to your heart's content in Sydney from mid-morning until far into the night, and some premises are licensed to stay open for twenty-four hours. Together with an abundance of good restaurants, which between them produce every variety of cooking known to man, and local wines that are among the best in the world, this city has been transformed from a depressingly limited place for revictualling into an epicurean delight, *pace* the loud young men at sporting events (and the mob that turned Bondi Beach into a battlefield during Christmas 1995) who haven't yet learned how to hold their beer. The transformation, moreover, has been effected without losing two of the most attractively basic Australian characteristics. No extremely upmarket restaurant in London or New York would welcome a family of six which included two small children scarcely out of nappies and in need of high chairs, but it happens here. And wherever you eat, the young waiters and waitresses are always unaffectedly cheerful and courteous, without a flicker of deference, and without a hard-nosed 'Have a nice day' either. Although it's still not really done to say this in Australia, they invariably make you feel like tipping them for their genuine good nature alone, without worrying about whether you ought to or not.

But no transformation has been more astonishing than the one which now annually sanctions the week of Mardi Gras festivities, culminating in that gaudy pageant of extroverts through the middle of town. Homosexuality is not only no longer anathema here, the vice above all vices that must not be spoken of; it has become in some strange and fundamentally generous way blessed by a majority of the citizens, so that now the deviants seem to be the Rev Fred Nile and his supporters. The blessing has included the compassion to sustain a Candlelight AIDS Memorial March during the Mardi Gras festivities, though it has most obviously been extended to the great parade itself, in all its palpable sense of liberation, in all its gay abandonment, in all its fantastic extravagance, in all its overweening triumphalism, in all its ineffable vulgarity. Sydney has recognised at last, as much as anywhere on earth, that these people have committed no crime greater than hi-jacking an immensely expressive and attractive word which once had a wide application, but which no one can now use in any other context than this, except at the risk of sniggering ridicule.

CHAPTER EIGHT

Warts and All

One of the most piquant experiences this city has to offer starts in the early evening with a ramble round old Sydney, which eventually brings the tourist to the top end of Macquarie Street and the Hyde Park Barracks. This, as we know, was built in 1817 on the eponymous Macquarie's orders, to accommodate six hundred convicts who spent their days in hard labour for the government. And Francis Greenway designed a very handsome brick building, delicately austere, with one of his employer's obligatory clocks set into the pediment—not at all like the grimly overpowering prisons the Victorians would shortly be putting up back home. Were it not for some barred windows, from the outside it would quite easily pass for a rather commodious Georgian market hall, or an ambitious Methodist chapel with a remarkably prosperous congregation. The barracks and its outbuildings, either jointly or severally, have been through many vicissitudes during the course of their working lives, becoming—after the few remaining convicts were rehoused on Cockatoo Island in 1848—in turn an immigration depot for single women, a government printery, a district court, a headquarters of the New South Wales Volunteer

Rifle Corps, an asylum for elderly and poverty-stricken women, the Patents, Coroner's, Weights & Measures department, the offices of the Clerk of the Peace, the Public Trustee and the Master in Lunacy, the Legal Aid Office, and the place where Parole Board hearings took place, as they still do, in chambers on the eastern side of the barracks courtyard.

Mostly, however, the Hyde Park Barracks these days is one of Sydney's several highly imaginative museums. It mounts exhibitions, like a heartbreaking display of convict love tokens, which men left with their wives or their sweethearts or their mothers or some other relative as a parting gift before they were transported. They fashioned them from coins which they had defaced by grinding and rubbing them until they were smooth discs, before scratching a tenderly anguished message on the blank surface. 'Forget me not. J. Riley 1832' says one, with a heart, two birds and a straggle of flowers pricked out round the message; and, on the reverse, 'Token of love from your Unfortunate Nephew J. Riley Sept 16th 1832'. There's a long gallery on the top floor of the barracks which has been left in its original condition, with slits in the walls through which the gaolers could peer to see that all was well inside, where the convicts slept in hammocks, side by side just like sailors, seventy of them to a room. And it is there that the curious visitor may spend the night at the end of his tour if he wishes, listening to the half-crazed mutterings that come quietly through a sound system, before he is sent on his way after a deliberately frugal breakfast, in a distinctly reflective mood.

There is much to reflect on after a night in Hyde Park Barracks: on the detritus that was saved for posterity because rats make nests of anything that comes to hand, and a lot of this was uncovered during restoration work some years ago—bits and pieces of undergarments, socks, aprons, bonnets, menstrual rags and soiled bandages—and the curators have made an interesting historical (and zoological) point with it. On a beautiful quilt that has been created from similarly small pieces of fabric, to remind us that the women confined here after the penal times were required to work as seamstresses. On a computerised database, where you can find out if you have a convict ancestor, where he or she came from, what job if any that person did before conviction, the offence, the penalty, the sentence and where it was passed, and the ship used for the transportation. The only trick that anyone appears to have missed is in the courtyard surrounding the main barracks, where the triangles used to be arranged. Convicts were tied to these as a punishment, and were then flogged with a cat-o'-nine-tails, up to 100 lashes at a time, until the skin of their backs was flayed and sometimes flesh, too, right down to the bone. When Ernest Augustus Slade was superintendent here in 1833–4, the floggings were notable for 'that peculiar art in the flourish of the scourge, which ... so greatly adds to the pain'.[1] That bit the museum's curators have left to our imagination, for there isn't a triangle in sight.

The history of Australia's penal origins is disgusting, even allowing for the fact that the accepted values of two centuries ago were at scarcely any point civilised by today's standards, and allowing for the mitigating humanity of men like Arthur Phillip and Lachlan Macquarie (and, after them, Sir George Gipps and Alexander Maconochie), who were very far from sadistic, who did their best to make life as tolerable as possible for their charges, not least in offering them the prospect of early redemption, and who were even-handed in everything they ordered for the convicts, their guards and the civil population alike. Nor can the essentially wicked System be exonerated on the grounds that some of the convicts were indeed evil and viciously cruel men themselves: the vilest crimes against the Aborigines, especially in Van Diemen's Land, were perpetrated by convicts or by those who had served their time and were greedy for land and other advantages. The truth is that the majority of those transported, who were subjected to the most dreadful conditions in transit and remained exposed to the possibility of savage punishment after they stepped ashore, were pathetic no-hopers, or people whose infractions of the law might warrant nothing more than a police caution today, or they were troublemakers, which meant Chartists and suchlike in England, Scotland or Wales, seditionists in Ireland; and most 'political' prisoners, in fact, were Englishmen, not Irish. Their story needs no résumé here, for it has already been magnificently told by Robert Hughes, whose account describes not only what happened in early Australia, but what it was in British society that produced this degrading epoch.*

It is possible to see the origins of many Australian characteristics in the penal settlement. Mateship almost certainly began with the behaviour of convicts to each other, as did its less attractive corollary, the levelling tendency. Anyone who ratted on a fellow convict to authority would later be killed by other prisoners, even if it meant biding their time for revenge (or they would at least bite off an ear or the tip of his nose); but anyone who defied authority could be sure that lips would be sealed when authority tried to identify the culprit. There are cases of the most powerful inducements—up to a free pardon, a free passage back to England and a cash reward—being ignored in a display of convict solidarity. The popular disdain of authority, conveyed among other ways by the traditional reluctance of Australian soldiers to salute their officers except in the most pressing circumstances, quite clearly comes from the same relationship that fostered mateship: and so does the authoritarian streak that has always run through this democracy, and which has promoted a number of unedifying habits like police brutality and intimidation in various forms, both secular and religious, though the Roman Catholic insistence on hierarchical imperatives has clearly played its part in the latter case.

It is possible also to see the thrust of the Australian entrepreneur, the man of humble origins who eventually makes it big at the bank, as a continuation of something that began to happen

---

*Hughes found that seven out of ten convicts were tried in England, one in five in Ireland. On this evidence, the most lawless place was London, and after that Lancashire, Yorkshire, Warwickshire, Surrey, Gloucestershire and Kent, counties which supplied four transportees in every ten (see *Fatal Shore*, p. 163).

almost as soon as the First Fleet sailed in. Although not a single convict could have left the English Channel without a sense of dread hopelessness, many soon came to the conclusion, after they had found their feet on the great continent, that they could, with some perseverance, be much, much better off here than ever would have been possible at home had they never been convicted. Peter Withers, a Wiltshire farm labourer, who had been transported for rioting against miserable conditions and increasing mechanisation on the land, wrote to his brother two years later: 'all the Bondage I am under is to Answer my Name Every Sunday before I goes to church, so you must not think I am made a slave of, for I am not, it is quite the Reverse of it. And I have got a good Master and Mistress, I have got plenty to eat and drink as good as ever a gentleman in this country has, so all the Punishment I have in this Country is the thoughts of leaving my friends, My Wife and My Dear Dear Children....'[2] That was a very big but, of course; yet the fact is that in 1826, a few years before that letter was written, no more than 7 per cent of the convicts who had become eligible for a free passage back to Europe took advantage of this statutory right.

Some convicts became notable figures in the community, an unlikely prospect at home had they remained on the right side of the law. If Francis Greenway hadn't made a hash of forging a contract, he would never have been anything more than an obscure provincial architect in Bristol. Had there not been a mutiny at the Nore, William Redfern would have been just another diligent naval surgeon until he retired to tend his garden wistfully within sight of the sea; he would not have become a revered figure in the medical history of a new nation. Samuel Terry, an illiterate labourer from Manchester, transported for stealing some stockings, would not otherwise have won prizes at the first Easter Show in Sydney for breeding stallions, nor would he have prospered enough to be subsequently hailed as the Rothschild of Botany Bay. If he hadn't been transported for seven years, James Ruse would have remained a struggling small farmer in Cornwall, instead of becoming known as the father of Australian agriculture. If Solomon Levey hadn't been sent to New South Wales for stealing a chest of tea in 1814, he wouldn't later have become a merchant, a banker, a landowner and a philanthropist, wealthy enough to subsidise the new settlement in Western Australia. If, in 1790, thirteen-year-old Mary Haydock had not been transported for joyriding on the squire's horse in Lancashire, she would not have married the young merchant Thomas Reibey in Sydney and, when he died, taken over his shipping and sealing business, which she expanded until she owned seven farms along the Hawkesbury River and much property in town as well.* Those half-dozen were not the only convicts who prospered because they had skill and energy which they put to good use the moment they had served their time: there would have been at least scores of others who also worked their way from fetters to riches in New South Wales, while 'scores of thousands of emancipated convicts [went] on to build happy, productive and law-abiding lives for themselves and their children in Australia'.3

As potent as anything in the continuum that stretches back to 1788, however, is the sense of shame that many Australians felt because there was a convict somewhere in the family's history. A friend of mine in Sydney, an acknowledged expert in her profession, is something of a rarity because she is descended not merely from one but from two people who were transported in the First Fleet. Both ancestors were sentenced to seven years at Manchester Quarter Sessions in January 1787 for stealing six pieces of fustian, one piece of yellow canvas and half a gross of white filleting and, after being held for a while in the forbidding Lancaster Castle (which is still used as a prison today), they were despatched aboard the transport *Prince of Wales* in Arthur Phillip's convoy, leaving their

---

*In a sense, her greatest achievement didn't come until late in the twentieth century, when her picture was printed on Australian currency—first on the A$5, later on the A$20 notes.

children behind, though no one now knows where or with whom. The husband worked as a blacksmith in Sydney Cove, and was notable for his surliness, which earned him twenty-five lashes on one occasion for insolence ('You may kiss my arse!' he said) to a Marine sergeant, and at another time he was put in irons. He was also a heavy drinker, who preferred to take payment in rum for any extra work he did in his own time; and this is thought to have contributed to his early death in 1791, but not before the couple had produced two more children, thus siring the line that flourishes in Sydney today. Yet, until shortly before her mother died a few years ago, my friend had no knowledge of any of this. It was the dirty little secret that one of the generations between then and now had been too ashamed to pass on: it was the Stain of convict ancestry in the eyes of 'respectable' people to whom, until the 1820s, the word 'Australian' was an expression of condescension (and some Australians choose to believe that the habit has not yet died among the British, which is perhaps another reflex dating back to the earliest days). Happily, this story has a better ending. It is now such a matter of pride among people of this lineage that a Fellowship of First Fleeters exists and circulates new titbits of information, as they crop up, in a newsletter; while my friend and her husband have in their bathroom a framed poster, bearing the names of everyone who sailed with Arthur Phillip, where their own children can study it and feel good about their highly exclusive pedigree.

You'd be pushed to make a case that Sydney's penal origins were responsible for its long and sometimes frightful criminal record, but there can be few other cities whose misdemeanours great and small have been meticulously logged in an unbroken line from the very first day of their existence. And nothing much, except penological attitudes, appears to have changed in that time: the offences for which the convicts had been transported, the crimes some of them and others committed after their arrival, have all been repeated endlessly in this city over the past two hundred

years, which suggests nothing more than a wretched flaw in human
nature, almost enough to make anyone believe in a doctrine of
original sin. What's interesting about Sydney is that the crimes
have sometimes crossed the boundaries of such proprieties as
criminals themselves have generally observed at a given time.

Since the Middle Ages, for example, murdering a clergyman has
been subject to a powerful taboo in all Western societies (except
in South America). Yet in Sydney a parson was an early victim,
after arriving from the missionary outpost of Tahiti in 1798. The
Rev. Mr Clode was simply awaiting a passage back to England,
and in his charity he lent some money to a soldier named Jones,
obviously expecting to be repaid before his vessel sailed. He was
told that the loan would be ready for his collection if he turned
up at a shanty on George Street which was occupied by Jones, his
wife and two other Redcoats. He was never seen alive again but,
the day after, a workman found Clode's body in a sawpit, its head
bashed in and its throat cut. Suspicion obviously fell on Jones, but
he was a convincing liar and a more than passable actor, even after
the discovery in his hut of an axe with blood and brains still sticking to it, together with a knife and a discoloured blanket. Taken to
the sawpit where the body still lay, he offered to kiss it to demonstrate his innocence for, he said, he had loved Mr Clode like a
brother and couldn't possibly have done him any harm. No one
believed him and eventually one of the other soldiers told how the
murder had been carried out, with Jones cutting his victim's throat
after his axe had failed to do the job outright. Governor Hunter
decided that this and its attendant squalor—a jovial drinking
party was held in the hut after the mess had been cleaned up—
merited an exemplary punishment. The Redcoat who turned
King's Evidence was spared the gallows but Jones, his wife and the
third soldier were hanged in front of as many inhabitants of Sydney, convict and free, as could be mustered in time. Their gibbet
was erected over the ashes of the hut, which the Governor had ordered to be razed as a preliminary to the execution. Mrs Jones's

corpse was handed over to a surgeon for dissection, the other two bodies were left to hang in chains until they had putrefied. And on the following Sunday the colony's first chaplain, the Rev. Richard Johnson, preached a sermon in his wattle-and-daub church on a text taken from the Book of Samuel: 'Is this thy kindness to thy friend?'

If we're looking for an equally gruesome example from the many murders that Sydney has known in the twentieth century, a notorious case from the 1930s will serve. The caretaker of a yacht in the Harbour disappeared on the night the boat sank at her moorings. When the police investigated, they found that he had in fact gone down to a cottage on the coast after the boat sank, but had not been seen since. They were getting nowhere with the case until a local aquarium shortly afterwards acquired a shark from somewhere out at sea and put it into a tank for public display. Strangely, it refused to eat at feeding times and swam round and round as though it was out of sorts. One day it was seen to be vomiting and a startled keeper recovered from the contents of its stomach a man's arm. At first it was assumed that the unfortunate chap had been attacked while swimming, but a doctor who specialised in treating shark bites examined the evidence and told the police that the creature was entirely innocent: the arm, in fact, had been hacked from a torso so crudely that, if the body had been alive when this happened, it certainly wasn't alive now. It was noticed that some tattoo marks had survived the butchery and the shark's digestive system, and after all the tattoo shops in the city had been canvassed, police were able to work out that the arm belonged to the missing caretaker. Further detective work resulted in an arrest and a trial. Before the arrest, the water police had a high-speed chase down the Harbour before they collared a terrified man in a motor-launch. He was the registered owner of the sunken yacht, and the police decided to put him up as the chief witness for the prosecution. The night before the trial began, he was shot dead on one of the wharves at Dawes Point, at the southern approach to the Harbour Bridge. The accused was not convicted because there wasn't enough evidence, and whoever was responsible for the two murders was never officially identified, though the police were eventually certain that both had something to do with a smuggling ring.

Gangs of various compositions have been another constant in the life of this city. Towards the middle of the nineteenth century several were operating at the same time, each with its own well-defined territory. The so-called Forty Thieves had the suzerainty of the Rocks, the Iron House Mob ruled Woolloomooloo, while Bristley's Mob ran the show between George Street and Darling Harbour. In common, they picked pockets, roughed people up and terrorised law-abiding citizens simply by rampaging through the streets, smelling of violence. Bristley's Mob was the most interesting of them, some of its members being regular customers of the Royal Victoria Theatre, where they evidently took a shine to the darling of the local matinées, the actor Francis Nesbitt; to his good fortune, as it later turned out. In 1849 he decided to try his luck on the Californian goldfields. He didn't have much of that until the day he was stripped and robbed by a bunch of bandits—who not only put him on his feet again and returned his money when one of them remembered where he had seen their victim before, but actually passed the hat round to compensate him for their behaviour. They were Bristley's Mob, now known as the Sydney Ducks in San Francisco, and they had gone to California to seek their fortunes too. In its paradoxes, this is a very Australian story.

The twentieth-century mobs provide no such warming memories. Before the First World War there were razor gangs in Woolloomooloo and at Millers Point, while North Sydney's residents could well have done without the larrikins who banded themselves into the Gore Hill Tigers and the Blues Point Mob and conveyed sheer menace wherever they roamed the streets. The target areas have changed since then, and a great deal of gang violence in recent years appears to have become concentrated in the city's Asian communities. The past decade has seen many examples of such families being bound, gagged and robbed in their homes, especially in the Vietnamese suburb of Cabramatta, after these had been broken into by groups of thugs armed with machetes, sawn-off shotguns and knives: in 1992 alone, more than thirty families were violated in this way. What's more, triads spawned by Hong Kong have started running crime in the Chinese quarter of the city, and a few years ago a leading local businessman was murdered by them. He was Stanley Wong, President of the Dixon Street Chinese Community, who had played host at a lunch honouring the visiting Chinese Prime Minister Zhao Ziyang, for which the local Special Branch provided food tasters, just to be on the safe side. But the prospect of loot rather than political agitation was what got Wong killed by two young men who, when they were arrested, were found to have identical key rings bearing the 14K triad insignia.

Or consider fraud; compare and contrast the cases involving the rogue who called himself Count von Attems when he arrived in Sydney in 1868, and that of Peter Geoffrey Huxley, the banker who was sentenced to twenty years in 1970. The Count, a slight figure wearing a monocle, disembarked from the steamship *Northampton* with a manservant and drove straight to the best hotel in town, the Royal. Within a day or two he had become the talk of local society, which was given to understand that he was an officer in the Austrian Imperial Hussars, so close to the Emperor Franz Josef himself that a warship was even now on its way to the southern hemisphere to take him home after his inspection of Australia. Invitations to dinner, to balls, to regattas and whatnot began to pour in and even the Earl of Belmore asked him to sup at Government House. The management of the Royal were quite happy at the prospect of their bills being paid by drafts on various London and Viennese banks, and even cashed one of the Count's cheques for £200, a tidy sum in those days, without demur. This was not the last money he extracted from gullible people, though no one in the end ever quite worked out how much he owed. After a couple of months, he left for Brisbane, to await the arrival of his warship and, while he was waiting, persuaded the Prussian Consul in Queensland to part with £2,000, bought a schooner and victualled her with, among other nourishments, six crates of champagne. After hiring a captain and a crew he sailed off into the Coral Sea, but was later arrested by the Dutch in Batavia and imprisoned for fifteen months. This somewhat mollified Sydney and Brisbane when they discovered that Count von Attems was an impostor, a former valet to the genuine article, who had died some years earlier.

The modern parallel is no laughing matter, alas. Huxley was the secretary of the Rural Bank, which was owned by the New South Wales Government. Like many men in such a responsible and trusted position, he was asked to become honorary treasurer of various charities, which included the United Nations Greeting Card Fund, the Art Gallery Society of New South Wales, and the Australian Freedom from Hunger Campaign. In common they had high cash turnovers, and Huxley began milking them in order to finance his gambling. He admitted later that he frequently bet $50,000 on one race and more than once had lost up to $300,000 in one day. When he was brought to court and charged with 129 offences, he reckoned he had lost a total of $1.8 million, that most of the money had gone to one Sydney bookmaker in particular. His twenty years was an unprecedented sentence for such a crime in New South Wales, though in fact he served only nine years before he was released. The Rural Bank made good the stolen money, but the lasting damage was that people were reluctant to give to local charities for a long time afterwards.

And then there is corruption, whose history is as long as anything, for it began with John Macarthur and his partners in the rum monopoly, and has led to Sydney in recent years being defined as 'the most corrupt city in the Western world after Newark,

New Jersey, and Brisbane, Queensland'.[4] The mantle of Macarthur and the Rum Corps fell upon the men who ran the city after it was incorporated in 1842 and the first municipal elections were held, and from then on local government was a regular source of scandal, few years elapsing between one rumour of bribery or defalcation and the next, though not all of them stood up to proper examination. By the 1870s, Sydney was agog at the disclosures coming out of the Town Hall about the Inspector of Water Works, David Robertson. The most titillating of these concerned his activities with a Town Hall employee named Polly, which Alderman J. D. Young at a subsequent inquiry described as 'enough to make every man blush'.[5] More seriously, it emerged that workmen in Robertson's department not only sometimes reported for their day's instructions to the Cricketer's Arms, where he and Polly had a love-nest, but that the men periodically arranged testimonial dinners for Robertson, together with a whip-round when Polly needed hospital treatment. Their generosity became less remarkable when it was revealed that Robertson habitually gave them large amounts of overtime pay, which often found its way into his pocket not only through the testimonials, but in repayments for land he had sold to some of the men.

He was also at the centre of a racket involving water meters. Sometimes these were resold when property changed hands, and the money certainly did not finish up in the Corporation's account: sometimes they were deliberately adjusted to swindle either the customer or the ratepayers in general, the books again being falsified in each case. Yet remarkably, when these matters were brought into the open, the City Council decided to take no action other than to issue a reprimand. This, it seems, was because the City Engineer reckoned Robertson's legitimate skills were such as to make him effectively irreplaceable. Not only was he not prosecuted or even sacked, but in a reorganisation of Sydney's water and sewage department he was, after a brief suspension, dignified with the new title of Inspector of Water Services.

Matters were no better as the twentieth century got under way, when the allocation of stallholding licences, a Lord Mayor who took weekly backhanders for giving people jobs, electoral fraud, cartage contracts, coal contracts, the regrading of a road and even the erection of a petrol pump all had an airing at one time and another; and the Civic Reform Party won an election in 1921 on the issue of municipal corruption. Much worse was to follow in 1927 when the council was dismissed by the state government, three commissioners being appointed to run the city in its place. The issue which brought about this sensational event was the council's decision to build a power station at Bunnerong, just above Botany Bay. A royal commission which was later appointed to investigate the matter found that the English firm of Babcock & Wilcox, in tendering for the power station contract, which was worth £667,000, had given Sydney's Deputy Electrical Engineer, Silas Y. Maling, £10,000 to help him make up his mind in its favour. He kept £2,000 of this for himself and passed on the rest to Alderman Frank Green, who shared it with several Labor Party colleagues. Another firm, the International Combustion Company, attempted to bribe its way in too, and several aldermen were said to have profited from this separate approach. Criminal proceedings were started on this occasion, but not before Maling did a bunk to New Zealand, where he was trying to get a visa that would allow him to proceed to the United States when the New South Wales police arrived and extradited him. He was, of course, convicted, fined £300 and gaoled for six months, though he refused to give evidence against Alderman Green, who as a result walked away without punishment. Babcock & Wilcox's manager in Sydney, who had arranged the bribery, escaped, too, after turning King's Evidence against Maling; but his firm was fined £10,600 for creating temptation in the first place. Not until 1930 were fresh municipal elections for a reconstituted city council permitted by the state government, and when these took place not one of the aldermen whose names had been mentioned in the royal commission's report bothered to offer himself to the electorate.

Politicians higher up the ladder have also been caught in compromising positions. There was a period in the 1930s when people wanting favours in the New South Wales Parliament—a well-placed question to a Minister or a telling intervention in a debate—could generally get them for an outlay of £10 a time. Much worse than that has happened since, most notoriously during the ten years when Sir Robert Askin was state Premier after his Liberal Party took office in 1965. He is remembered for many things, not least for something he said when President Lyndon Johnson visited Sydney in 1966 and demonstrators let him know exactly what they felt about the war in Vietnam by trying to block his motorcade. 'Run over the bastards,' Askin instructed his chauffeur. It also became common knowledge that he took about $100,000 in bribes each year from the gangsters running illegal gambling dens, that he had very close links (as they say in all the most cautiously reliable crime reports) with three major criminals in the city. Shortly before Askin died in 1981, an Independent MP went so far as to declare that 'under the Askin Government in the 1960s, the real penetration of organised crime by overseas gangsters, mobsters and the Mafia took place. I have no doubt that ex-Premier Askin knew and may have encouraged these activities.'[6] Nor did the rot stop with Robert Askin. Since his time, a Minister of Prisons in New South Wales has spent seven and a half years in one of his own gaols for taking bribes to arrange the early release of prisoners, because he owed vast sums in gambling debts.

As for the police, another of Lachlan Macquarie's bequests to Sydney... That upright man would turn in his grave if he knew half the goings-on in the apparatus of law enforcement that he created with thirty-five properly paid constables in 1810.* Every

---

*This was nineteen years before Sir Robert Peel founded the Metropolitan Police in London. In Sydney, policing of a sort before 1810 was carried out by convicts who were thought to be more trustworthy than their fellows, and who were paid for their services in rum and remissions.

police force on earth has been suspected of corruption at one time or another, and the police in Sydney have probably been no worse than those of any other great city for most of their existence; but in the last two or three decades their low reputation has placed them securely among the most reviled constabularies in creation. Robert Askin wasn't the only person taking a hundred thousand bucks a year from criminals in the 1970s; the New South Wales Police Commissioner was at it as well, and a number of other senior police officers have not come well out of close scrutiny. One man at the end of his career was given a substantial cheque at a farewell banquet attended by three hundred of Sydney's most shady customers, and another was retired early and in disgrace on the pension of a sergeant when he'd actually reached the rank of Deputy Police Commissioner. Matters had become so notoriously bad by 1994 that Parliament set up yet another royal commission (they have been a recurring feature of Sydney's life since the nineteenth century) and Judge James Wood's report rocked this city, whose cynicism about its police is proverbial even by Australian standards, and whose citizens believed that they had long ago heard everything.

'Corruption in New South Wales', the Wood Commission concluded, 'embraces receipt of bribes, green-lighting, franchising, protection or running interference for organised crime, releasing confidential information and warning of pending police activity, quitting or pulling police prosecutions, providing favours in respect of bail or sentencing, extortion, contract killings, stealing, supplying drugs, and other forms of direct participation in serious criminal activity. And that is without being exhaustive.'[7] Part of the trouble was a sub-culture in which there were rewards for officers who refused to report corrupt colleagues, punishments for those who did, yet another throwback to the penal times. During the commission's three-year existence no fewer than 1,020 New South Wales policemen resigned and another 320 were prosecuted.

The rottenness was so extensive, from top to bottom of the constabulary, that the Government took the extraordinary step of appointing an Englishman to lead its police force into straighter ways, his first priority being to clean it up before he turned his attention to other forms of criminality. This was a daring thing to do, and Police Commissioner Peter Ryan, sometime Chief Constable of Norfolk and senior officer in both the Metropolitan and Greater Manchester forces, from the outset faced the hostility of the New South Wales Police Association, whose members heckled him on one occasion with shouts of 'Go home, Pom!' Not long afterwards, eleven of them committed suicide, when they were threatened with exposure for corruption. The good Commissioner has been sacking people at intervals ever since and, as we have already seen, another by-product of his appointment was the appearance of homosexual officers in the Mardi Gras parade, an unthinkable event before 1998, with homophobia more widespread and powerful in the police force than in any other section of society. Ryan, who quickly decided that he'd taken on the most demanding police job in the English-speaking world, discovered that vast sums of money were swilling round the Sydney underworld, most of it related to drugs and to a number of ethnic groups in the city, to people who in the past thirty years had migrated from Lebanon, from Hong Kong, from China, from Vietnam and from parts of the old Soviet Union.

It is a sobering thought, in fact, that the recent past has seen crimes committed in Sydney that this city had never known before, even though its repertoire has always been broader than most. There had been no kidnapping for ransom in this country until the tragedy which took place after the Opera House lottery winner's name was declared in 1960. There had been no political assassination until 1994. There had been an attempt in 1868 on the life of Queen Victoria's son Prince Alfred, Duke of Edinburgh (he who planted *Martiusella imperialis* in the Botanic Gardens), when an Irishman's bullet failed to do the job properly because His Royal Highness's braces got in the way, and he was merely wounded (the Irishman, nevertheless, was hanged in Darlinghurst

Gaol). And someone took a pot shot at the Labor leader Arthur Calwell in Mosman a hundred years later, again unsuccessfully.

So the first assassination was the shooting of a state Labor MP, John Newman, outside his home in Fairfield, which is part of the Cabramatta constituency he represented in the Legislative Assembly. Newman had made a name for himself as the man who proposed to cleanse his patch of the Asian gangs who had begun to terrorise its largely Asian inhabitants; and three Vietnamese, one of them a prominent local businessman and councillor, were eventually, three and a half years later, charged with Newman's murder. The day after the shooting, the *Sydney Morning Herald* carried a banner headline, 'Cabramatta's Days of Innocence Have Died', and there was another story entitled 'MPs Reflect on End of a Good Natured Country'. One of these politicians dramatised the shock widely felt in Sydney when she said, 'If this means Australia has become a member of the world community, I don't want to be part of the world. I want to be Australian, where people can speak out for what they believe.'[8]

Nor had there ever been anything before like the bombings that shook the town in the 1970s. The first happened with separate explosions outside two Yugoslav travel agencies in George Street, which injured sixteen people, and for which no culprits were ever found. Much more serious was the bomb that went off outside the Hilton Hotel, again on George Street, six years later in 1978. This explosion occurred just after midnight, when two council workers were emptying a garbage can, and both were killed, together with a policeman who was standing near by. The target seemed obviously to be inside the hotel, where delegates to that year's Commonwealth Prime Ministers' Conference were staying, among them Margaret Thatcher, Morarji Desai of India and Malcolm Fraser, head of the Government in Canberra. The politicians next morning set off on their planned excursion to the Bradman museum down at Bowral, whose oval was where the great man had played his first cricket, but Mr Fraser took the precaution of having 500 troops guarding their train, while three RAAF gunships flew discreetly behind it to keep an eye lifted for further trouble in the countryside.

At first, it was assumed that Mr Desai might be the target (he was not very popular in his own country at the time) and three members of the dissident Ananda Marga movement, all Australians and Sydney residents, were arrested soon afterwards and sent to prison for sixteen years apiece, but following a Supreme Court inquiry they were released after only seven years. Someone else had confessed and was sent down for twenty years, yet several disquieting features in the case have never been answered to the satisfaction of sceptics whose instinctive reaction is to question anything involving the police in New South Wales. The man found guilty changed his evidence fifty-two times during the trial; the evidence of a Special Branch agent was found to be untrustworthy by the judge; a student who was subpoenaed to give evidence subsequently committed suicide. One theory has been that the federal security services and the police were themselves responsible in a public relations exercise that disastrously backfired; that they had planted the bomb and intended to 'discover' it in order to demonstrate their efficiency and have their budgets increased by a grateful government. The case has rested ever since.

Nothing has nagged at the public conscience, however, so much as the most alarming unsolved crime in Sydney's history, which rates the superlative because of its wider implications. It was committed in 1975 when the great struggle to save Woolloomooloo and its immediate hinterland from rape by the property developers was still raging. As we have already seen in Chapter 5, Sidney Londish was eventually seen off by the residents and their supporters, but his rival tycoon Frank Theeman appeared at one stage to have a better chance of getting what he wanted. Theeman's past was never quite clear to anyone outside his family. Some people understood that he was born in Holland, others in Austria: what's certain is that he got out of Europe in 1938, when the Nazis started seizing Jewish businesses, including Theeman's lingerie factory. With his wife he sailed for the Antipodes and, *en route*, had the most remarkable slice of luck when an Australian racehorse owner, Timothy O'Sullivan, befriended him and lent him £1,000 to make a fresh start as soon as he reached Sydney. With this, Theeman founded another textile business but, as soon as he became wealthy enough, he sold it and moved into property development. And while Sidney Londish was embroiled in the Battle of Woolloomooloo, Theeman was attempting to bring off a similar coup on higher ground just above the 'Loo. He had targeted, in particular, an area between William Street and the escarpment overlooking the naval base and those comfortable old houses that Jack Mundey and Fr Campion and the local residents were trying to defend.

William Street is one of Sydney's broadest thoroughfares, always deafening with traffic and lined for some of its length with car showrooms, as it plunges out of the city centre in a long switchback which presently sets its course for the eastern suburbs and South Head. Before ever it reaches the open suburbs, as it were, it skirts both the 'Loo and King's Cross; is, in fact, the boundary separating both of them from Darlinghurst and Paddington. With Bondi, King's Cross is the only name in Sydney that rings a bell with people who have never been within ten thousand miles of the place, and that is because it has always, even when it was Queen's Cross, been the place where the city's nonconformists have congregated, especially the more raffish ones. It is to Sydney what Soho is to London, what the Village is to New York, an area which has a decent open-air café life during the day but which at twilight is transformed into something that mixes sleaze and a touch of criminality with the allure of illicit adventure in a particularly garish fairground. Strip joints, massage parlours, shops selling blue movies, doorways that lead to heaven knows what, arcades where you can lose a fortune on poker machines—these are King's Cross's stock-in-trade and until recently, until (it is said) the action shifted to Cabramatta, this was also where all the big deals in hard drugs took place.

But just beyond this lubricious locality you could be in a different city, another world, and its name is Victoria Street. There are backpackers' hostels here, and you can pick these out a hundred yards away because outside on the street are parked dusty and almost clapped-out pickups and cars, with wire grilles to prevent windscreens being shattered by flying stones on dirt roads in the Outback: each has probably been round Australia a dozen times already, and its latest owner is anxious to sell it on before he goes home. The hostels are superseded by domestic properties, together with the odd cosy-looking hotel, but what every building here has in common is a distinct period charm from the nineteenth century, with a fine sense of proportion, steep-pitched roofs, cast-iron railings and balconies, with Virginia creeper running across the walls, and the foliage from tub plants dripping down from the upper floors. In its own modest way, this could reasonably claim to be the most handsome street in all Sydney. Frank Theeman wanted to demolish it and to replace those buildings with high-rise blockhouses that would, if his ultimate ambition was realised, stretch all the way to the Rocks, which is something over a mile away. He was prepared to invest A\$60 million in the first phase of this development.

Like his friend Sidney Londish, he was opposed by the local residents and by Jack Mundey's men, but in April 1975 the Builders' Labourers' Federation in New South Wales was taken over by its federal headquarters, where green bans had never been popular because they had nothing obviously to do with the advancement of the membership. The green ban on Victoria Street was consequently lifted, which left the residents to fight on their own. One of them was Juanita Nielsen, a young woman of means which she had inherited with one of Sydney's biggest department stores, Mark Foy's. She was an unconventional heiress, however (the fact that she lived on Victoria Street when she could have afforded Darling Point had she wanted it says enough about that side of her character), who had started her own local newspaper, *NOW,* which began to campaign loudly against the Theeman development. She not only didn't like what he was trying to do; she despised the way he was going about it. Theeman's 'security men' were simply a bunch of thugs trained and led by a karate expert, who intimidated residents one by one into relinquishing their properties, but Nielsen told them where to go when they came knocking on her door. There were also a number of other murky characters in Theeman's background, including a corrupt former policeman and the people who owned and ran the Carousel Bar in King's Cross. One evening in July 1975, Ms Nielsen, for reasons her friends have never understood, went alone to the Carousel to discuss an advertising deal for her newspaper. She was never seen again, and her body has never been found. She had, in fact, stopped Frank Theeman in his tracks, because he pulled out of the Victoria Street development after calculating that it was still costing him $3,000 each day after an already overlong campaign. But, if he knew who Juanita Nielsen's murderer was, he took that knowledge to his own grave in 1989.

So Sydney, you see, is not always the buoyantly attractive metropolis full of essentially good-natured citizens that its admirers everywhere secretly long for it to be. It has its vices too, its amorality, its cruelty, its corruption, its viciousness, its ruthless greed. It has even acquired the 'gated community', the sophisticated laager whose prosperous inhabitants feel a lot safer for their neighbourhood's expensive security arrangements, as patented in the United States: guards, chain-mesh perimeter fences, massive iron gates and—who knows?—quite possibly landmines and booby-traps as well. And, oh yes, there's another thriving scam, which in 1998 resulted in a murder in front of the victim's missus and their kids; something to do with rival tow-away trucks which all like to be first on the scene of traffic accidents, where the crashed vehicles are in need of at least some serious and very profitable panelbeating. What all this amounts to, alas, is that in its criminal record Sydney is no different from every other metropolis in the Western world.

CHAPTER NINE

Politics, Too

A few hundred yards from the Hyde Park Barracks, a bit further down Macquarie Street, stands the building in which the fate of this city and this state is settled in a robustly knockabout fashion and in short bursts, by men who don't believe in overworking themselves. This is the New South Wales Parliament, which is architecturally distinguished by incorporating a wing of the old Rum Hospital, with its original balcony and verandahs: the other wing became the Sydney Mint Museum, whereas the middle section was demolished to make way for a new hospital, whose plans were vetted and approved by Florence Nightingale herself. Utterly Australian on the outside, therefore, the Parliament's innards (not to mention its procedures) give the visiting Englishman a queasy feeling that he has seen something like this before, when he too, just like your average Sydneysider, has frequently wondered whether the taxpayer's money is always spent prudently.

Though a Legislative Council of officials was formed in 1824, another eighteen years elapsed before elected representatives sat on it, and it was not until 1856 that New South Wales acquired a second chamber, a lower House, which they called the Legislative Assembly. The model, naturally enough, was the British Parliament, but, instead of Lords and Commoners, the honourable members of this legislature were simply distinguished by their different terms in office: elected every four years to the Assembly, there for the duration of two Parliaments if the voters sent them to the upper chamber.

The moment you walk through the front door of the Assembly, you are confronted with a number of imperial bygones. Here is an oil painting of the last British monarch but two and his queen (the picker-up of unconsidered trifles, and we have met her before); and there, by George, is a massive canvas depicting Queen Victoria passing the Westminster Houses of Parliament in state, on the occasion of her Diamond Jubilee. Advance to the debating chamber and the first thing to catch your eye is the royal coat of arms above the Speaker's chair; and after that the seats on which the honourable members arrange themselves, the green-leather upholstery being copied from originals in the House of Commons (in the Legislative Council, they go in for red, just like the House of Lords). The imitations of Westminster extend not only to the Rules of Debate, but also to some of the trappings of ceremony, to two baubles in particular. There is an Usher of the Black Rod, who has an important function in the Council, which he discharges with the assistance of a wand whose pedigree began in the fourteenth century with Edward II: they have already worn out two of these on Macquarie Street, and the present Black Rod goes back only to 1974, when it was presented to the politicians by the Bank of New South Wales. Yet Sydney never had a Speaker's Mace, which is now carried into the Assembly by a Sergeant-at-Arms in the best Westminster tradition, until that same year, when the Jewish Board of Deputies decided that it was not going to be outdone by any bank.

The Assembly contains another painting and a memorial, which are reassuringly Australian and could belong nowhere else. The painting is of William Charles Wentworth who, conceived at sea in the Second Fleet by a convict girl and an emigrating surgeon who had four times been acquitted of highway robbery, was author of the first book ever written by someone born in Australia, which argued the case for a parliament in New South Wales: he was also the man who led the first successful expedition across the Blue Mountains in 1813. The memorial is in bronze, and it is dedicated to Lieutenant-Colonel George Frederick Braund and Sergeant Ed Rennix Larkin, representatives of Armidale and Willoughby in that Parliament, 'who, being among the first among the legislators of Australia to volunteer for service with the Australian Imperial Force in the Great War, fell gloriously in action in the Dardanelles in the month of May 1915'. That plaque tells you as much as anything ever could tell you about the very best in Australian democracy.

The very worst—or, at least, something getting close to it—is all too often in the air when the MPs are assembled, as they are for brief periods every year with long intervals in between. Politicians generally are regarded as a species of low life in Australia (it's a toss-up whether they or the police are at the very bottom of the pile in public esteem) and the reasons for this are not hard to detect.* One is that the state assemblies probably do put in fewer hours than elected representatives in other Western societies, and so they are commonly accused of laziness, of getting rather well paid for doing not very much. Another charge is that they have too often been caught with their hands in the till, and while major corruption—such as Robert Askin and a later Minister of Prisons practised in New South Wales—is relatively uncommon, far too often MPs are guilty of grubby little pocket-lining practices.

---

*There have been well-respected battlers in Parliament, however, and none has ever been more popular than Dawn Fraser, whose first experience of public scrutiny came when she was a champion swimmer, the fastest woman in the world for many years and the first person to win gold medals in three Olympic pools in succession (Melbourne '56, Rome '60, Tokyo '64), after which she made her name all over again by getting herself elected to the Assembly as Independent MP for Balmain, which is where she was born and bred in a large working-class family.

A banner headline in Sydney in 1998 was 'Like Thieves in the Night', above a story about MPs deliberately prolonging a debate until midnight so that they qualified not only for free taxis home, but back again next day, all at the taxpayer's expense; and the debate, as it happens, was on an Opposition motion to censure the Fair Trading Minister for lying about some of his travel expenses.[1] The politicians are also despised for the way they too often behave politically, inside and outside Parliament. One of the *Sydney Morning Herald*'s most distinguished editors would have spoken for many people, before and since, when he wrote: 'As he listens to a succession of fourth-rate speeches, almost all delivered at great speed in a raucous, ill-educated voice without any attempt at wit or originality or even construction, he feels something like despair.... As the debate drones on, the student (of politics) may reflect that the old saying that a country gets the politicians it deserves cannot possibly be true of Australia. No country deserves politicians as bad as these.'[2]

That man was familiar with politics in Westminster, where ill-educated voices can also be heard from time to time, but these have always been counterpointed by speech which has been partly formed in the Oxford Union and other places where smooth slander and silken innuendo are developed as normal skills of the sophisticated orator. Sir Robert Menzies was widely disliked by his fellow countrymen for many things and one of them was that he, too, had the gift of the witty put-down that left his adversaries spluttering impotently.* He was certainly one of the few men in Canberra or in the state assemblies who could have matched, for example, Michael Foot's polished piece of abuse in the House of Commons, to the effect that a notably unpleasant Tory minister

---

*Menzies rates a second footnote in this book for one of his Parliamentary thrusts after an Opposition windbag had bored everyone else stiff. The Prime Minister heard him out patiently, then got up and observed that 'The conducted tour we've just been given of the honourable member's mind would have been a great deal more instructive if it hadn't taken place in gathering darkness.'

'has all the virtues of a semi-housetrained polecat'. At which even the insulted Norman Tebbit was, for once, left speechless.

Here, however, is Neville Wran QC MP, Premier of New South Wales, and supposedly one of the most articulate speakers of his time, doing his best in the Legislative Assembly. He was taking part in a debate about compensation for retiring members of the Legislative Council:

MR WRAN: The honourable member is a low cur like his Deputy Leader. He was aided and abetted by the defrocked member for Dubbo, the Leader of the Opposition, who made a direct reference to my wife. It is a curious thing that we who are not born to rule seem to have some respect for the position of women in the community, but not so our colleagues of the Country Party, not so the Leader of the Country Party and the Leader of the Opposition.*

[*Interruption*]

MR SPEAKER: Order! I call the Leader of the Opposition to order.

MR WRAN: I repeat, the honourable member for Oxley is a despicable cur.

MR PUNCH: That is praise from you. The Premier is a sensitive man.

MR WRAN: I am sensitive about the women in my family. I had better not say what I am tempted to say or we might get back to the broom cupboard. I shall continue with the claims of the greedy grubs of the Country Party, aided and abetted by the Liberal Party, as they appear at page 33 of Mr Justice Selby's report....[3]

It was Neville Wran who, within a year of gaining office, taunted the City Council with the gibe that 'it has no more power than a crippled praying mantis' and that he intended to keep it that

---

*The 'defrocked member for Dubbo' was, in fact, a former Methodist minister who had resigned in order to become a politician. The Premier was not invited to withdraw his remark.

way, particularly as it was controlled at the time by the Civic Reform Party.[4] The history of Sydney is littered with frictions between the Town Hall and Macquarie Street, though maybe no more than between parliaments and municipalities in other parts of the world: what's striking here, however, is the fact that repeatedly the operations of the one have been summarily suspended by the other. We have seen how this happened in 1927 in the wake of the Bunnerong scandal, but a precedent had already been established in 1853, when the City Council was sacked for failing to provide an adequate water supply or sewage system, even though it had a strong case for arguing that these failings were the result of underfunding by the Government.*

Another spasm of bossiness came in 1969, when Robert Askin's Liberal Government dismissed the Labor-controlled council and restored some electoral boundaries that had been altered once before, to Labor's benefit for an uninterrupted twenty years. 'The passing of this legislation was accompanied by a protest meeting which filled the Town Hall, and a march of 2,000 workers on Parliament House, where members hurled abuse at each other in rowdy scenes played to a packed public gallery.'[5] Yet another twenty years down the track, and three commissioners were once more running the city on behalf of the Government, this time because a number of development plans were threatened in council, including the construction of the overhead monorail which nowadays conveys tourists and hardly anybody else past a lot of people's privacy on its way to the Darling Harbour pleasure park.

The tussles between the politically left and right in this city have rarely been conducted from dangerously extreme positions, though Sydney went through a nasty phase during the Depression,

---

*Sydney has never quite kept up with the times in such matters. As late as 1976, only 67 per cent of the city was sewered, and the dunny man (known as the midnight mechanic in northern England before the Second World War) was still emptying non-flush lavatories in the small hours of the morning.

in an antipodean version of the simultaneous conflict in London between Oswald Mosley's British Union of Fascists and the Communist Party. The Reds were also involved in Sydney, where the Australian Communist Party was founded in 1920 and where its bitterest enemies called themselves the New Guard, a paramilitary organisation of ex-Army officers formed by a Turramurra solicitor, Eric Campbell; and there were street battles between the two factions, in which men tried to blind each other with cayenne pepper.* But the thing the New Guard would eventually be remembered for most of all came close to farce. They were so hostile to J. T. Lang's Labor Government in New South Wales that they decided to demonstrate their extreme displeasure with it at the opening of the Harbour Bridge. The man chosen for this mission styled himself Captain Francis de Groot, though his business was making repro furniture in Rushcutters Bay. From somewhere he acquired a horse, got out his old uniform, his sword and some medals, so that he would look the part of an outrider in the official Bridge-opening retinue; but he wore an ordinary khaki cap, as an observant journalist reported later, 'instead of the usual cocked hat' which was customary on all the best ceremonial occasions. He wangled his way (with the assistance of a kindly policeman) to a position in the official enclosure just behind the Governor-General's escort, where he saluted His Majesty's representative (who amiably returned the salute) and then waited for the ceremony to begin, after all the appropriate speeches had been made. 'The Premier's voice was carried by amplifiers to the dais where the ribbon stretched across the bridge and, shortly after he had finished his speech, and while Mr Davidson (Minister for Works) was speaking, the man spurred his horse up to the ribbon and,

---

*A more serious threat arose in Victoria, where a White Army was formed and mobilised several thousand men who were plainly ready for action against a Labor state government, though the order never came, probably because the Hogan administration collapsed and was replaced by something more to the White Army's taste.

with an underhand swish with his sword at the ribbon, shouted: "On behalf of decent and loyal citizens of New South Wales, I now declare this bridge open." '6 Then and there, however, officials tied the severed ribbon together again so that Mr Lang could do the job authentically. Groot was, of course, arrested and later charged with 'being a person deemed to be insane, and not under proper care and control', though the insanity charge was dismissed and he was merely fined £5 with £4 costs for offensive behaviour in a public place.

New South Wales is, by instinct and tradition, a Labor Party fiefdom, although control of the City Council in the twentieth century has swung back and forth between Labor and its political opponents. But since 1910, when a state Labor government was elected for the first time, Labor has been in office for almost twice as long as its various opponents, and it once had a run that very nearly lasted a quarter of a century (from 1941 to 1965). This is in spite of the fact that Sydney was a bit slow off the mark in marching to the political beat of organised labour's drum, both Melbourne and Adelaide having taken some first steps in the movement before a Labour Electoral League was founded in Balmain in 1891—and won the first election it contested in New South Wales shortly afterwards. But the conference that resulted in the certificated birth of the Australian Labor Party did take place in Sydney Trades Hall nine years later, when the twentieth century was not yet a month old.

One of the ALP's founders was Billy Hughes, who became the most controversial figure Australian politics has ever known. Though of Welsh descent he was actually born in London and emigrated at the age of twenty-two, working in the Queensland Outback as a labourer before coming to Sydney in time to win a seat in the Parliament on Macquarie Street in 1894. He was a combative bantam of a man who was working his way up through the local party machinery and through the trade union movement to distinctly higher things, which he reached when he was elected to the new Federal Parliament in 1901. By 1915 he was Australia's Prime Minister, and that was when the controversies began.

Hughes came to office just two months after the Australian Light Horse had suffered its most frightful casualties in two misguided and criminally mismanaged charges against the Turks on Gallipoli, and a few weeks before all Allied troops were evacuated at the end of a disastrous nine months in the Dardanelles. Yet at this very moment, when the country was reeling with grief at the avoidable butchery of young Australians, blazing with anger at the incompetence of British generals, Hughes went to London and was fêted there for speeches he made in support of imperial solidarity. Worse, when he returned he proposed conscription for the rest of the war, and many Australians assumed that he had simply succumbed to the manipulative flatteries of the British Government. They defeated Hughes's grand design in two consecutive referendums, and another result of this rebuff was a split in the Labor Party, which was not healed as long as Hughes lived. For instead of resigning over conscription, he stayed in office with a few loyalists and formed a new National Party with what had lately been the Opposition. Many never forgave Billy Hughes for that, because he had done by far the most odious thing in the philosophy of the Australian working man: he had ratted on his mates when the chips were down.

Hughes had not really been toadying to London. But he needed to stay onside with the British because he reckoned the young nation was not strong enough to go it alone after the war, not with all those Chinese and Japanese and Indians and whatnot just to the north of it. White Australia was an important part of the Labor Party ethos, and Hughes subscribed to it as much as anyone. He also wanted to ensure that his adopted country, by its valour in arms, would be heard respectfully in its own right when the peacemaking time came round; as, indeed, it was. At Versailles in 1919, Hughes did not shrink from pointing out to the sanctimonious Woodrow Wilson that Australia had left many more dead men on the battlefields of Europe (not to mention Gallipoli) than ever did the vainglorious US of A. He was reincarnated as something of a hero to many when he came home after that, but remained a controversial figure to the end of a very long life, still committed to most of the principles—including public ownership and government control—with which he had launched his political career: he always reckoned that he had stayed put politically, that it was Labor that had changed. His epitaphs were varied when he died in 1952, still representing a Sydney constituency in Canberra, and one of the most memorable was composed by the cartoonist David Low: 'He was too small to hit, too deaf to argue with, and too tough to chew.'[7]

Jack Lang was never quite in Hughes's league as a national figure, and he had no international standing at all, but neither was he ever regarded as a villain who had betrayed his own people to the enemy. He was the son of a Sydney watchmaker and jeweller, and made his own way at first as an estate agent before entering the New South Wales Parliament in 1913. Thereafter his upward progress in the state Labor Party was steady rather than spectacular; Treasurer in 1920, Leader in 1923, Premier from 1925 to 1927, and again from 1930 to 1932. His first term in office was marked by a number of reforms that were the beginning of his reputation as a local champion: he introduced a widow's pension to the state, a workers' compensation act and a system of child benefits that the rest of the country wouldn't catch up with for another sixteen years, and he restored the forty-four-hour week that Labor had introduced in 1921 and which had been abolished twelve months later by an incoming coalition government.

His reputation was further enhanced during his second term as Premier, most of all by his stance in a classic case of the plucky colony rebelling against the overbearing Motherland, which was, in fact, the position that got him re-elected. The London banks had started leaning on the Federal Government for the payment of interest on loans at an extortionate rate, and they had the backing of Westminster. Lang went to the polls with an agenda that was partly economic and partly an insurrection. He would lead

New South Wales out of its Depression—which was as bad as anything the United States and Europe were also experiencing in the wake of the Wall Street Crash—and one of his instruments would be a refusal to pay the British interest rates: he also called upon the Federal Government to abandon the London gold standard altogether, which could easily be construed as downright republican talk. It was this last item that resulted in the formation of the New Guard, whose own position was made clear in the first issue of its house magazine:

> In the hour of this State's need the New Guard has arisen. To convey to all people the message of our great patriotic movement is the aim of this journal. The message is one of protection from the designs of the disloyal. . . . And under the cloak of a free democracy we, a people of pure British stock, are under the domination of a band of imported agitators of a low type, openly professing the revolutionary principles of Karl Marx. This band controls with an iron discipline the elected representatives of the people. . . . Nor can this discipline be unwelcome to a Premier who openly glories in flouting the sanctity of contract, a principle for which sixty thousand of the cream of our manhood died in far-off lands.[8]

Lang had, as most people knew, purged his party of communists some time before that was written, but he knew exactly what Eric Campbell and his associates were on about. Oswald Mosley himself couldn't have stated their case more eloquently.

In the event, the Big Fella's time was ended by the Crown, whose Governor of New South Wales, Sir Philip Game, dismissed him for illegally circulating among public servants an instruction to put all taxes and other forms of income into the state's coffers instead of following normal procedure and depositing these monies in banks, where they could be seized by the Federal Government. The grounds for the dismissal were never tested in the law courts but, to the chagrin of his supporters, Lang meekly accepted the diktat anyway and backed down; which was one reason why Labor was thrown out of office again in 1932. Whereupon the New Guard disbanded, Captain de Groot stabled his horse for good, and Sir Philip went home to become Commissioner of London's Metropolitan Police.*

There are several reasons why New South Wales has been such a Labor stronghold with its heart firmly planted in Sydney, why the party has dominated local politics for so long. One is certainly the incidence of Irish Australians in the city, with their long resentment of authority deeply embedded in the local working class; and its corollary, the political engagement of the Roman Catholic Church. Eight of the twenty-four Labor members of the Legislative Assembly at the turn of the century were Catholic, but by 1922 the figure had risen to twenty-two out of thirty-six; and that proportion has never been seriously disturbed. These men and their supporters and their priests were bonded not only by their religion, but by hard times which had started with the early settlement and would continue unabated right through the Depression to the beginning of the Second World War; also by the resentment that saw in most forms of authority a thinly veneered extension of British sovereignty.

This animosity reached its height during the conscription debates in 1916 (which came shortly after the Easter Rising in Dublin) and 1917, but it was still raging in 1920, when the Labor Lord Mayor of Sydney, Alderman W. P. Fitzgerald, whose party had conspicuously refused to join in the peace celebrations in 1919, or even to fly flags from the Town Hall, gave an official luncheon for Dr Daniel Mannix, Archbishop of Melbourne, who was about

---

*The dismissal of Jack Lang, dramatic though it was, did not create nearly as great a sensation as the dismissal of the Labor Prime Minister, Gough Whitlam, by the Governor-General, Sir John Kerr, in 1975. The reasons in this case were much more complicated than in Lang's, but centred on two different interpretations of the Australian Constitution: whether or not a government could stay in office when its fiscal policies were consistently blocked by the Federal Parliament's upper House. Ironically, the Labor leader came from the upper middle classes of New South Wales, the Queen's representative who dismissed him having started much lower down the social scale in Balmain. The psychological implications of their confrontation are intriguing.

to embark on his first *ad limina* visit to Rome, where he would submit the customary report on the state of his diocese. Mannix was unsurpassed in his hostility to conscription and to imperial attachments generally, and no one had any doubt that this civic hospitality was a snub aimed at London, especially when the top table pointedly refrained from proposing the loyal toast to King George V. And yet the Catholic Church in Australia has not always been the politically monolithic structure that the universal reputation of the Vatican suggests: it, too, has had its differences of opinion, just like the Labor Party. When the Archdiocese of Melbourne in the 1950s backed the breakaway Democratic Labor Party (Archbishop Mannix wearing his anti-communist mitre on this occasion), the hierarchy in Sydney stood by the ALP, concluding that reformation from within would be more expedient than sniping from without.

At bottom, and most obviously, Labor acquired its grip because, like social democratic parties everywhere, until quite recently it identified itself exclusively with the preoccupations and aspirations of the local working class. These have been as attractive and as rebarbative in turn as the reflexes of manual workers and artisans everywhere. Always, however, there has been something singularly Australian about the positions adopted here, often touching extremities that no one else has quite reached. It is hard to imagine any Labour Prime Minister in Britain, past or present, doing what Joe Cahill regularly did during the years of his Premiership: wait his turn with everybody else in one of Sydney's department stores until the barber was ready to give him a haircut, a lifetime habit he saw no reason to change just because he had made it to the highest position on Macquarie Street. Nor is it likely that British workers would down tools in support of a boss figure, as happened on the occasion of that first concert at the Opera House, which almost didn't take place because, by an oversight, no tickets had been issued to the contractors' supervisors and their wives, and the blokes blacked the lighting, the air-conditioning and everything else in the building until the foremen had been invited along with everybody else. On the other hand, the racism of British workers has never been as vicious or as implacable or as nearly unanimous as the antipodean variety that obliged every government to pursue a White Australia policy from the end of the nineteenth century until long after the Second World War. The ALP didn't disown it until 1965.

Attitudes such as these were being formed in New South Wales long before working men banded together as a parliamentary force, from the time that trade unions were formed. Some early steps in this direction were taken in Sydney at about the time the British Government repealed Pitt's Combination Act at home in 1824, though this didn't stop the transportation of the Tolpuddle Martyrs from Dorset ten years later. They, hapless fellows, were consigned to a land which had recently proclaimed its very own Masters' and Servants' Act, that promised six months' imprisonment to anyone who neglected his work or spoiled or lost his master's property. At the same time, anyone who took as little as an hour off work without permission from the boss stood to spend an unspecified period on the treadmill. Nevertheless, by 1849 there were a hundred or so combinations of workers in Australia ready and willing to find a way round such intimidations, and to challenge the legislation if necessary (they did, in fact, succeed in getting the enacted penalty halved). These included the Society of Compositors, whose members had gone on strike in Sydney twenty years earlier, thereby holding up several editions of the country's first independent newspaper, the *Australian.* The gold rushes, bringing in men who could tell of increasingly organised labour in both Europe and America, and who would have encouraged imitation, may very well have played their part in the rapid growth of unions between 1850 and 1869, when another four hundred were formed. Between those two dates, building labourers in Sydney had secured the first eight-hour working day in the world, and their mates across the entire continent very quickly obtained the same benefit. Long before the nineteenth century was done and before the ALP was a going concern, an all-Australian congress of trade unions had taken place in this city, and virtually every workman in the country was represented there. Among others, seventy thousand sheep shearers had sent their spokesmen to town.

If we want a paradigm of Australian trade union history, trade union outlook and trade union power, from the beginnings of working-class solidarity up to the present day, the Waterside Workers' Federation will serve as well as any other, especially as it is probably the union above all others that has been closest to Sydney's heart. As early as 1837, wharf labourers and seamen who were outfitting whaling vessels in the port combined to stop work for another shilling a day and, although they didn't get it, this was a first stirring of the militancy to come. The wharfies didn't organise themselves properly for another thirty-five years: they didn't really need to during the gold rushes, when the Australian ports were crammed with shipping and labour was almost able to name its own price. But in 1872 the Sydney Wharf Labourers' Union was launched 'in the Oriental Hotel last Tuesday night. There were between 4 and 5 hundred present. The object of the society is to benefit the conditions of the labourer socially, morally and politically. A committee was elected. The meeting adjourned to enable the committee to frame the rules.... The utmost order and decorum prevailed and from the enthusiasm manifested there is no doubt that the society will become successful.'9 By the mid-1880s, this was the biggest union in Australia catering for men who did not (like the shearers) earn their living in the countryside.

In 1890 a federation of wharfies was formed by delegates from eight Australian ports (and one from New Zealand) meeting in Sydney, but it was virtually stillborn because that same year brought the first in a long sequence of industrial battles that have been lumped together as the Maritime Strike, though it involved shearers, miners, carters and other tradesmen as well as seamen and wharfies. At bottom, this was an attempt by employers to crush all the trade unions, whose gains over the previous two or three decades had become a serious threat to profit margins, especially as the boom time of the gold rushes was long since past. The strike was, in fact, started by the belligerent Shearers' Union, which was determined that all agreements between its members and graziers should be nationwide and not be made individually. The wharfies, refusing to handle blacked wool, were quickly involved: violently in Melbourne and in Sydney, where four thousand men confronted police trying to get wool to ships waiting at Circular Quay, and several people were injured when mounted constables charged the mob after the Riot Act had been read. After just three months of conflict, the dispute came to an end, and so very nearly did all the unions. Both sides had been well prepared as they fought each other (sometimes literally), but the shipowners, the coalowners and the graziers gained the upper hand because there was a large reservoir of unemployed labour to be tapped in Australia, and police forces which would protect such men from union intimidation when they were recruited to break the strikes: the Government of New South Wales alone enrolled hundreds of special constables to defend them, and from that moment the employers controlled the Sydney waterfront. For the wharfies, the dispute had been a disaster. 'A week after the strike's end a meeting of the SWLU was a stark contrast to the union's pre-strike circumstances. Where formerly it had nearly 2,000 financial members anticipating full employment at increased rates for reduced hours, its membership was now splintered with at least 800 former members debarred from the union because they had worked with non-union labour.... The union's five guinea membership fee quickly slipped to a paltry one shilling.'[10] Before olive branches were waved, and outcasts were readmitted in 1896, the SWLU membership was down to a hundred men.

Billy Hughes helped to put it on its feet again. The constituency of Lang, which he represented in the Legislative Assembly, incorporated many of the families whose breadwinners worked on the Sydney waterfront, and in 1899 he became the Secretary of the SWLU, five years after he had been elected to Parliament. His value was immediately obvious when, at his inaugural meeting, he was accompanied on the platform by the Premier, the Minister for Works, several other parliamentary colleagues and a couple of clergymen. At a stroke, the wharfies' union had become respectable, and an improvement in the economy meant that its members were in some demand again. But the Australian Steamship Owners Federation was newly formed and it had the ear of many people in both the state and federal parliaments.

So there were still things to be fought over, quite apart from the matter of pay and the number of hours a man worked in the course of a day or a week. There was the sheer irregularity of employment on the wharves, for one thing, of not knowing when your wage packet would be in your hand, and how many more there would be before you had to manage again on whatever you had saved. A man might be labouring for thirty hours or even more in one shift at the height of the wool season, clocking on and being discharged at any time in twenty-four hours, depending upon several factors which included the state of the tides: but in winter he could be without work for weeks on end. He could await work for hours at a time, even when he had been mustered because it was imminent, and his waiting in a Sydney monsoon might be without the benefit of any shelter. It would, moreover, be waiting for work according to the 'bull' system, by which a foreman would choose his team according to personal preferences that too often left the less muscular, the troublesome or the ones who didn't stand him a drink often enough waiting indefinitely.* Convict overseers, who had been transported too, used to operate according to similar principles, except that in their case the penalty was some other

---

*The 'bulls', of course, being physically stronger than their mates and competitors, could work longer and harder than the others. This same system of casual labour on the docks was also the rule in the English ports of London and Rochester—where it was known as the 'free call'— until the late 1960s.

form of punishment. From this time on, the wharfies knew the length of the Sydney waterfront, from Circular Quay round to Darling Harbour, as the Hungry Mile. The bitterness with which they ever after remembered it was perpetuated in some verses that one of them composed during the Great Depression:

And blood shall blot the memory out—of Sydney's hungry mile.
The day will come, aye, come it must, when these same slaves shall rise,
And through the revolution's smoke, ascending to the skies,
The master's face shall show the fear he hides behind his smile
Of these his slaves, who on that day shall storm the hungry mile.[11]

It was Billy Hughes, by this time in the new Federal Parliament but still union Secretary, who persuaded all the dock workers in the country to amalgamate into the Waterside Workers' Federation of Australia in 1902. More than that, he persuaded some of his ALP colleagues in Melbourne (the temporary capital, where the Federal Parliament met until 1927) to sit on the union's governing body, which sealed for ever an already developing relationship between the wharfies and Labor politicians. There was a period of strain after Hughes became Prime Minister and tried to bring in conscription, which was seen by the wharfies (and other unions) as non-negotiable on two counts. Not only did many of them not want to fight what they saw as an Englishman's war: they also reasoned that, if men were turned into soldiers and sent overseas, the way would be open for immigrant labour to take their place at home—and immigrant in this context meant 'coolies' and 'niggers', words which were freely used at meetings of the WWF. The upshot was that, on a motion from the Sydney branch, Billy Hughes was stripped of his position in the union, which thereby became the first (and is perhaps even now the only one) in the world to throw a Prime Minister out of its company.

No sooner had he gone than a General Strike brought more upheaval in 1917, after rail and tramways employees in Sydney downed tools in protest against a new regime on the production lines, which had been imported from America. As more and more workers, including wharfies, were pulled out in sympathy, there were protests the like of which not even this city had seen before: forty thousand men marched on one occasion and, on another, one hundred thousand people assembled in the Domain to hear a number of rousing speeches, including one from the local wharfies leader which denounced 'All kings, governors, bosses and parliamentarians' as 'parasites fattening off the backs of the workers'.[12]

There was to be at least one other gathering of that size in the Domain, when Jack Lang addressed his people on the topics that would, twelve months later, result in his removal from office by the state Governor. By then, Sydney was in the depths of the Depression, and many citizens were dependent upon cash handouts, food vouchers or free issues of shoes and clothing from Lang's Government. Soup kitchens were set up in Martin Place and elsewhere, and the Domain was one of the places where homeless men and women camped out for the night, with their billies for at least a brew-up of tea, newspapers that served as blankets, and humpies improvised from bags to give some sort of shelter when it rained. An Unemployed Workers' Movement was formed by the communists and, for the second time in its history, Railway Square outside Central Station became the scene of a pitched battle when the police and UWM demonstrators clashed. The misery of those years was graphically captured in a *Sydney Morning Herald* article:

> During recent months the growth of begging in Sydney's streets has been a feature of the city's life. Many of those who have swelled the ranks are obviously victims of the financial crisis, honest unfortunate beings reluctantly driven to the quick charity of the passer-by as a last resource.... Most of the tales are as old as begging—tram fare to a job, sick wife, last square meal a week ago, war injury. Some are true, many false. Lurking in an alleyway, a man pushes his stunted child forward to offer onion pickles, home-made toffee.... Thin faces dart from doorways—ties, handkerchiefs, face cream, shoe laces, posies, fish that waggle fins; unshaven chins, unwashed necks, collarless, shirtless, sockless, tense faces ... some offer nothing, some

sing, make pretence at playing violins, clarinets, anything. Some just stand and look with hunger in their eyes. When the sun dips, the still lower orders rake the garbage bins—hooking, stirring; 'nothin' 'ere, Jack'; banging of lids, the prowl beyond the lights. By the time the theatre crowds are home, they have all gone—somewhere. [13]

The Second World War rescued Sydney from all that, as it rescued working people in Europe and North America. The wharfies, who had suffered as much as anyone in the 1930s, got to their feet again and, even before general hostilities had begun, went on strike to make a political point, by blacking cargoes of pig iron that were destined for Japan, which was then warming up for the big one in its preliminary war with China.* Like other unions, the WWF was never reluctant to involve itself in the plight of others even if those it helped were people who, in other circumstances, were dismissed and patronised with expressions of racial contempt: Australia is full of paradoxes like that. Although the Canberra Government supported the American war in Vietnam, to the extent that it sent Australian troops to fight there, the wharfies decided that their own act of solidarity would be with the North Vietnamese. In Melbourne they refused to load a cargo of barbed wire destined for Saigon, and received a message of thanks from the transport workers' union in Hanoi: in Sydney they twice blacked a vessel bound for Vietnam, and brought the port to a standstill for twenty-four hours when one of their representatives was suspended by the port authority. So obdurate were they in this matter that the vessel, which was owned by the Australian National Line, was recommissioned as a naval auxiliary, so that Her Majesty's sailors could be pressed into service as stevedores.

Jim Healy didn't quite live to see that happen, though it was

---

*The union was threatened with sanctions by the Attorney-General, R. G. Menzies, who thereby earned himself the imperishable nickname Pig Iron Bob. By one of Australia's great political ironies, Billy Hughes became Attorney-General when Menzies formed his own first government in 1939.

perfectly in line with his philosophy. He was a Manchester man who had emigrated with his wife and children after being wounded in the First World War, and he joined the Communist Party at the same time as putting himself up for Billy Hughes's old union job in 1934. He succeeded and, from the national headquarters on Phillip Street, he set the wharfies on the course they have pursued ever since—pragmatic but inflexible, often reasonable but always militant. When Healy died in 1961, more than three thousand people on foot, together with a hundred cars and five trucks full of flowers, followed his hearse slowly through the city's main streets, which were lined with spectators four and five deep, and policemen who saluted as the cortège rolled by; and two thousand of those mourners made their way to Rookwood, Sydney's sprawling municipal cemetery, ten miles out into the western suburbs. Right across Australia, the day's work came to a halt in fifty-eight ports. All this for a Pom, who had become one of their own.

Some things have changed on the Sydney waterfront since Jim Healy arrived from Lancashire. No longer are the union bosses corpulent fellows who wear braces to camouflage the size of their girths, and trilbies tilted flataback so as to look easygoing and affable, the very image of the middle-aged Aussie who is seriously out of shape: now they are likely to be as trim and dapper as any other executive with a mobile clipped to his belt, they doubtless pour wine from time to time as a change from the everlasting inundations of beer, and they are probably a bit younger than their predecessors were, at least when they reach high office, if not when they retire. The men they represent no longer have to carry heavy sacks of grain or flour or cement on their shoulders, which could produce deformities over a number of years, they do not risk being brained because a sling has broken and dropped its load, nor do they finish a shift badly stained with lampblack or some other noxious substance that penetrates the pores, sometimes permanently: machinery does most of the donkey work nowadays, while hard hats and other forms of protective clothing have become obligatory by law; and these are advances the union gained bit by bit, from the time of Billy Hughes.

But in some ways nothing at all has changed, and the Maritime Union of Australia—as the WWF became when it amalgamated with the Seamen's Union a few years ago—continues to fight its corner as it always did and still needs to, periodically. Sydney was reminded of this in 1998, when the company manning the city's waterfront and the port at Botany Bay sacked fourteen hundred wharfies and found itself with mayhem on its hands for weeks; and this was what most onlookers would never afterwards forget, especially as the rights and wrongs of the dispute were not cut and dried, involving as they did cold calculation by the employers and restrictive practices by the men. Day after day the news bulletins showed hundreds of wharfies bellowing abuse at scab labour across the picket lines, and (a tactical blunder as it turned out, which seriously backfired) some of them took their children close to the action, in order to curry sympathy with the television audiences. But, frightening as these confrontations were in their obduracy, their anger, their hatred, their incipient violence, their ruthlessness, they told a great truth which has been unchallengeable for a hundred years or more, and was demonstrated in a kinder way at Jim Healy's funeral. It is that when push comes to shove, and in spite of the numerous silvertails who come somewhat higher up the social scale, this is above all a working man's town, as London and New York—which do not have waterfront strikes because they no longer have waterfronts to speak of—are not any more. This truth includes all the bloody-minded camaraderie, all the bitterly unforgiven memories, all the crude defensiveness, all the fundamental decency and all the occasional cruelty that goes with the working man's territory. Here is a place where such people fight for what they've got and never, never back down, even though they risk being broken and cast aside. No one can really understand Sydney unless he grasps this fact.

CHAPTER TEN

The One Day

Anzac Day was announced in the middle of the night by the sound of alarm clocks going off all over the place. Some people may not have gone to bed at all if they lived in the outer suburbs, where public transport was moving before three o'clock so as to get everyone to Martin Place on time. The Dawn Service was not due to begin there until 4.30 a.m. but, an hour before that, men, women and even some children were taking their places behind barriers in front of the old GPO, so as to get a good view of the wreath-laying and the dignitaries in their special enclosure opposite the Cenotaph. And 4.30 a.m. it had to be, for that was the very moment when the 3rd Brigade of infantry stumbled ashore to their beachhead at Ari Burnu all those years ago, and began to create the great legend of Australian valour on Gallipoli.* In a sense, the entire twelve months since the last 25 April had been a waiting for the small hours of this day, and certainly no one in Sydney for

---

*In the confusion of that dawn, the Australians landed on either side of Ari Burnu instead of, as intended, on two beaches to the south of the headland. Some of the tows put their troops ashore on the northernmost of these bays, which consequently became known as Anzac Cove.

some time beforehand could have been unaware that the memory of the Australian and New Zealand Army Corps in 1915 was about to be reconsecrated yet again. At the top of George Street, outside the Anglican cathedral, small wooden crosses had been sold every day for a couple of weeks and then stuck into a plot of grass, each with a sprig of rosemary bound to it with an elastic band ('There's rosemary,' said Ophelia, 'that's for remembrance'). Across the street, a corner shop had hung its own talisman, a banner, conspicuously above its front door: 'Woolworth's Salute ANZAC,' it said. 'Lest We Forget.'

By four o'clock there would have been several hundred people in Martin Place, and grandparents with small girls and boys were being helped to the front of the barriers by everyone else so that the children could have an unobstructed view of this great testimony to their nationhood. Old chaps in their best suits, with medals on their chests, were marched up in small platoons and took their positions close to the Cenotaph, whose bronze guardians—a soldier and a sailor standing at ease and back to back at either end of the low granite block—gleamed dully when the television arc lights were switched on. A younger man strolled up, wearing the uniform of the Light Horse, with its hackle of emu feathers fastened into the famous old Digger's hat, and a row of medals pinned over his right breast. 'They must've belonged to his dad,' an old lady explained to the boy at her side. 'You're only allowed to wear them on the left if you've won them yourself.' As the Premier of New South Wales and the other notables arrived and sat down in front of the Post Office, Scouts and Guides were working their way through the crowd, with baskets full of rosemary cuttings, which they distributed methodically to everyone there. A couple of sailors appeared and bent Australian flags to the two tall poles rising above the Cenotaph. Autumn leaves drifted down from the trees now and then. By this time, the lower end of Martin Place was packed, and hundreds more spectators had arranged themselves on the other side of Pitt Street, where the precinct sloped up towards the Sydney Hospital. There may have been more than a thousand people between George and Castlereagh when the Dawn Service began.

It began precisely on time but an hour or so before dawn actually broke upon a warm and pitch-black night, which is exactly the way things were when the Anzacs landed on the peninsula. It began with everyone singing 'Abide with Me' and, apart from the culminating national anthem, it ended with Rudyard Kipling's recessional hymn; and these two solemnities encompassed a ceremony that was never for one moment diverted into a triumphant nationalism. It was a lamentation, just that, such as only New Zealanders could also comprehend.* A naval chaplain read prayers, an admiral gave a brief address, the state Governor recited the Dedication to 'the comrades who went out to the battlefields of All Wars, but did not return'; and that great concourse of people stood with their heads bowed as the words were spoken for them, and sometimes took a deep breath, and occasionally dabbed their eyes with a handkerchief. But they stood upright again when the Last Post was sounded by a naval bugler, when Laurence Binyon's melancholy lines were proclaimed, and when Reveille rang and rang and rang again along the mourning thoroughfare. Small parties came out of the gloom and laid wreaths along the Cenotaph's plinth, and the children watched as motionless and as silently as everybody else; and in this way a torch was handed on to another generation of Australians. And then good nature, warmth, humour even, took over again, and sadness was dissipated in the dawn. A loudspeaker informed us that the Hyde Park Barracks canteen would be open for breakfast forthwith, and that anyone who wanted to inspect the museum there could do so free of

---

*This is not quite literally true, in fact. The small English town of Bury turns out for its own version of Anzac Day on the nearest Sunday ('Gallipoli Sunday') to 25 April each year. Bury was the home of the Lancashire Fusiliers, which landed at Cape Helles at the same time as the Anzacs were going ashore further up the peninsula: the regiment left nearly two thousand dead there before 1915 was over.

charge until 8 A.M. Another announcement advised drivers to shift their cars out of Pitt Street before six o'clock, 'otherwise they will be towed away in the nicest possible manner'.

There was then a hiatus in Anzac Day, and people filled it by wandering up to the barracks or to some of the near-by cafés that were laying on bacon and eggs earlier than usual. But soon the pavements along George Street started to attract newcomers who had given the Dawn Service a miss, but who certainly intended to be there when the big parade began. Which it did at nine o'clock when the sun, rising across a cloudless sky, promised Sydney another unseasonable scorcher in the autumn of its year. As unbroken lines of watchers formed along both sides of the street, the Scouts and Guides returned and handed out more rosemary to anybody who reached for it, which presently appeared to be everyone along a good half a mile of George. Many of them also had Australian flags, and these were waved in a rippling salute as a huge fleet of taxis rolled up the road, each carrying disabled ex-servicemen on a free ride to Hyde Park, where the parade would eventually end; but not for a while.

The marchers and their musicians had been mustered in Martin Place after breakfast was done, and the first contingent now leftwheeled into George behind a pipe band playing 'Waltzing Matilda' with a confident skirl and a bonny swing of the kilt. First up were a mass of cadets, each with a flag, and these were brandished enthusiastically at the growing crowds waving back on either flank. Then the old sweats came into view, men who had been at Tobruk and on Crete, in Singapore and along the Owen Stanley Range, though no one any more who had been at Gallipoli: the last of the original Anzacs who made that first landing on 25 April, Ted Matthews of Leichhardt, had died only five months earlier at the age of 101, and they had given him a state funeral with full military honours on Macquarie Street.

Old soldiers from the Second World War, some of them great-grandads by now, were not by any means the only men marching between the thickening crowds. Old matelots came along behind placards identifying the ships in which they had served—HMAS *Australia, Perth, Canberra, Yarra, Ballarat, Bundaberg* and many more. There were old airmen, including a group who called themselves the Odd Bods, because they had enlisted in the RAAF but had fought most of their war with the RAF. There were men in white berets who styled themselves the Polar Bears, Australian ratings who somehow or other had found themselves at the wrong end of the world, sailing with the Royal Navy in the terrible Arctic convoys to Murmansk. Nobody, it seemed, had been forgotten. Not the Poms, who had Dunkirk veterans on parade and even (you wouldn't want to read about this!) some expatriates who had fallen in behind a banner declaring their affiliation to the Brigade of Guards. Not the Salvation Army (the 'Salvoes'), not the war correspondents, a small posse of men marching behind a green banner, not the immigrant communities: Estonians, Czechs, Greeks, French, Italian Combat Partisans, Serbs (but no Croats that were obvious), Vietnamese and even former members of the Soviet Army, who jangled with many more medals than anyone else in sight. Three men from New Guinea were there, wearing head-dresses above collars and ties that made them look like visiting Sioux businessmen, who were referred to more than once by Australians who owed their lives to them, as Fuzzy-wuzzies; but this was said in such an affectionate and obviously grateful way that it was stripped of all offensiveness.

It was a very Australian quasi-military parade, quite apart from its wonderful inclusiveness: smartly turned out but very relaxed, the marchers waving, grinning and chatting among themselves as they strode and limped along, endlessly, doggedly, laboriously, breathlessly, in the mounting heat of the day, no longer always in step and sometimes in wheelchairs. They sang 'Kiss Me Good-night, Sergeant-major' when one of the bands struck up the tune, and they looked as pleased as Punch when friends and relatives rushed impulsively out of the crowd to shake their hands, pat their backs, hug them and kiss them from time to time. One old codger (and he was not the only one) had his grandson walking alongside him, just in case, and the lad couldn't have glowed more if he'd been at Kohima himself. There he was, enfolded in that astonishing display of affection from the biggest gathering of people he could have seen in his life. The television commentators kept track of the numbers, though goodness knows how: by ten o'clock there were an estimated fifty thousand along George Street and Bathurst, as the long column made its way to Hyde Park. By eleven the figure had grown to eighty thousand, and three-quarters of an hour later the nation was told that a hundred thousand citizens had turned out in Sydney this Anzac Day. Certainly, wherever the cameras panned, people were standing four and five deep on both pavements, without interruption, all the way from Martin Place.

It took three hours for that parade to pass a given point, and when the last squad of marchers moved off from the GPO, all the people on the sidewalks fell in behind them and stepped out for Hyde Park too, until the length of George Street bobbled with the movement of surging humanity. They were glad of the trees when they reached the park, for the sun by then was at its height, and there was still a little way to go before this day was officially done. Another service was conducted from the threshold of the great Anzac monument, where a notice beside the soaring entrance to a Hall of Silence reminds everyone who comes here that 'This memorial is sacred. No smoking or noise.' It was reflected, with the building itself, the vestments and the uniforms and the density of onlookers gathered there, in the long Pool of Remembrance that lies straight down the middle of the park. And when the service was over, when Reveille had once again died away, a sense of vigilant constancy, over and done with for another year, was almost palpable. People were gossiping as they drifted off and, until then, they hadn't done that since the parade began. They reached for their fags and lit up as they put some distance between them and the sacred place, and often made a beeline for the nearest pubs. The old sweats headed for their regimental or squadron or mess-deck reunions, which had all been carefully listed in the newspapers; or they fell back on their local outpost of the Returned and Services League, as they did week in and week out in the course of a year. Some of them would be playing two-up within the hour; most of them would probably have thick heads before the next dawn. But Anzac Day would have been honoured yet again in the only way possible.

It is impossible to exaggerate the importance of this unique mixture of pageantry and sorrow. There are several clichés attached to the events of 1915 on Gallipoli and all are perfectly valid. It *was* the time when Australia and New Zealand came of age, the moment of acknowledged nationhood, the heroically dreadful epic that set them apart from the British at last, the passage of arms which told the rest of the world that these were extraordinary warriors. The price of this maturity was far too high, and anyone who goes to Gallipoli without shedding tears is a very cold customer indeed. Nearly nine thousand Australians lie there still, and you can count a lot of them (though not all, for some vanished without trace) in the row after row of neat headstones beside Anzac Cove, in Shrapnel Valley, on Plugge's Plateau, at Johnston's Jolly and Lone Pine and Hill 60 and many more places on the peninsula. 'My Jim Gave His Life For Freedom. Loved & Remembered By His Dad', says the inscription on one; and there are many other such messages, composed by broken-hearted people reaching out from ten thousand miles away. Young Australians, boisterously rowdy by nature, become very quiet when they arrive in their battered old transit vans and begin to wander through the graveyards of Gallipoli. The one at Lone Pine shelters 2nd Lieut. Digges La Touche, whose life and death typified the unswerving imperial patriotism that sent many to the killing grounds of the peninsula. He was an Anglican priest and theologian in Sydney, an Irish Protestant by origin, who believed that this was a holy war against sheer evil and went off to it 'with one proclaimed purpose in mind: to die for the Empire'.[1] Shortly after landing, leading his men into an attack with cane and revolver in hand, he was very badly wounded and died after bleeding continuously for twenty-four hours.

The young have not always wanted to know about that year in the Dardanelles, and what it signified for their country. Their impatience with Anzac Day, and especially their revulsion at some of the attendant goings-on, were perfectly captured in *The One Day of the Year*, the play Alan Seymour composed between the French and the American wars in Vietnam, when a batch of Australian Army 'advisers' had just left for Saigon, with students at Sydney and other universities starting to take a dim view of it all.* Young Hughie dismisses Anzac Day contemptuously: 'Because we're sick of all the muck that's talked about this day...the great national day of honour, day of memory, day of salute to the fallen, day of grief.... It's just one long grog-up.' And Alf, the old Digger, after a deal of angry sparring with his son, finally blurts out why this day above all others is special to him: 'All them blokes like Wack 'n' me and the lot of 'em get out there for somethin' there's not too many men in not too many countries in this world'd want to do. That's not a victory we're celebratin', son. It's a defeat.... They lost. But they tried. They tried, and they was beaten. A man's not too bad who'll stand up in the street and remember when 'e was licked.' Then, at the very heart of it: 'Boys I've known all me life. Went through the Depression with me, then the War. They're nothin' much, either. Nothin' much.... But for one day they're somethin'. They make a fuss of y' for once. The speeches and the march...and y're all mates. Y're mates an' everythin' seems all right. The whole year round I look forward to it. Me mates, some grog and—and the feelin' y're not just...not just...'[2] Some

---

*The play was thought to be so contentious that the Adelaide Festival Board banned it for fear of offending the RSL, which has always been one of Australia's most powerful pressure groups.

people will dismiss that as an embarrassing sentimentality, but it is a great deal more besides; it is another way of putting the Australian working man's most guarded and most precious truth.

Hughie Cook was right about one thing, though, and the republicans nowadays go to some lengths to emphasise it. Australians are not a warlike people: they are less warlike than almost anyone else in the world, and Donald Horne may have put his finger on one of the reasons why when he wrote, 'Several generations of Australians were taught to venerate not lions or eagles or other aggressive symbols of nationalism; they were taught to venerate sheep.'[3] Yet no nation on earth has ever produced better or braver warriors, much admired even by their enemies. The peculiar thing about this is that their reputation has usually been earned fighting other people's wars and not their own, the one exception being their engagement against the Japanese in the Second World War, which was certainly in their own best interests. Otherwise, they have responded to the bugle's call out of a strangely steadfast loyalty to some far distant government, or in a misplaced spirit of adventure, or a mixture of both.

They first got into this habit in 1885, when news of General Gordon's death in Khartoum reached Sydney and, within days, a contingent of volunteers, vivid in red tunics and white pith helmets, embarked at Circular Quay for the Sudan, whence they returned three months later, after but one skirmish, which produced three slightly wounded soldiers and seven deaths from fever or dysentery. Much more seriously, 1899 saw over sixteen thousand Australians off to the Boer War, a high proportion of them mounted troops, for whom the British had particularly asked. Banjo Paterson covered their doings for the *Sydney Morning Herald*, and was able to report the first half-dozen of many Victoria Crosses Australians were to win in the next fifty years; also the fact that six hundred of them wouldn't be coming home this time. Imperial Bushmen were still leaving Australia for the high veldt when a naval contingent sailed from Sydney to help a medley of Europeans and Americans put down the Boxer Rebellion in China. And then there were the two World Wars, about which nothing more need be said here, apart from the fact that, between them, they cost 93,168 Australian lives: this from a country whose population was less than five million on the brink of the Great War, and only just over seven and a half million by 1947. And even this carnage did not stifle the Australian reflex to stand up and be counted when someone else's battle lines were formed. The Diggers were fighting in Korea and in Malaysia before ever they buckled to again on behalf of the Americans in Vietnam: fifty thousand of them had been there by the time Saigon fell, with another three thousand men dead or hurt.

But, then, although these young men and their forefathers had been brought up to regard the sheep and not some nobler (and predatory) creature as a symbol of their country's ambitions and true nature, they were also reared upon a tradition of martial imperatives; and anyone who inspects this metropolis carefully can see how deep-seated that was. No other Australian city contains such a wealth of fortifications dating back to the first days of settlement, and two military survivals from the nineteenth century are still going concerns: one is the handsome Victoria Barracks in Paddington, which has been occupied by the Army ever since its completion in 1848; the other is a sail loft and other buildings inside HMAS *Kuttabul* at Garden Island, where horticulture was relinquished for naval purposes in 1856. Both of these are obviously out of bounds to civilians, but anyone can have a field day of military archaeology at a number of other sites around the Harbour.

One of the first men ashore as soon as Governor Phillip's fleet had dropped anchor off Sydney Cove was a young lieutenant of Marines aboard HMS *Sirius*, William Dawes, who had been appointed official astronomer in the First Fleet, particularly charged with observing the transit of Maskelyne's Comet when it passed over New South Wales some months later. On rising ground at the western end of the cove he pitched his tent, and subsequently built a hut, to house his telescope and other instruments; and this was the predecessor of the Observatory which still stands there today. Seven months later, having discharged his primary function, he supervised the building of earthworks near by, in which he positioned eight guns taken from *Sirius.* In time, after the young Lieutenant had returned to England (eventually becoming Governor of Sierra Leone and then of Antigua), the Dawes Battery had its firepower increased to thirteen 42-pounders and five mortars, with a magazine, a barracks for the gunners, and quarters for their commanding officer. This little military complex was, unfortunately but inevitably, demolished to make way for the southern pylon of the Harbour Bridge in 1923, but five pieces of its artillery stand *in situ* to this day, in a small park which is massively dominated by the tremendous shape curving overhead. The cannon on their cumbersome carriages point straight down the Harbour, ready to loose off a salvo at anything sailing within reach. One of them is trained to put a shot across the bows of the Opera House, while another could almost certainly wreck several rows of its orchestra stalls.

They also have the range of Pinchgut, which was Rock Island when Thomas Hill was consigned to it for a week on bread and water, because he had stolen biscuits from another convict less than a month after the First Fleet arrived. Its penal purposes were underlined some years later when Francis Morgan was hanged there for murder; and, brutal as the crime was, Morgan deserved to be immortalised if it is true, as folklore insists, that when he was asked for his last words before the sentence was carried out, he breezily surveyed what there was of the young colony and said, 'Well, it certainly is a fine harbour you have here!' Penal Pinchgut remained until Governor Gipps ordered a fort to be built on the rock in 1839, though that took some years to accomplish, which is why the tiny island was translated into Fort Denison, rather than Fort Gipps, to commemorate the Governor who supervised the construction in 1855. The idea for the fort took shape after a couple of American warships arrived without warning to pay a courtesy call on the British authorities. Captain Wilkes, commanding the *Vincennes*, logged their landfall like this: 'At half past ten pm we quickly dropped anchor off the Cove in the midst of the shipping without anyone having the least idea of our arrival.... Had war existed, we might, after firing the shipping and reducing a great part of the town to ashes, have effected a retreat before daybreak in perfect safety.'[4] No wonder the British decided they ought to put some 8-inch muzzle-loaders on the rock, to augment the guns mounted on the Dawes Battery and on Bennelong Point: and one of these still fires a blank cartridge every afternoon, so that anybody within earshot can synchronise watches with Pinchgut's timing of one o'clock.

Most of the old fortifications are much further downstream. There are old gun emplacements just behind North Head, but as these were subsumed into the Army's School of Artillery they, too, are off limits to the rest of us. There's better luck inside the opposite entrance to the Harbour at Laings Point, better still a few feet above the adjacent Camp Cove. That is where Europeans first set foot in this Harbour, when Arthur Phillip sent a boat ashore to see what the landing there was like; but, deciding that it wasn't much of an improvement on Botany Bay, he sailed on a few more miles until he found what he was looking for at Sydney Cove. At Laings Point, some of the old nineteenth-century emplacements are still detectable in the vegetation, but at Camp Cove there is a hefty artillery piece as well, which left the Armstrong ordnance factory at faraway Newcastle-on-Tyne in 1872, and which ever since has been poised to put ball into the stern of any craft proceeding on its unlawful occasions towards an unsuspecting city centre.

And then there are the two fortifications on the north side of the Harbour right opposite the Heads, which are the most determinedly belligerent in the entire defensive strategy of Sydney. It's not just that their guns commanded the entrance to the Harbour, and could in theory have blown out of the water anything that sailed in from the world beyond, long before it even sighted Circular Quay. It is that the gun emplacements and the subterranean passages, the magazines and the other chambers servicing them were constructed on such a scale, and to such a thickness of masonry, that they could have withstood aerial bombardment in the Second World War, let alone nineteenth-century cannonfire. Until these two vast stone and concrete strongholds were tunnelled out of the cliffs at Middle Head and Georges Head in the early 1850s, Sydney's defences were limited to the Dawes Battery, to Bradleys Head and to a handful of other small emplacements at the top of the Harbour. But then a couple of generals, newly arrived from England, decided that this wasn't good enough, especially in view of the deteriorating international situation. They were worried that the Russians might be about to invade Australia.

There had always been a certain amount of British paranoia about foreigners attached to the foundation of the penal colony, but for many years this was caused only by their long-standing nervousness about the intentions of the French; understandable enough, as there was nothing to choose between these next-door neighbours when it came to territorial aggression. So when two vessels commanded by Jean François de La Pérouse sailed into Botany Bay after Arthur Phillip had only just arrived himself, the British assumed that hostilities had broken out yet again between the two old enemies. La Pérouse immediately disarmed all suspicion by explaining that Louis XVI had merely despatched him to the South Seas on a voyage of curiosity, much the same sort of thing that Captain Cook had embarked upon. The two commanders, indeed, were extremely cordial to each other, before one of them made off to take possession of the finest harbour imaginable, and the other sailed out into the Pacific, never to be seen again: not for another thirty years did the French discover that, shortly after this encounter, both *La Boussole* and *L'Astrolabe* were lost with all hands in the New Hebrides.

The British, however, were now alerted to a potential threat that had always plagued them wherever they colonised; and they occupied Van Diemen's Land in 1803 specifically to forestall the French, who had sent two further expeditions on 'voyages of curiosity' in these waters by then, with more to come before 1826. So New South Wales continued to brace itself for trouble from the most familiar quarter, as local newspapers periodically reminded their readers. 'Lest some chance French frigate or letter of marque should, in the event of war, think fit to pay us a sort of Paul Jones visit in Sydney, our active and spirited officers have already made preparations for giving them a warm reception, such as they may little expect.... Last week, we observed the Government launch actively employed in taking a number of heavy guns to the battery at Bradleys Head, sufficient to blow out of the water the largest ship of the line that may attempt to force a passage.'[5] The French were not the only potential source of danger in 1841, however. The Spanish had also been nosing around the Australian coast, and it was always conceivable that the Dutch interest might be reawakened, even though they appeared to have found what they were looking for in the spice islands of the Java Sea. There were several good reasons for building defence-works around this magnificent anchorage in New South Wales some time before the middle of the nineteenth century.

Back in the northern hemisphere, the British (and, ironically, the French) had also been viewing uneasily the growth of Russian power and the Czar's territorial gains in Central Asia, and they could see this great rival in the East profiting even more from the gradual disintegration of the Ottoman Empire, which had begun at the start of the century. The Russian Army had emerged from the Congress of Vienna in 1815 as by far the strongest in Europe, a lead it held for the next forty years, and there was no telling where that power and the Czar's ambitions might take his soldiers next; or his sailors, another force to be reckoned with ever since the time of Peter the Great. On no fewer than seventeen occasions before 1830 had Russian warships visited Australia, starting with the arrival of the *Neva* at Port Jackson in 1807. It may, even so, at this distance seem strange that Australia should have worried overmuch, given its remoteness from the most likely area of conflict. But this is to ignore the fact that the colonists still saw the rest of the world through British eyes. The newspapers in Sydney and elsewhere followed daily events in the Westminster Parliament as closely and in as much detail as the London *Times:* when they reported that 'the news from abroad announces that on the 28th March Hersova was taken by the Russians' they meant news from anywhere that wasn't part of the British Empire. They really did think of themselves as an offshore island, much larger than any of the others maybe, but still within hailing distance of the Home Counties. If London felt threatened, Sydney must look to its defences too.

'If indeed the course of hostilities', declared the city's principal journal,

> should unhappily involve these colonies in a share of the actualities of war, we entertain not the slightest doubt that the people of Australia... would rise as one man to repel invasion and to sustain and perpetuate in this fifth quarter of the world the glory of the British name. It is not in the hour of need that we shall desert the standards of our country, and exchange for an unglorious and utterly unsafe neutrality the possible dangers but the strong security arising from our connection with the Crown of England. When the day of separation comes, as come it must in the course of time, we trust that great act will be achieved without involving a single sacrifice of honour, or a single feeling of shame.[6]

In the antipodean autumn of 1854, the American warship *Golden Age* (Capt. D. D. Porter) sailed into Port Jackson with tidings that were conveyed to the city by the *Sydney Morning Herald*'s shipping correspondent, who had been granted an interview as soon as the vessel dropped anchor. The news was that the British and French navies, sailing together from Constantinople, had captured the entire Russian fleet off Sebastopol, that the Allies had declared war on Russia, that the Hungarian patriot Louis Kossuth had landed in his homeland with thirteen hundred men to assist the Turks, that the British Mediterranean squadron had been recalled, that ten ships of the line and fourteen steam frigates were being fitted out to blockade the Baltic. In an editorial supplementing this news, the paper declared, 'We will admit that a Russian squadron of considerable force is collected in the China seas, and that it has been collected there with some definite purpose of making it available in case of war...'; and it went on to estimate how long it might be before such a squadron was liable to sail in through the Heads ('several months').[7] Only after the paper hit the streets did it dawn on the editor that he was the victim of an American hoax, and great was his irritation when he found out. 'The attempt to excuse and palliate the transaction under the cover of Saturday being the 1st of April is far from dignified and respectable in a commander belonging to the United States Navy.'[8]

Hostilities had, in fact, broken out on 27 March, though Australia wasn't to know about the Crimean War until several weeks later. But the temper of the times was such that from early April onwards there was very serious discussion in the *Sydney Morning Herald* about how the city should be defended from a Russian enemy. Perhaps because he was still smarting from the April Fool's jape, the editor kept his own views very much to himself, but he opened his correspondence columns to anyone else who had an opinion; and these were numerous, and generally long-winded. The construction of the fortifications at Middle Head was well under way by then, but this would be inadequate in most people's view. One man, who obviously had some rudimentary knowledge of ballistics, pointed out that 'guns of iron are not essentially necessary to the formation of heavy batteries. Any substance sufficiently firm to resist the explosive force of gunpowder will project a shot a distance proportioned to the length of the bore and the strength of the charge, whether the tube be of wood or iron; indeed, for many years after the invention of gunpowder, the cannon were formed of leather, or of staves of wood bound with hoops of iron.'⁹ What this clever-clogs was proposing as a local adaptation was horizontal tunnels drilled into the rocky faces of both the North and South Heads, which 'are admirably adapted for the construction of those monster petards which have proved so destructive in Indian warfare'. Charged with a ton or so of powder and a number of granite boulders as substitutes for cannon balls, they 'would effect the destruction of the leading vessel of the enemy, if discharged by means of a sausage-train or a galvanic battery, the moment she came within the line of fire'. You couldn't say our man was afflicted with tunnel vision, however, for he had thought of other necessities—the removal of the light vessel from the Sow and Pigs, and the conversion of the revolving light on South Head into a fixed or reciprocating beam 'which would be sufficient to warn strangers that something was wrong, and that it would be advisable to remain outside the Heads until daylight'.

Someone else concurred, and supplied a number of drawings that filled nearly a column of newsprint, to illustrate the practicalities of such tunnelling: best line the cavities with the funnels from scrapped steamships, he suggested, and cover the apertures with canvas painted to resemble the adjacent rock face, so that foreign mariners would not notice them and thereafter spread the word about these additions to Sydney's defences. Other correspondents rubbished the idea and put up their own fancies to stimulate the authorities. Shallow-draught vessels crammed with artillery were proposed, because these would be mobile enough to dart in and out of an enemy fleet and could put themselves out of range if necessary, by scuttling to safety up the nearest creek. Or how about filling a number of metal containers with gunpowder and submerging these mines at intervals across the Harbour, where they could be detonated one after the other, as enemy warships sailed overhead? Perhaps the best thing might be a huge chain strung at sea level between the Heads, or a boom stretching from Bradleys Head to Watsons Bay. But if we're going to rely on fire-power from fixed positions near the entrance to the Harbour, let's be sure that each gun has a little furnace close by, on which the cannon balls could be stoked until they were red hot. 'Although I doubt a vessel could escape the fire of such guns, I would mount two or three on every available point up the harbour. All should fire red hot shot and chains etc.... Should you think these few remarks worthy of occupying a space in your valuable paper, I should feel obliged by their insertion. And remain, Mr Editor, Yours, obediently WM.'[10]

The Russians never did reach Sydney, of course, though there was a scare that August when the SS *Great Britain* arrived at Port Phillip with smallpox on board and, having been discharged from quarantine, let off a quantity of fireworks, which caused a rumour to fly round Melbourne that the city's outskirts had just been invaded. The fortifications were completed at Port Jackson (minus the horizontal tunnels at the Heads) and a boom was eventually put across the Harbour in 1890, between Green Point on the southern shore and Georges Head. This had to wait over half a century before it was required for serious duty, and then it conspicuously failed to stop the enemy.

The Second World War was nearly three years old when the Japanese attacked Sydney. The city had been at battle stations from the moment Australia dutifully followed Great Britain in declaring war on Germany, which meant the gradual introduction of various emergency measures, like rationing (of both food and clothing), the building of air-raid shelters and the establishment of a Disasters Centre, whose downtown location is, even now, an official secret of the Federal Government. From the start, Sydney played an important part in naval strategies, as a refuge where damaged vessels could be repaired, and by the time the graving dock at Garden Island was completed the Harbour had become the principal base

of the British Pacific Fleet: in 1945 eight of the Royal Navy's capital ships—five aircraft carriers and three battleships—docked
here for revictualling and overhaul. The United States Navy also
regarded it as a home port after the Japanese had brought America
into the war, and eight thousand GIs who arrived in March 1942
aboard the *Queen Mary* were the first of many who trained and relaxed here before being shipped out to fight their way from one
Pacific island to another.*

The first air raids on Australia had taken place a few weeks earlier at the Top End, when Darwin, Broome and Wyndham were
bombed: Darwin would be raided more than sixty times before
the war was over, and aerial attacks were also carried out at various
times on Townsville, Port Hedland and Exmouth Gulf. Sydney's
anti-aircraft guns were fired only once, in 1943, and the plane they
were shooting at never dropped a bomb. But the gunners would
have been ready to have a go at anything that moved by then, for
the city was still getting over the shock of what had happened the
year before.

On the night of 31 May 1942, just three months after the Japanese had captured Singapore and taken fifteen thousand Australian
prisoners, an assortment of Allied warships were berthed around
the naval base at Woolloomooloo. They were well upstream of the
boom, whose gate was opened and shut at intervals by a recommissioned ferry-boat stationed there for that purpose, so that the
Manly traffic and any other authorised shipping could pass up
and down the Harbour as usual. Somewhere out in the Tasman
Sea was a large Japanese 'I'-class submarine, which was principally
there to act as mother ship to three midget vessels, each crewed by
two men and carrying torpedoes. Two of these craft got through
the boom, undoubtedly by sailing below a surface vessel that was
being admitted through the gate. Some vigilant watchkeeper a

---

*This transatlantic liner was pressed into service as a troopship early in the war, the only vessel
big enough to carry so many men and fast enough to do so safely without needing to sail in
convoy.

little later spotted one of the periscopes and raised the alarm, and a sort of disciplined chaos then ensued, with searchlights blazing, depth charges dropped and guns firing at putative targets which could have been anywhere. One of the intruders was sunk before it was able to release a torpedo, but the other surfaced and fired twice at the American cruiser *Chicago*, which was moored to a buoy. One of these torpedoes was a dud which failed to explode, but the other passed under a Dutch submarine and sank an auxiliary vessel tied up at the wall. She was the former ferry *Kuttabul*, which had been pressed into service by the Navy as floating accommodation, and nineteen ratings sleeping aboard that night were killed when the torpedo detonated.* It was never established whether the submarine responsible was sunk there or not—though she certainly didn't return to her mother ship—because only one lot of debris was ever found on that part of the Harbour floor, with more wreckage much further downstream where the third submarine had blown itself up after getting tangled in the boom. One other casualty in this engagement was Fort Denison, which was winged by a shell fired by the USS *Chicago*'s gunners. A week later, however, a large Japanese submarine (possibly the one that had launched the midgets) surfaced from the sea off Bondi and, before she was driven off by shore batteries, put seven shells into Rose Bay, where the RAAF maintained a flying-boat base. Five of the shells didn't go off, but a passer-by suffered a broken leg when one of the other two landed near by.

There was, almost inevitably, a moment of farce in the original attack on Sydney: there usually is, somewhere not far from warfare's tragedies. The Japanese mother ship belonged to an unusual class of submarine, whose vessels carried a small reconnaissance seaplane in a watertight compartment abaft the conning tower.†

---

*The Garden Island base was subsequently given the name HMAS *Kuttabul* in memory of the dead sailors.
†Unusual but not unique. The world's largest submarine at the time, the French vessel *Surcouf* (2,880 tons) also carried a spotting plane and two 8-inch guns.

Some time before the midget attack vessels were launched, this aircraft was released into the night to inspect the target area and report on the deployment of the Allied shipping. For some time the pilot flew around the Harbour and its surroundings, and the sound eventually attracted the sympathy of the air-traffic controllers down at Mascot, who assumed that this was some friendly pilot having trouble (well, it couldn't possibly be a Jap plane, could it, because everybody knew that their range limited them to attacks in the north of Australia?). They therefore obligingly switched on the landing lights along the runway so that the poor bloke could come in safely; and were understandably mystified when presently he just flew away again.

Grimmer by far is something that the National Parks guide points out to visitors who trail along after him at the Middle Head fortifications. It is a brilliant day on the Harbour, and the heat of the afternoon beats back from the heavy masonry of the gun emplacements, while frogs rasp in the undergrowth, and kookaburras and currawongs dash from tree to tree and cackle to each other when they've made it deftly to another branch. A Manly ferry steams down the channel past the headland, and the little boy in every man watching her estimates the distance between the *Collaroy* and the embrasures, visualises the ideal trajectory, and wonders if he could register a direct hit with his first salvo, were he the master gunner in charge of the batteries up here. A voice calls him down some stairs into the gloom of the magazines and the subterranean passageways, and he is told that the artillerymen wore special shoes devoid of nails or any other metal, so they wouldn't accidentally kick a disastrous spark into life off the stone that would blow them all to kingdom come. The guide pauses by the deepest chamber, which was originally a generating room, and invites everyone to peer inside: it is murky, smells awfully of grease and something rotten, and there's often three feet of water on the floor because it generally floods badly during heavy rain. This, says the guide, is where Australian SAS soldiers were brought for part of their training thirty years ago, before they were despatched to Vietnam. It was known as the Tiger Cage, and they loathed it and feared it more than anything else that they were put through before going to war. In turn, and for several days at a time, they were interrogated and tortured here, sometimes suspended upside down, half drowned, unable to stand, so that they would know what to expect, and how to survive it mentally, if they were captured by the Vietcong.

That is one of the memories that dog you long after leaving Sydney behind. So is the much more recently awful tale of the Australian submarine that was exercising in heavy seas outside the Heads, and which submerged without anyone noticing that two of the crew were still stowing tackle on deck, probably tethered to it as a safety precaution in that weather. So is the memorial service which is held each year at Garden Island as 31 May comes round again, when two wreaths are cast upon the water. One is for the Australian and British sailors who were killed when the original *Kuttabul* blew up, the other for the Japanese submariners who also perished in that attack. This country has a very large and generous heart; just occasionally, as at the time of White Australia, it has forgotten where its heart is.

But what sticks in the memory most of all, what will linger in your being to the end of your days, is the bawl of the bugle in the darkness before dawn, the autumn leaves gently twirling down from the trees in Martin Place, the wide-eyed concentration of children watching their history unfold, the sound of the pipes and 'Waltzing Matilda' along George Street, the tramp of all those dogged old feet in the heat of the day, the cheerfulness and the pride of everybody on that Anzac Day parade. And a hundred thousand sprigs of rosemary.

CHAPTER ELEVEN

❧

Uptown, Downtown . . .

Like that of most cities in the Western world outside America, Sydney's appearance has changed more in the past half-century than ever before in its history. True, the most startling transformation came between the two World Wars with the building of the Bridge, which altered the skyline dramatically. Apart from that, though, everything had gradually evolved over long periods—by Australian standards—of time, and would continue to do so for another twenty-odd years. People became accustomed to relatively small adjustments in the pattern of buildings and streets and, because these happened piecemeal and with intervals between each, many citizens were scarcely aware that they were happening at all. It was municipal development by stealth, if you like; or you could say that it was change and evolution without violence to the general aesthetic of the place.

If you study paintings and photographs from the nineteenth and early twentieth centuries, it is quite striking how often much of Sydney around the Harbour is as familiar in appearance to us now as it was to those who composed their pictures long before the great transformations took place. Just occasionally you wonder if the artist had been looking at the same scene, even allowing for the passage of time. Maria Scott in 1868 managed to make Circular Quay and the adjacent shore look like something overlooking the Ganges at Varanasi, where very large buildings rise precipitously above the ghats: and although it is true that Sydney is quite a hilly place, sometimes severely so (anyone who doubts that should try climbing from George to Cumberland along Essex Street), nowhere has its waterfront ever been as steep as that painting suggests. More typically faithful to the topography is Eugène von Guerard's view looking towards the Heads from Point Piper in 1865, when scarcely anything that far out of town had been built: yet in spite of the homes that are nowadays spread across the foreground and the far distance where Manly sprawls, enough of the natural landscape is as visible to us now as it was to von Guerard then. Other pictures of the Harbour and its surroundings from a little way below the Bridge make the same point: it is in downtown Sydney and its North Shore counterpart where the big differences have occurred.

A sepia photograph from the turn of the century shows ferries coming in and out of Circular Quay, with two much larger passenger vessels berthed alongside Bennelong Point, the earthworks of the Dawes Battery still firmly intact, and an untidiness of buildings which would be wiped out a few years later when the southern approach to the Bridge was going up. The skyline behind the Customs House is not very exciting but, like Woolloomooloo on the eve of its great battle, it fits and it looks comfortable. Which is more than you can say about it today. When that photograph was taken, the tallest buildings in sight were the GPO tower, half-way up George Street, and the Town Hall, right at the top. And, with a solitary exception, this remained so until a dozen or more years after the Second World War. Neither of those buildings is any longer visible until you get within a few yards of it, because they have become obscured by skyscrapers.* The classical form of the

---

*Much the same thing happened in New York, but a lot earlier. When the Brooklyn Bridge was completed in 1883, the tallest building in Manhattan was Trinity Church on Wall Street. Fifty years later it had disappeared from view except in close-up, browbeaten almost to death by the financial monsters surrounding it.

Customs House has also been hidden from the ferry passengers until they emerge from the wharves: the Cahill Expressway and the overhead railway saw to that.

The critical moment for Sydney's appearance came in 1957. Until then, all construction in the city had been limited by a Height of Buildings Act which was passed in 1912 after the Culwalla Chambers went up and alarmed the city fathers who, visionaries that they were in this respect, could see their city being disfigured by mere imitations of the new skyscraping craze sweeping America.* Henceforth, they declared, no building could exceed 150 feet above the pavement (which Culwalla had topped by twenty feet) but what they really meant was that no roofline could rise higher than that. Towers built simply for architectural effect were allowed to continue upwards beyond the specified limit, presumably to avoid dismantling the GPO and the Town Hall, two distinguished landmarks which already climbed to 262 feet and 187 feet respectively. This was a loophole that a cheeky newcomer would exploit in 1939, when the Amalgamated Wireless Company completed its head office, whose roofline restricted itself to a lawful 150 feet (which represented twelve floors) before being craftily extended by a latticework radio beacon, which very nearly doubled the total height and made the office extremely conspicuous.

The regulations were administered jointly by the New South Wales Government, which sanctioned plans aiming above 100 feet, and the City Council, which invigilated everything below that figure. And this demarcation line was still effectively in force when, in 1956, the powerful Australian Mutual Provident Society began to lean on the authorities to change the legislation to its advantage. Other developers were also sniffing around but it was the AMP, with its financial base well founded in insurance premiums, which

---

*The Culwalla's architects, Alfred Spain and Thomas Cosh, had toured America and introduced many devices they came across there, including fireproof construction and internal fire escapes, high-speed lifts, a postal-box system and rooftop water tanks.

had the clout to pull the thing off and establish a precedent that reshaped the heart of Sydney more drastically than anything that had happened before, even including the Harbour Bridge. The City Council's protests were ridden over roughly by the State Government (though both were controlled at the time by the Labor Party) to the extent that the council was 'learning perhaps more regarding possible legislative amendments from press reports than from the Chief Secretary's Office. Amid the shambles, an Advisory Committee was appointed by the State Government to recommend appropriate changes to the Act.'[1] These amendments became law the following year, and in 1959 the AMP building began to rise just behind Circular Quay, Sydney's first genuine skyscraper as they understand the word in North America, complete with the fashionably new curtain walls of tinted glass. It eventually topped out at 377 feet, twenty-six storeys above the pavement, but that wasn't the worst of it. The crucial matter of floor-space ratios was manipulated as well, increased so generously from the norm that Sydney's ratios ever since have been about twice what is permissible in European cities, exceeded only in the United States and Hong Kong.* To make way for the new structure, the very decent old Farmers and Graziers building, which nicely complemented the adjacent Customs House, was torn down, leaving its old neighbour in the fullness of redevelopment to be visually crushed by the loaded arriviste.

From now on, it has been acutely observed, 'City planning in Sydney was to take a back seat to the needs of capital. Playing on a political field, the rules of town planning were supremely mutable and the goalposts, often numerous, were eminently movable. Indeed, entire teams, several of which might be playing at once,

---

*The floor-space ratio is essentially the relationship between the building height and the building area: the higher you are allowed to go, the greater will be the area occupied on the ground, for the sake of stability. Various external considerations are generally taken into account when settling the ratio—traffic, width of street, exclusion of light to other buildings, the general aesthetic of the vicinity—all of which were ignored in the case of the AMP.

could be sent off without warning, and referees, also numerous, replaced.'[2] It is appropriate that caustic comments on the doings of politicians and their hidden persuaders in this place should be phrased in sporting metaphors. And certainly the surge of eager capital and political acquiescence from then on resulted in a spate of building that before long left the AMP looking, if not exactly dwarfed, perhaps a little stunted. Towering above George and Pitt and Phillip and all the other central streets, the skyscrapers steadily rose, clump after clump of them, and soon had imitators on the other side of the Bridge. There, another insurance company, Mutual Life & Citizens, in 1956 had built Australia's largest office building (which incorporated Australia's first curtain walls) before the embargo on height was lifted the following year. In 1967 the AMP's height was exceeded by that of the State Office Block on Phillip Street, thirty-five storeys of it, widely known as the Black Stump and standing on land that was part of the original Domain. Another twelve months and the cylindrical Australia Tower Building had risen to forty-six storeys, which accommodated offices, shops and a tapestry by Le Corbusier: it had a near-miss from another art form shortly after completion, when an eccentric showman announced that he was going to cover it in swaths of canvas during some well-publicised weekend but, coming to the conclusion that it was too much of a challenge even for his intrepid genius, he did his thing instead on a much smaller building in La Pérouse.

Miffed by the superior elevations of these rivals, the AMP tried again on a site just behind its first skyscraper, and succeeded in topping the Australia Tower by some sixty feet in 1975. The brash mentality that masterminded most of these developments was clearly revealed in a full-page advertisement that AMP ran the week its new possession was opened:

There's more to the new AMP Centre than Australia's best view.... Australia's tallest building is well worth hard-nosed consideration by many a board of directors. . . . Look at the location: Sydney Cove. There's more to that than historical prestige. Sydney Cove means it's a minute's walk to ferries, trains and buses. Good employees stay with companies for life for slimmer reasons than that. The centre is just three minutes' lunch-time stroll from the Opera House . . . sunny terraces and fine stores, eating places, coffee shops, a tavern and banking facilities. . . . Nobody needs to go uptown, because now this is uptown, downtown. Below the terraces is parking for 270 cars. . . . If you would like a tour on a sunny day, or just to chat over the possibilities and the price, have your girl ring our leasing agents. . . .[3]

The AMP didn't hold its record for long after 1975. That same year saw the demolition of the Theatre Royal and another elegant old favourite, the Hotel Australia, to make room for more entrepreneurial push, this time by Mutual Life; not quite such an appalling act of authorised vandalism as the destruction of the Farmers and Graziers had been, but getting close. And by 1977 the owners of the MLC Building, all sixty storeys of it, were able to announce that this was the world's tallest reinforced-concrete office tower. At the same time, North Sydney acquired its Northpoint, with room for five thousand office workers spread across forty-five floors. By 1981 the slender column of Sydney Tower had climbed into the sky, its principal sales pitch being the view from the top—which is a thousand feet above the pavement, making it visible, so it's said, from as far away as the Blue Mountains. It is the tallest structure in Australia, though the building from which it springs is very lowdown. Tell it not in Sydney Square, but—psssst!—the two highest proper buildings are in the other place.

After the Tower there was a pause in the building boom until Sydney was chosen as the place where the XXVII Olympiad would be held, which triggered another frenzy of downtown redevelopment. Big business moved in yet again, picked its sites, knocked things down and brought in soaring and precarious derricks (they swayed in the wind) to pluck huge beams of steel from the ground and place them precisely where they were wanted in tensile patterns that rose inexorably towards the sky. In the dying fall of the twentieth century, the central thoroughfares of Sydney looked as if they had been blitzed, with vast cavities in the ground, gigantic frameworks without walls, improvised duckwalks, and hordes of dusty men with helmets on their heads. George Street became a death trap to anyone who didn't pick his feet up properly, as he stumbled from one lopsided paving stone to another, and hoped not to trip into that great pond of ditchwater or scalp himself on yet more projections of scaffolding.

The wonder is that it took them so long to mutilate the General Post Office. The old landmark had escaped the first violations of this city after 1957, though it soon became an example of the first class dominated by the second-rate, as high-rise nonentities were thrown up on every side. For more than a hundred years it had splendidly flanked one side of Martin Place between George Street and Pitt, a Venetian palazzo of a building with a distinctive tower that just might have owed something to Christopher Wren. With some courage and at vast expense, it was raised in 1891 on top of the Tank Stream, long after that watercourse had become nothing but an enormous underground drain. Inside, the central hall was vast and echoing, with a marble floor and with tremendous counters of polished wood and gleaming brass, an interior which made you feel that posting a letter or buying stamps was a matter of almost Victorian consequence; and it is likely that only the GPO's counterpart in Dublin confers such gravitas any more. Someone has suggested that the building symbolised this city in the way the Houses of Parliament have always symbolised London, or the Eiffel Tower has been Paris's great totem; that it was 'Sydney's Opera House of the nineteenth century'.[4]

In 1996 it was announced that the GPO was to be gutted, to make room for two more high-rise additions to Sydney's commercial prospectus. One would be an office block of twenty-four floors, the other a hotel of thirty-two floors, run by an American company which already owned over a hundred 'resort hotels' all over the world. There would be a basement food court and, at ground level, there would be restaurants and shops, all nicely arranged around a glass-covered courtyard. Some A$500 million were to be sunk in this project, and it had the blessing of Australia Post, which had granted the developers a long lease on what might be left of the old building after they had dismantled most of it. In the bland language of people who do not intend to reveal their true intentions before they have managed a *fait accompli*, and who wish to stifle any conceivable hostility, it was said that the GPO would be retained as 'a significant presence . . . very much part of the civic environment' in the middle of the new complex: the courtyard would be 'the heart and soul of the development, as public and accessible as we can make it'.[5] As the great demolition began, and yet another canyon was blasted and drilled out of Sydney's rocky foundations, it became apparent what this boiled down to: the frontage on Martin Place would be retained, together with the main staircase inside, as a classy entrance to the hotel, *en route* to some very expensive accommodation. But this dear old truncated thing would be diminished yet again by two more monoliths towering over it. Citizens in need of stamps and aerogrammes, from now on, could go round the corner and do business across the plastic counters of an anonymous little shop. Some of them wondered how much longer the Anzac Day bugle would be heard in the Martin Place dawn before the five-star guests overlooking the Cenotaph began to complain.

Environmental pressure groups never stood a chance of saving the GPO intact when even the City Council had been kept in the dark until the last minute, and when the Commonwealth postal authorities were themselves a party to the deal. So the dissidents concentrated their attention instead on Circular Quay, where yet another insurance company (Colonial Mutual Life this time) had as far back as 1986 been given the go-ahead to redevelop the eastern curve of land leading to Bennelong Point and the Opera

House. From the 1860s, this had long been lined with buildings which separated the original Sydney Cove from the Botanic Gardens. In the first place these were individual wool stores and warehouses, good Victorian industrial stock bearing names which had resounded through the history of Sydney's commerce: Dalgety & Co.; Burns, Philp & Co.; Pitt, Son & Badgery; Wily, Trenchard & Co.; and one or two others. They didn't form an uninterrupted slab of building, but left gaps through which the trees of the Gardens could be seen, and they were low enough for the castellations of Government House to retain their place on the skyline. Once shipping began to abandon East Circular Quay in the early years of the twentieth century, however, their days were numbered, but a few survived to be hemmed in by modern slab buildings in the wake of the 1957 ruling, until they too were squeezed out of existence by market forces and public indifference.

The building of the Opera House probably had something to do with the end of indifference, for it reminded Sydneysiders for the first time in the twentieth century of what was possible, how beautiful architecture could be, how it could fit perfectly into a natural environment, how they didn't have to put up with the mediocre, the cheap and the downright ugly just because someone could improve his balance sheet by spending not a penny more than the absolute minimum required to get any building off the ground. The first (and surprisingly extravagant) proposal for East Circular Quay looked like 'a wingless 747 about to hit the Opera House' and was hooted out of court by public derision.[6] The politicians began to lose their nerve as the protest groups shaped up, and querulously asked if anyone had any better ideas. More than 200 organisations and individuals responded, and the real killer to the men and women who ran the supervising Central Sydney Planning Committee (which is dominated by the state Government) must have been submission No. 179. It came from an architect and it consisted of two words: 'Trees Please'. So the politicians and the planners began to wring their hands in the face of this great disapproval, and cry 'What Have We Done?' CML became so horrified at the prospect of losing tens of thousands of insurance premiums from families who were incensed at what it was planning that it passed the parcel to a Chinese company and retained only a 5 per cent stake in the enterprise. Nobody was louder in his self-abnegation than Sydney's Lord Mayor, Alderman Frank Sartor, but he was the first to point out that there was no way planning permission to build up to 155 feet could be revoked except by paying the developers a prohibitive A$200 million in compensation from public funds. As a result, it became inevitable that, unless hard-nosed business made an unprecedented gesture and backed off in sheer goodwill, the Botanic Gardens were going to be completely screened from East Circular Quay by an uninterrupted wall of glass and steel, in which would be set yet another hotel and/or some very pricey apartments.

By then, many citizens had become downright cynical about the way such things had been handled over a long period of time. But even they were dumbfounded by a report that was published towards the end of 1998. This compared Sydney with seven cities in other lands (Atlanta, Frankfurt, Singapore, New York, London, Kuala Lumpur, Vancouver) after compiling questionnaires that were answered by local functionaries, each of them adjudicating on their own patch, not coming to conclusions about anybody else's. The Australian response was in the hands of a recently formed Committee for Sydney, a hotchpotch of businessmen and professional experts, led by the lawyer who had been in charge of the successful bid for the Olympic Games. The questions covered such areas of civic concern as economic development, quality of life, all aspects of the environment, and what the jargon refers to as 'infrastructure development'. When all the submissions had been handed in, ticked, tagged and evaluated, it was found that Sydney had done extremely well in some respects. It had easily the best weather, its people were safer from criminals than other places, and more of its citizens had specialised skills than anywhere else: it also had the outstanding telecommunications network, which could have surprised no one who has observed that every other Sydneysider appears to have a mobile phone these days, including old bodies in cardigans who don't look as though they are accustomed to handling anything more sophisticated than a leagues club poker machine. But then came the stunner. When the various committees were asked what they thought of planning and organisation in their cities, the average mark they awarded was 80.1 per cent. Sydney's score was not quite zero, but it was near enough at a breathtaking 1.7 per cent. This provoked a local headline the morning after the report was published: 'Sydney—Red Tape Ruin'.[7]

Only the absolute depths of that score surprised anyone, for most people had long since doubted that anywhere else could possibly lurch from one urban disaster to another with quite the same myopia they attributed to their own administrators. For years there had been periodic newspaper campaigns against a transport system that sent long convoys of buses, each vehicle driven closely behind the one ahead, to the same destinations, followed by intolerable gaps between one departure and the next, a system which also left many western suburbs without any buses at all. Regularly, the gridlock caused by too many private vehicles incensed the same journalists who, like other car drivers, had too often been stuck in the rush-hour jam on the roads leading on to and off the Harbour Bridge or the Tunnel underneath. All this on top of developments that too often seemed to be part of a very short-term strategy, or some extremely doubtful proposition, or with no motivation at all except financial gain. The same complaints, it is true, can be heard in many other cities across the world. But Sydney lays itself wide open to criticism because, although supreme power is invested in the Government of New South Wales, the city's destiny is in the hands of too many other bodies as well, frequently competing with each other, often ignoring what a rival has already achieved. There are forty-two local councils in Greater Sydney, for a start, and then there are fifteen more authorities with their fingers in the pie—the CityWest Development Corporation, the Darling Harbour Authority, the South Sydney Council, the Heritage Office, the Opera House Trust and others, all added to the Sydney City Council and the Department of Urban Affairs and Planning. This is not a new confusion: in 1918, when the heart of Empire was governed by a single body, the London County Council, Sydney's future depended upon fifty-three civic authorities of one sort and another. Complaints that the left hand did not know what the right was doing have been heard periodically since 1845, when Alderman Edward Flood noted a 'list of streets being opened by the Government at the north end of the town, of which the Corporation and their Surveyor had no knowledge whatever'.[8]

Sydney has been lurching for quite a long time, and some would say that the city's last chance of being properly planned went with the departure of Lachlan Macquarie in 1821. He had grown up with an understanding of and appetite for civic design, as practised most notably by John Wood and his son in eighteenth-century Bath, and he had the vision to pursue the same ideal in Australia: 'No governor before him was so attuned and none after him enjoyed the power and authority to do anything about it. Only in Macquarie was the spirit willing and the flesh able.'[9] The briefest comparison of the order in everything Macquarie touched, with the general disorder that was sanctioned after him, is enough to suggest the nature of what was lost and what might have been. A recent study of the planning that has and has not happened here since 1788, the haphazard sequence of improvisations, the lack of a long vision into the future of this place, was significantly entitled *The Accidental City*, and its text very clearly demonstrates why.

Sydney is, of course, many other things besides a metropolis that has grown and been shaped almost by happenstance. It has become Australia's principal financial centre, leaving Melbourne bereft at the loss of a title which it had held for most of the twentieth century, and a fair piece of the nineteenth as well, when its loftier citizens were wont to think of Sydney as Sleepy Hollow. The change has occurred over the past twenty years, and Sydneysiders who take some pleasure in scoring off the other place can reel off the relevant facts and figures as knowledgeably as they can tell you anything. Out of ninety-four foreign banks with offices in Australia, they say, seventy-three have headquartered themselves in Sydney and only six in Melbourne; forty-one out of fifty-five Australian merchant banks are based here and sixteen of the top twenty-four finance companies; fifty-seven of Australia's hundred biggest companies are nowadays Sydney's own, including Woolworth's, AMP, Qantas, the international transport giant TNT and News Corporation, which belongs to Rupert Murdoch who, once upon a time, was proud to acknowledge that he came from Melbourne and has since located himself nearly everywhere but. The reasons for this change in the fortunes of the two cities are doubtless complex but one powerful factor is Sydney's closer proximity to Tokyo, Singapore, Hong Kong and the other major cities of businesslike Asia; Japanese banks have been particularly keen to gain a foothold in the city. And it evidently matters in this hectic age of the microchip and the satellite dish, more than the untutored might think, that Sydney is situated at 151° 17′ 30″ East, because this means that here is the first international trading centre to open each day; whereas poor old Melbourne lags a full six degrees behind the Sydney sunrise—which, symbolically speaking, denotes time and money as well as longitude.

A by-product of this shift in the balance of commercial and financial power may be a further change in the social composition of the city. The great influx of Asian immigrants in the past generation, as we noted earlier, has already altered Sydney's character and will continue to do so in the future. It may also be that an increasingly higher proportion of white-collar jobs available in the newly inflated service industries will dilute Sydney's reputation as a town whose prevailing values are those of men who work with their hands rather more than they are required to work with their heads. Not that this ever was a classless society, in spite of an Australian mythology that has generally reckoned otherwise. To some extent, the mythology was constructed by passing acquaintances like D. H. Lawrence, who lived briefly at Thirroul, just above Wollongong, and then wrote *Kangaroo* in six weeks flat. 'There was really no class distinction,' his character Somers believed. 'There was a difference of money and of "smartness". But nobody felt *better* than anybody else, or higher, only better-off. And there is all the difference in the world between feeling *better* than your fellow-man and merely feeling *better-off*.'[10] True, perhaps, as far as it goes. But Henry Lawson, whose knowledge of his country was much greater than Lawrence's, had vehemently looked forward to the day when 'the curse of class distinctions from our shoulders shall be hurled. . . . When the people work together, and there ain't no fore-'n'-aft.'[11]

Sydney can still provide choice examples of the Australian class system in action, and one of them is on show every winter weekend, when *hoi polloi* watch and play rugby league football, while the rah-rahs and the silvertails pleasure themselves in the rugby union tradition: and the epithets measure the social suspicions separating the two groups. See those boys coming out of a commemorative service in St Andrew's Anglican Cathedral, the ones wearing straw boaters instead of caps above their uniforms? They're from Knox Grammar which, like Sydney Grammar School, prides itself on sharing many of Eton's and Harrow's values, including a sense of social distinction (but, it has to be said, if you really want to be sure your son will prosper in this world, put him down before he's born for Geelong Grammar—where Pommy Prince Charles once spent a term—even though that means he'll have to go to you-know-where for his education). Any number of social surveys in the recent past have demonstrated that 'at least half of Australian men and women regard themselves as middle class, about a quarter to a third regard themselves as working class, and about a tenth regard themselves as upper class or upper-middle class'.[12] Politicians are notoriously nervous of referring to the topic because the slightest nuance of any kind on any subject can upset the voters, but an exception has been the sometime Premier of New South Wales, Neville Wran QC, nowadays resident of polished Woollahra, but originating in Balmain when it might have been in another world rather than at the other end of the same city. It was Wran who once memorably said that 'Balmain boys don't cry,' to illustrate the toughness of the suburb into which he had been born. More recently, in his political heyday, he found it expedient to declare that he didn't really think of Balmain and its inhabitants as working class so much as the home of 'working people': and then, in the next breath (blood will out), he couldn't help blurting, 'But let me tell you, the very best thing about the working class is getting out of it!'[13]

Sydney is a city that should matter to all of us for a number of reasons, some more obvious than others. One of them is that here the fond outsider senses that this is our very last chance to get the urban thing more or less right, which some would say is a very Australian way of looking at things. We can still hope here that a tremendous mishmash of nationalities, a mixture that has happened only once before in the modern world and can never happen again, will grow into a people whose differences of origin and physique matter not at all, but are seen as something to glory in; which has not happened anywhere yet. We can still hope that the appearance and the operation of this city may yet approach something closer to an ideal than any other huge community has managed so far, a combination of the organic and the organised which avoids the chaos latent in the one and the soullessness inherent in the other: the next generation of Sydneysiders deserves something better than what they will inherit if their parents are not more careful than their grandparents, but nobody in his right mind would wish upon them the planster's sterile vision, as expressed in

Ankara, in Chandigarh, in Brasília, in Islamabad, and even in Canberra. In spite of all the unforgivable things that have been done already, and despite the fact that some of them are unlikely ever to be undone, the present confusion is not completely beyond redemption. If it is not too late to try, the redevelopment of Boston's waterfront—where the demolition of an overhead expressway has been under serious consideration recently—would be an excellent precedent for Sydney to follow for a start. It is no less than it deserves, and it is within its grasp. No city, as John Pringle once remarked, was ever born under so cruel a star; but no city now gives the impressionable visitor such a feeling of still boundless optimism.

CHAPTER TWELVE

...Downstream

What else is there that tells of this city's essence? Sydney is where the principal morning paper refers to the deity as a capitalised Him, even in a piece by an agnostic about bringing up her children without exposing them to any religion; whereas secular publications elsewhere in the Western world which find it necessary to refer to Christ or God, tend to print the divine pronoun entirely in lower-case nowadays. It is a city whose most celebrated cemetery has gravestones with marvellously insouciant inscriptions like 'Strewth!' and 'Be ready mates, that's all!' It is one of those few cities which enjoy clear blue skies so many days in the year that sky-writing by advertisers is still a going concern, which is a commercial tactic without much point in the cloudy northern hemisphere. It is an opera house with a high proportion of the audience dressed for comfort rather than effect, whereas their grandparents would have worn evening gowns and best suits simply to go to the cinema, just as opera-goers still do at Covent Garden and the New York Met. It is where children are allowed into the main reading room of the Mitchell Library and, so long as they don't fidget and chatter enough to disturb the concentration of the ticket-holders, nobody dreams of suppressing them. It is where even the best restaurants—and they are as good as you'll find anywhere—are apt to serve the ingredients of the main course balanced on top of each other, in the manner of a club sandwich but without the bread. It is where theatre reviews and other critical notices can descend to a cruelty rarely found anywhere outside New York. It is a sub-lieutenant RAN, in all his gold-braided and peak-capped smartness, striding along Market Street with an egalitarian rucksack on his back. It is a bus driver applying fresh nail varnish when she is stuck behind a line of other buses in a rush-hour traffic jam on the hill leading up to the Town Hall; and it is one of her mates, in a similar plight at the bottom of Parramatta Road, passing time by scanning the job vacancies in his *Sydney Morning Herald*. It is the wharfies dropping whatever they are doing to go and fight bush fires that threaten someone else's property, and turning out for other emergencies when the call for help comes through.

It is the memory of that icy Parliamentarian Enoch Powell, who was Professor of Greek at Sydney University for a couple of years before the Second World War, then went home to enlist as a private in the Warwickshire Regiment, when what he really wanted to be all the time was Viceroy of India. It is also the memory of Gilbert Murray, another classicist, a Sydneysider who was destined to spend his life on an international stage as scholar and indomitable worker for peace: he was also 'a capable boxer in youth, a fearless glacier-walker in his sixties', according to the *Dictionary of National Biography*, who finished up in Westminster Abbey. It is Laurie Nicholls, Balmain supporter incarnate, who has never been known to miss a match or to wear anything but a bushman's black singlet above his slacks: and has done so, what's more, following the Kangaroos round northern England in the depths of its winter, when he was lucky not to catch terminal pneumonia. It is Mark Taylor, of Northern District, New South Wales and Australia, one of the finest men ever to stride on to a cricket field, who, when about to overtake Don Bradman's Test record for an

Australian, and with the world's top score well within reach, deliberately declared his innings closed so as to give his team a better
chance of winning a match against Pakistan. It is a city which no
longer trails behind Melbourne in the frequency, the quality and
the popularity of public lectures given by distinguished experts on
anything from architecture to biodiversity, with the Sydney Institute, the Art Gallery and the State Library each mounting a hundred or more such events in the course of a year, almost all of
them oversubscribed by citizens eager to improve themselves. It is
a community balanced between competing cultures, which measures everything according to the metric system, which drives on
the left like the British and pays lip-service at least to several forms
of royal this and that, but which has also adopted the American
practice of NightSafe areas on lonely CityRail platforms, and the
habit, on certain solemn occasions, of placing the right hand
across the left breast during the national anthem, just like all those
patriotic major league baseball players. The famous old *Bulletin*,
which for most of its life exemplified and extolled Australian
working-class values, including the motto 'Australia for the White
Man' (not abandoned until 1960), now appears only as a local
edition of *Newsweek*, into which it has for several years been
incorporated.*

Which brings us back to the Harbour, as everything does,
sooner or later, for it is indisputably the alpha and the omega of
this place. If you ask your friends and acquaintances to nominate
the most memorable or most significant things about their city,
they come up with a great variety of preferences which tend to be
sensual on the whole: it's uncommon for someone to propose, let
us say, Sydney's warmth and tolerance or the *Morning Herald*'s dis-
putatious letters page, though such uplifting notions are certainly
not forgotten by the way. But much more likely is the rich birdlife

---

*Founded in 1880, the *Bulletin* has been Australia's principal weekly ever since. For many years, its
motto was 'Australia for the White Man and China for the Chows'.

of the city, most of it as colourful as anything you might expect to encounter in the Amazon rainforest, or the weather, which is indeed mighty impressive in whichever of its two forms it pours down. Someone puts forward the Fish Market beside Blackwattle Bay, where great banks of everything from barramundi to Balmain bugs, from John Dory to succulent prawns are not only Dutch-auctioned to restaurants and other traders, but sold over the counter to you and me; and where vast quantities of octopus and squid are tenderised in concrete mixers while the retail customers kill time with a plate of sushi or good old fish 'n' chips. Someone else says, hey, did you know that this is one of the great jazz cities of the world, the only place apart from Los Angeles and London where (so Frank Sinatra used to insist) you can be sure of a quality backing band? And then there's the local café culture, with its endless search for the perfect cappuccino, in places that serve coffee in seventeen different ways. Or how about the wonderful colonial architecture, the major stuff along Macquarie Street, the engagingly domestic over in Paddington?

Your friends do not, oddly enough, agree on many topics that make Sydney such a stimulating place: except one. No one fails to convey that this city without its Harbour would not only be unimaginable but absolutely unbearable. And then they beg to differ again on what it is about the Harbour that excites or soothes them most, or simply leaves them spellbound. This votary is captivated by the light, by the way it gleams upon and seems to purify the water and makes the surrounding bush and the pink pantiled suburban roofs glow in the heat of one day, but transforms everything into mysterious, spectral, ominous and very lonely patterns in the low cloud and driving rain of the next. One man has never got over the thrill of the view as he drives to work along the Warringah expressway, though he's been enjoying it now for the best part of thirty years. Another obtains the same lift by exploring the bushy slopes of the Middle Harbour or by simply strolling along the great curving promenade at Balmoral before taking lunch at the Bathing Pavilion. And then there's Nielsen Park, full of trees, with a fine netted beach, and its own breezy headland where you can sit and gape at the views across to Chowder Bay and Georges Heights; and afterwards backtrack to Vaucluse House, the Tudor Gothic mansion that Charles Wentworth built between crossing the Blue Mountains and composing an Australian Constitution. Everyone says that in the inconceivable event of having only one day to spare from business in their city, the visitor should not fail to take the ferry to Manly from Circular Quay.

As our mariner prepares to put to sea again, he may reflect that not many ports of his acquaintance offer such a splendid run ashore, providing not only everything a sailor could look for, but wonderfully spontaneous hospitality as well. If he commands a cruise liner and is leaving before the evening tide, he will announce his departure with two or three blasts of the horn, whose deep diapason, with the wind in the right direction, will carry for miles along Parramatta Road, where it will still be heard above the hubbub of the most intimidating traffic south of Teheran. As his vessel casts off and he keeps a wary eye on the other craft coming in and out of Circular Quay (for the law of the sea insists that he is still in command, even though the port pilot is now in charge), he will notice that the eagerness of the commuters to get into the city is such that many of them do not wait for the gangways to be let down, but jump ship over the gunwales, to the exasperation of the ferry crews. His own vessel goes astern very gingerly until she is well out into the stream, then comes round handsomely under the Bridge and loses way with Milsons Point on the port quarter. This, our captain recalls (for repeated visits to Sydney have given him a feeling for and some small knowledge of the local history), was named after James of that ilk, who was one of the first free settlers when he came here in 1806, intending to farm the fifty acres he secured from Governor King; but, finding them too rocky for words, made a virtue out of necessity and began to sell the stone as ships' ballast—excavated and hammered into pieces by assigned convicts, of course—and thereafter prospered exceedingly.

As the tugs release the vessel from their gentle clutches, with her stem well and truly headed downstream, she sits motionless for a moment with the supreme Opera House on the starboard bow and the unforgettable Bridge right overhead, two of the half-dozen most recognisable constructions of the modern world*— and, dear Lord, everyone by now must know that Paul Hogan worked as a painter on one of them before he became Crocodile Dundee. Our ship gets under way and her captain, well aware of what this water conceals, reflects yet again that you'd have to be a lunatic to go swimming outside the shark netting here, though there are at least two certified sightings of note. Young John Robertson is supposed to have done so quite regularly as a boy, going into the water below Mrs Macquarie's Chair with his clothes tied to his head, having a breather on Pinchgut, then carrying on across the Harbour until he reached home on Cremorne Point. He survived to become Sir John Robertson, Premier of New South Wales five times between 1860 and 1886, and a luckier man than Frederick Ward. Otherwise known as Captain Thunderbolt, Ward was a bushranger who, between Robertson's first and second terms in office, escaped captivity by swimming ashore from Cockatoo Island, and was not seen again until, seven years later in 1870, police shot him dead up at Uralla in northern New South Wales, where the sympathetic (and understandably impressed) townsfolk erected a statue to him which still stands beside the main street of the little place.

The vessel glides past the Opera House and, as she crosses the entrance to Farm Cove, anyone on the bridge with a good pair of binoculars might just catch sight, beyond the fig trees and the casuarinas and the flashing cockatoos, of Arthur Phillip's statue in the Palace Garden behind Macquarie Street. There the great man

---

*Such lists are obviously subjective but, if we exclude all monuments (especially the Statue of Liberty, which I take to be the most instantly recognisable structure in the world), my other four nominations would be the Eiffel Tower, the Chrysler Building in New York, Gaudi's church (La Sagrada Familia) in Barcelona and the Le Corbusier chapel (Notre-Dame du Haut) at Ronchamp.

stands, a musket in his left hand, the King's commission in his right, in the middle of a memorial fountain, surrounded by lazy-looking naiads and a Neptune who is brandishing a trident, while the bewigged Governor himself looks sternly across the rest of the Botanic Gardens and the Port Jackson that he brought to life after James Cook had passed it by. His eye has been caught, perhaps, by that brace of American warships slipping into Wool-loomooloo Bay, where Bennelong took Phillip to see his first corroboree. Presently the Yanks will be snugged down astern of HMAS *Darwin* and HMAS *Tobruk*, and their liberty men will doubtless sample soon afterwards the victuals on offer at Harry's Café de Wheels, a converted caravan which has been parked outside the naval base for as many years as even retired admirals can recall, and certainly since the days of the Second World War. Its sides are plastered not only with lists of what you can stand up and eat there, but with photographs of film stars and other notables who have been given to understand that no visit to Sydney is complete unless you've had your fill of Harry's fare (particularly esteemed is his Pie Floater, Garden Island's equivalent of the Cornish pasties, the mouth-watering oggies, that used to be sold outside the Devonport Dockyard gates on the other side of the world). And when the USS *John Young* and the USS *Reuben James* put to sea again, they will almost certainly do so to the strains of 'The Star-Spangled Banner'. The inhabitants of those smart apartments on the ridge above the base have become connoisseurs of many national tunes because of this tradition when foreign warships leave port. It has been perpetuated by everyone except the South Koreans, who once chose for some unfathomable reason to cast off to the earsplitting din of 'Rock around the Clock' instead.

There is no getting away from the naval activity of this port, mixed up as it is, day in and day out, with the comings and goings of vessels such as ours. When the ferries come jostling out of Mort Bay each morning on their way to work, it is very likely that the Navy will already be about its business under the rising sun: a small minesweeper backing and filling above the Bridge, maybe, or a frigate further down the Harbour with a taxing day ahead of her, a concentrated series of those exercises which the sailors know as 'evolutions'. And there is nothing braver than the sight of destroyers steaming down the Harbour in line ahead, off to intricate war games in the Tasman, their smokestacks cockaded with red kangaroos, vivid white identity numbers looming large upon their immaculately grey bows, signal lights twinkling to each other, bunting being run up and down the halliards, in one peremptory hoist after another.

As we approach the buoy where we make a great dogleg, in order to round Bradleys Head and set course anew for the run past the Sow and Pigs, our pilot explains for the benefit of anybody who doesn't already know, that the pillar sticking up from the end of Bradleys (rescued in 1875 from the demolished portico of the very first GPO) used to mark the end of the measured mile from Fort Denison, but it became redundant when speed trials were abandoned before the Great War because the volume of shipping round here by then had made them too dangerous to continue. Behind the pillar rises a famous memento of that war, the tripod mainmast and crow's nest of the battle cruiser *Sydney*, which fought the German raider *Emden*, scourge of Allied shipping in the Indian Ocean, and drove her on to the rocks of the Cocos Islands, in the Royal Australian Navy's first big battle honour.

From here on down the Harbour, until we turn sharply to starboard and a new bearing to the open sea, much of the North Shore is still military land, even though it is no longer used as such; and it occurs to you that so much of the bush has survived and made this haven so lovely largely because private speculators, the spiritual heirs of John Macarthur & Co., have never been able to lay a finger on it. The Army and the Navy between them have served this city well in their subsidiary roles of preservation societies (though it's time someone got rid of those ugly look-outs sprouting from the bush above Georges Head, additions to the defence-works after Pearl Harbor and December 1941). The southern shore has not fared quite so happily but at least those Harbourside suburbs are, by and large, let us say, inoffensive, sometimes even picturesque. A seaplane has just taken off from Rose Bay, water dripping from its floats, and a pelican shuffles along the deck in front of a rather good restaurant, whose staff feed him fish heads and guts so that he will stay put during luncheon, to amuse the diners while they wait for their house-smoked salmon, their snapper fillet and their blue swimmer crab.

There has been heavy rain these past few days, which accounts for that great khaki stain spreading across the North Harbour, the muddy outfall from Manly's stormwater drains. The city-bound *Queenscliff* is rolling like a barrel, her commuters bracing themselves a bit as she crosses the open mile of swell where the great ocean pours in between the Heads. Both her skipper and ours are much more concentrated on those tumbled waves surging about the Sow and Pigs, making some of Kenneth Slessor's buoys (which he remembered 'Tossing their fireballs wearily each to each' across the Harbour's night)[1] bob and bow in an agitated ring around the shoal. Safely past the greatest hazard Sydney can present to the mariner, our helm is put hard over until we have made a perfect turn through precisely ninety degrees, which brings our nose towards the open sea. On the port bow, North Head rises from the depths like a battered rampart, while to starboard some fishermen are on the ledges of the much lower South Head, casting into the surf for mulloway, kingfish and black bream. Hovering just behind them, eyes searching the scrub for their own sustenance, are a pair of hawks, mewing to each other in the wind. A few more revolutions bring our ship abreast of a stubby lighthouse and its magenta candy-stripes. The cutter comes bucking and splashing alongside to take the pilot back to Watsons Bay and, as soon as he is down the ladder and safely on to that hazardous deck, our engine-room telegraph clangs for full ahead both. Once past the Hornby light, we have officially left the most beautiful working harbour in the world.

In their haste to get from here to there (Let's go! Let's go!) Americans would have thrown ten bridges across this incomparable heirloom by now; and would have ruined it, utterly and for ever. Sydney must remember that.

Sources

CHAPTER ONE:
'One of the Finest Harbours in the World'
  1. Auchmuty, p. 23.
  2. *Sydney Morning Herald,* 8 July 1891.
  3. Quoted by Pringle, p. 12.
  4. Collins, p. 12.
  5. Mead, pp. 32–3.
  6. Quoted by Andrews, p. 157.
  7. J. C. Beaglehole (ed.), *Cook Journals,* vol. I: *The Voyage of the Endeavour 1768–1771,* pp. 310–11.
  8. J. C. Beaglehole (ed.), *The Endeavour Journal of Joseph Banks,* vol. II: *1768–1771,* pp. 58 and 60.
  9. Beaglehole, *Cook Journals,* vol. I, pp. 312–13.
  10. 'Phillip's Views on the Conduct of the Expedition and the Treatment of Convicts', 1787: *Historical Records of New South Wales,* vol. II, p. 53.
  11. Auchmuty, pp. 22–3.
  12. Ibid., p. 23.
  13. Collins, p. 8.
  14. Ibid., p. 25.
  15. Ibid., p. 94.

  16. Ibid., pp. 391–4.
  17. Ibid., p. 25.
  18. Ibid., p. 56.
  19. *Historical Records of NSW,* vol. II, p. 770.
  20. Hughes, *Fatal Shore,* p. 145.
  21. Barnard, p. 68.
  22. *Commonwealth Parliamentary Debates,* 8 October 1903, pp. 5933–4.
  23. *Australia and New Zealand,* vol. I, pp. 207–30.

CHAPTER TWO:
In the Beginning . . .
  1. Keneally, *Family Madness,* p. 298.
  2. Guide book quoted by Spearritt, p. 92.
  3. Berndt, p. 550.
  4. Ibid., p. 313.
  5. Ibid., pp. 302–3.
  6. Stanbury and Clegg, p. 3.
  7. Beaglehole, *Banks Journal,* vol. II, pp. 53–4.
  8. Collins, p. 311.
  9. Quoted by Willey, p. 38.

10. Quoted by Kenny, p. 9.
11. *Sydney Gazette,* 9 January 1813.
12. Quoted by Willey, p. 191.
13. Watling, pp. 7–8.
14. *Sydney Morning Herald,* 31 August 1987.
15. Ibid., 30 October 1997.
16. Ibid., 31 October 1997.
17. Ibid., 17 November 1997.
18. Ibid., 20 April 1998.

CHAPTER THREE:
The Last Melting Pot
1. *Sydney [Morning] Herald,* 23 May 1851.
2. Quoted by Dirks, p. 37.
3. Quoted by Fitzgerald and Wotherspoon, p. 55.
4. Ibid., pp. 54–7.
5. Quoted by Spearritt, p. 91.
6. Fitzgerald and Wotherspoon, p. 187.
7. *Sunday Telegraph,* 22 May 1955, quoted by Fitzgerald and Wotherspoon, p. 194.
8. Campion, *Place in the City,* p. 84.
9. Ibid., p. 160.

CHAPTER FOUR:
Merinos, Shipping and Botany Bay
1. Quoted by Cooke and Birkl, p. 44.
2. Ibid., p. 19.
3. Tench, pp. 80–1.
4. The best short but comprehensive summary of the Australian sheep industry, from its earliest days, is to be found in Ryder.
5. *Historical Records of Australia,* series I, vol. II, p. 11.
6. John Macarthur to James Macarthur, Macarthur Papers A2908 in the Mitchell Library.
7. Robert Scott to his mother, Scott Papers A2263 in the Mitchell Library.

8. The newly arrived botanist George Caley in 1800, quoted by Statham, p. 58.
9. Slessor, p. viii.
10. *Sydney Morning Herald,* 16 March 1998.
11. Beaglehole, *Cook Journals,* p. 305.

CHAPTER FIVE:
A Haven, a Battle and Endless Suburbs
1. Fitzgerald, *Sydney,* p. 284.
2. Campion, *Rockchoppers,* p. 209.
3. Fitzgerald, *Sydney,* p. 300.
4. Moore, p. 135.
5. Spearritt, p. 63.
6. *Sydney Morning Herald,* 7 March 1998.
7. Crow, p. 12.
8. The photograph, probably taken in the first half of this century, appears in Cashman and Meader, p. 169.
9. Quoted by Dale, p. 62.

CHAPTER SIX:
Have Fun, Sport!
1. Quoted by Birch and Macmillan, p. 352, from *Let's Go Sailing* by Lou d'Alpuget (1951).
2. Pringle, p. 116.
3. Pilger, p. 13.
4. Keneally, *Homebush Boy,* p. 95.
5. Moore, p. 306.
6. *Wisden Cricketer's Almanack* for 1931, p. 700.
7. *Tablet,* 29 August 1998.
8. NSW Legislative Council debate, 16 June 1997 (State Hansard, p. 10210).
9. Hughes, *Art of Australia,* p. 142.
10. Quoted by Robertson, p. 14.
11. Robert Hughes, Foreword to Robertson, p. vii.
12. Quoted by Norman Jeffares's essay *The 'Ern Malley' Poems* in Dutton, p. 408.

13. Ibid., p. 410.

CHAPTER SEVEN:
Mardi Gras and Tall Poppies
1. Report in 1846 by Robert Pringle Stuart, quoted in Hughes, p. 271.
2. Ibid., p. 272.
3. *Sydney Daily Telegraph*, 20 June 1948.
4. *Sydney Sun-Herald*, 10 March 1956.
5. Ibid., 11 March 1956.
6. *Sydney Morning Herald*, 23 March 1956.
7. Ibid., 12 April 1956.
8. Pilger, p. 103.
9. Conversation with the author, 1962.
10. *Sydney Morning Herald*, 10 December 1991.
11. Judd and Cable, p. 233.
12. Bligh to the Select Committee on Transportation, 1812, quoted by Hughes, p. 290.
13. J. T. Lang, *I Remember* (1956), quoted by Dirks, p. 96.
14. Birch and Macmillan, p. 322.

CHAPTER EIGHT:
Warts and All
1. Quoted by Hughes, *Fatal Shore*, p. 430.
2. Hughes, ibid., p. 200.
3. Ibid., p. 494.
4. Pilger, p. 260.
5. Fitzgerald, *Sydney 1842–1992*, p. 76.
6. Quoted by Pilger, p. 255.
7. Quoted by Phillip Knightley, *Independent on Sunday*, 29 June 1997.
8. *Sun-Herald*, 11 September 1994.

CHAPTER NINE:
Politics, Too
1. *Sun-Herald*, 5 April 1998.
2. Pringle, pp. 45–6. John Pringle was a Scot who edited the *SMH* 1952–7

and 1965–70. He had earlier been on the editorial staff of the *Manchester Guardian* during that newspaper's most illustrious days, and between his two stints in Australia he was Deputy Editor of the *Observer* in London.
3. *Proceedings of the NSW Parliament*, vol. 141, p. 453.
4. Ashton, p. 111.
5. Fitzgerald and Wotherspoon, p. 77.
6. *Sydney Morning Herald*, 21 March 1932.
7. Quoted by Dirks, p. 109.
8. *New Guard*, vol. 1, no. 1, July 1931.
9. *Sydney Morning Herald*, 19 September 1872.
10. Beasley, p. 17.
11. By Ernest Antony, quoted by Beasley, p. 78.
12. Quoted ibid., p. 50.
13. Quoted by Dirks, pp. 98–9.

CHAPTER TEN:
The One Day
1. Judd and Cable, p. 177.
2. Seymour, pp. 77, 94, 100.
3. Horne, p. 133.
4. Quoted by Messent and McGonigal, pp. 115–16.
5. *Sydney [Morning] Herald*, 12 February 1841.
6. *Sydney Morning Herald*, 13 March 1854.
7. Ibid., 1 April 1854.
8. Ibid., 3 April 1854.
9. Ibid., 8 April 1854.
10. Ibid., 27 April 1854.

CHAPTER ELEVEN:
Uptown, Downtown ...
1. Ashton, p. 76.
2. Ibid., pp. 79–80.

3. *National Times*, 21–26 July 1975, quoted by Spearritt, p. 249.
4. Jahn, p. 53.
5. *Sydney Morning Herald*, 29 May 1996.
6. Fitzgerald, *East Circular Quay*, p. 15.
7. *Sydney Daily Telegraph*, 28 October 1998.
8. *Sydney Morning Herald*, 10 January 1845, quoted by Ashton, p. 21.
9. Freeland, p. 30.
10. Lawrence, p. 21.
11. The Henry Lawson ballad from which this comes is 'For'ard'.
12. *Sydney Morning Herald*, 26 April 1997.
13. Ibid.

CHAPTER TWELVE:
... *Downstream*
1. Slessor, 'Five Bells'.

Bibliography

Historical Records of New South Wales (Mitchell Library)
Historical Records of Australia (Mitchell Library)
Commonwealth Parliamentary Debates
Proceedings of the New South Wales Parliament

Anderson, Ken: *Sydney's Suburbs: how and why they were named* (Kangaroo Press, 1989)

Andrews, Graeme: *Ferries of Sydney* (OUP and Sydney UP, 1994)

Ashton, Paul: *The Accidental City: planning Sydney since 1788* (Hale & Iremonger, 1993)

Auchmuty, James J. (ed.): *The Voyage of Governor Phillip to Botany Bay: with contributions by other officers of the First Fleet and observations on affairs of the time by Lord Auckland* (Angus & Robertson, 1970—originally published in 1789 as the official account of the founding of the Australian Settlement)

Baker, Sidney J.: *The Australian Language* (Currawong, 1966)

Barker, Anthony: *What Happened When: a chronology of Australia from 1788* (Allen & Unwin, 1996)

Barnard, Marjorie: *A History of Australia* (Angus & Robertson, 1962)

Barrett, David H. (ed.): *Crawford's Mariners Atlas: Port Stephens to Jervis Bay* (Crawford House Publishing, 1995)

Beaglehole, J. C. (ed.): *The Endeavour Journal of Joseph Banks 1768–1771* (Trustees of the Library of New South Wales in association with Angus & Robertson, 1962)

Beaglehole, J. C. (ed.): *The Journals of Captain James Cook*, vol. I: *The Voyage of the Endeavour 1768–1771* (CUP for the Hakluyt Society, 1955)

Beaglehole, J. C.: *The Life of Captain James Cook* (A. & C. Black, 1974)

Beasley, Margot: *Wharfies: the history of the Waterside Workers' Federation* (Halstead Press, 1996)

Berndt, Ronald M. and Catherine H.: *The World of the First Australians: aboriginal traditional life, past and present* (Aboriginal Studies Press, 1992)

Bersten, Helen: *Jewish Sydney: the first hundred years 1788–1888* (Australian Jewish Historical Society, 1995)

Birch, Alan and Macmillan, David S.: *The Sydney Scene 1788–1960* (Hale & Iremonger, 1982)

Blainey, Geoffrey: *A Land Half Won* (Sun, 1995)

Blainey, Geoffrey: *Triumph of the Nomads: a history of ancient Australia* (Sun, 1997)

Blainey, Geoffrey: *The Tyranny of Distance: how distance shaped Australia's history* (Sun, 1996)

Blombery, Tricia: *The Anglicans in Australia* (Australian Government Publishing Service, Canberra, 1996)

Brennan, Frank: *Sharing the Country: the case for an agreement between black and white Australians* (Penguin, 1994)

Broadbent, James: *Elizabeth Farm, Parramatta: a history and a guide* (Historic Houses Trust of NSW, 1995)

Campion, Edmund: *Australian Catholics* (Penguin, 1988)

Campion, Edmund: *A Place in the City* (Penguin, 1994)

Campion, Edmund: *Rockchoppers: growing up Catholic in Australia* (Penguin, 1987)

Cashman, Richard and Meader, Chrys: *Marrickville: rural outpost to inner city* (Hale & Iremonger, 1997)

Clark, Manning (ed.): *Sources of Australian History* (OUP, 1971)

Clune, Frank: *Saga of Sydney: the birth, growth and maturity of the Mother City of Australia* (no publisher given, 1961)

Coleman, Peter (ed.): *Australian Civilisation* (Angus & Robertson, 1962)

Collins, David: *An Account of the English Colony in New South Wales 1788 to 1801* (Whitcomb & Tombs, 1910)

Cooke, Anne and Birkl, Joanne: *Going to the Show?: images and memories of Sydney's Royal Easter Show* (Historic Houses Trust of NSW, 1996)

Cropp, Ben: *Dangerous Australians: the complete guide to Australia's most deadly creatures* (Bay Books, 1994)

Crow, Vincent: *Haberfield: distinctly Australian* (privately published, 1997)

Dale, David: *The 100 Things Everyone Needs to Know About Sydney* (Pan, 1997)

Davison, Graeme, Hirst, John and Macintyre, Stuart: *The Oxford Companion to Australian History* (OUP, 1998)

Dirks, Jo: *Sydney Downtown* (Kangaroo Press, 1993)

Drewe, Robert: *The Bodysurfers* (Picador, 1993)

Dutton, Geoffrey (ed.): *The Literature of Australia* (Pelican, 1964)

Fitzgerald, Shirley: *East Circular Quay 1788–1998* (City Council, 1998)

Fitzgerald, Shirley: *Rising Damp: Sydney 1870–1890* (Hale & Iremonger, 1987)

Fitzgerald, Shirley: *Sydney 1842–1992* (Hale & Iremonger, 1992)

Fitzgerald, Shirley and Wotherspoon, Gary (eds): *Minorities: cultural diversity in Sydney* (State Library of NSW Press, 1995)

Freeland, J. M.: *Architecture in Australia: a history* (Penguin, 1968)

Gilbert, Kevin: *Because a White Man'll Never Do It* (Angus & Robertson, 1994)

Grenville, Kate: *Lilian's Story* (Allen & Unwin, 1985)

Heads, Ian: *True Blue: the story of the NSWRL* (Ironbark, 1992)

Heads, Ian and Lester, Gary: *200 Years of Australian Sport: a glorious obsession* (Lester Townsend, 1988)

Horne, Donald: *The Lucky Country: Australia in the sixties* (Penguin, 1964)

Howarth, R. G., Slessor, Kenneth and Thompson, John (eds): *The Penguin Book of Modern Australian Verse* (Penguin, 1961)

Hughes, Robert: *The Art of Australia* (Penguin, 1970)

Hughes, Robert: *The Fatal Shore* (Pan, 1987)

Jahn, Graham: *Sydney Architecture* (The Watermark Press, 1997)

Johns, Elizabeth et al.: *New Worlds from Old: 19th century Australian and American Landscapes* (National Gallery of Australia and Wadsworth Atheneum, Hartford, Conn., 1998)

Johnson, Heather: *The Sydney Art Patronage System 1890–1940* (Bungoona Technologies, 1997)

Judd, Stephen and Cable, Kenneth: *Sydney Anglicans: a history of the diocese* (Anglican Information Office, 1987)

Keneally, Thomas: *A Family Madness* (Hodder & Stoughton, 1986)

Keneally, Thomas: *Homebush Boy: a memoir* (Hodder & Stoughton, 1995)

Kenny, John: *Bennelong: first notable aboriginal* (Royal Australian Historical Society, 1973)

Knightley, Phillip: *A Hack's Progress* (Cape, 1997)

Kohen, James: *The Darug and their Neighbours: the traditional aboriginal owners of the Sydney region* (Darug Link in association with Blacktown and District Historical Society, 1993)

Langford, Ruby: *Don't Take Your Love to Town* (Penguin, 1988)

Lawrence, D. H.: *Kangaroo* (Penguin, 1997)

Macdonald, Patricia R. and Pearce, Barry: *The Artist and the Patron: aspects of colonial art in New South Wales* (Art Gallery of NSW, 1988)

Martin, Stephen: *A New Land: European perceptions of Australia 1788–1850* (Allen & Unwin, 1993)

Mead, Tom: *Manly Ferries of Sydney Harbour* (Dolphin, 1988)

Messent, David and McGonigal, David: *The Complete Guide to Sydney Harbour* (David Messent Photography, 1994)

Miller, J. D. B.: *Australian Government and Politics* (Duckworth, 1964)

Moore, Andrew: *The Mighty Bears!: a social history of North Sydney Rugby League* (Macmillan, 1996)

Morris, Jan: *Sydney* (Penguin, 1993)

Murphy, Peter and Watson, Sophie: *Surface City: Sydney at the millennium* (Pluto Press, 1997)

Park, Ruth: *The Harp in the South* (Penguin, 1975)

Pilger, John: *A Secret Country* (Vintage, 1992)

Pringle, John: *Australian Accent* (Chatto & Windus, 1958)

Proudfoot, Peter: *Seaport Sydney: the making of the city landscape* (University of NSW Press, 1996)

Radford, Ron (ed.): *Tom Roberts* (Art Gallery of South Australia, undated)

Reynolds, Henry: *Frontier: reports from the edge of white settlement* (Allen & Unwin, 1996)

Reynolds, Henry: *The Other Side of the Frontier: aboriginal resistance to the European invasion of Australia* (Penguin, 1995)

Rintoul, Stuart: *The Wailing: a national black oral history* (Heinemann, 1993)

Rivett, Kenneth (ed.): *Immigration: control or colour bar?* (Melbourne UP, 1962)

Robertson, Anne: *Treasures of the State Library of New South Wales: the Australian collections* (Collins, 1988)

Rowlinson, Eric et al.: *Aboriginal Australia* (Australian Gallery Directors Council, 1982)

Ryder, M. L.: *Sheep and Man* (Duckworth, 1983)

Scott, Geoffrey: *Sydney's Highways of History* (Georgian House, 1958)

Seymour, Alan: *The One Day of the Year* (Angus & Robertson, 1962)

Shaw, A. G. L.: *The Story of Australia* (Faber, 1961)

Slessor, Kenneth: *Selected Poems* (Angus & Robertson, 1988)

Smith, Geoffrey: *Arthur Streeton 1867–1943* (National Gallery of Victoria, 1995)

Smith, Keith and Irene: *Smith's Guide to Sydney City* (Smith's Guides, 1988)

Spearritt, Peter: *Sydney Since the Twenties* (Hale & Iremonger, 1978)

Stanbury, Peter and Clegg, John: *A Field Guide to Aboriginal Rock Paintings* (OUP, 1996)

Statham, Pamela (ed.): *The Origins of Australia's Capital Cities* (OUP, 1990)

Taverne, Caroline, Casimir, John and Greenwood, Helen (eds): *Timeout Sydney Guide* (Penguin, 1997)

Taylor, Griffith: *Sydneyside Scenery: and how it came about* (Angus & Robertson, 1958)

Taylor, Kevin: *The Sydney Swans: the complete history 1874–1986* (Allen & Unwin, 1987)

Tench, Watkin: *A Narrative of the Expedition to Botany Bay: with an account of New South Wales, its productions, its inhabitants etc* (1789)

Thompson, John, Slessor, Kenneth and Howarth, R. G. (eds): *The Penguin Book of Australian Verse* (Penguin, 1958)

Trollope, Anthony: *Australia and New Zealand* (London, 1873)

Troy, Jakelin: *The Sydney Language* (Australian Institute of Aboriginal and Torres Straits Islander Studies, 1993)

Turbet, Peter: *The Aborigines of the Sydney District Before 1788* (Kangaroo Press, 1989)

Ward, Russel (ed.): *The Penguin Book of Australian Ballads* (Penguin, 1964)

Watling, Thomas: *Letters from an Exile at Botany Bay to His Aunt in Dumfries* (1794)

Willey, Keith: *When the Sky Fell Down: the destruction of the tribes of the Sydney region 1788–1850s* (Collins, 1979)

Willmot, Eric: *Pemulwuy, the Rainbow Warrior* (Bantam, 1988)

Wilson, Edwin (ed.): *Royal Botanic Gardens Sydney* (RBG, 1982)

Yeomans, John: *The Other Taj Mahal: what happened to The Sydney Opera House* (Longmans, 1973)

Index